CONFESSIONS OF A MAIL ORDER BRIDE

CONFESSIONS OF A MAIL ORDER BRIDE

American Life Through Thai Eyes

Wanwadee Larsen

NEW HORIZON PRESS
Far Hills, New Jersey

Library of Congress Catalog Card Number
89-043331

Wanwadee Larsen
Confessions of a Mail Order Bride

ISBN 0-88282-051-6
New Horizon Press

AUTHOR'S NOTE

The book you are about to read is meant to portray my experiences as recorded in a diary covering several years of my life. I have taken the liberty of changing all names and identifying characteristics of people and disguised certain situations to preserve the privacy of those involved. In some cases, the people in this book are composites, and in a few instances the chronology has been altered. But the essence of the book is true, and I have tried to be candid in revealing the experiences upon which it is based.

CONTENTS

PROLOGUE

The narrative that follows is based upon a diary in which I began making entries in Thai early in 1976, when I was just beginning to think about leaving Thailand. And I inked my last in summer 1985. I kept at it until I felt satisfied that I had become a full-fledged American. Then I mysteriously stopped —well, not so mysteriously: what had to be said, simply, was said. I was accepted as, had accepted myself as, a citizen of my brave new world of freeways, Fourths of July, and fast food.

My writing began during terribly stressful months of my life, as will be described, and it continued (increasingly in English) through nearly a decade of encounters with and adjustments to American life that at times resembled the moves of a matador, at times those of his bull. As if to maintain those charges and challenges, Fate had me moving over the map, to

1

four totally different corners of the country. During these years I found myself in New York City, Atlanta, Los Angeles, and—for a complete change of pace—semi-rural Arkansas.

And all the while my penmarks upon that small, sturdy, vinyl-bound diary *(buntuk prajumwan* in Thai) kept humming and clicking along. It was a quiet confidante, an escape valve, my unmarked block of marble, the blank white page of my day to be filled in every night as if it were some sort of magic runestone onto which my minutes and hours had, eventually, to be etched in order to be real. Without succumbing to that almost nightly impulse, I wonder how else I might have grown.

What was it that had to be said, and to whom?

For years the "whom" was always myself, writing away in the dark in Thai at first, then in English as I struggled to master it. (Writing in the diary was in fact an almost nightly exercise in mastery.) Once my American husband, who in my present life as a sculptress is also my manager, had fully uncovered what I was doing, he insisted on its value and that I should find readers—a lot of them. I felt inordinately proud, but doubtful enough to question vigorously: readers of what sort, and from where?

But, at my husband's request, I shyly shared the diary with other people; friends and family alike, who also insisted that the story I had been telling myself was unique, with the long-term result being this book. Outwardly I am thrilled to the core over it, but inwardly still full of doubt. Self-efface-ment, you see, is a hard Oriental habit to break: you can take the girl out of Thailand, but you can't take Thailand out of the girl.

The "what" of what had to be said is not merely the experience of *being* Asian in America—small boned, slant-eyed, patient and beige in a predominantly large-boned, round-eyed, hurrying white world—that is a part of it to be sure. But it is far more the *learning* that took place beneath the skin and be-

PROLOGUE

hind these (to most Americans) inscrutable Oriental eyes. Yes, far from being "kitchen appliances with sex organs," Asian-American women are as full of questions about life as anyone else. We do indeed have egos, flickering candles capable of flame.

If you divide and sub-divide people by race and gender, there is hardly a slice of humanity as diminutive in stature and all-but-invisible as Oriental women. I am not so much complaining as calculating here: as no one else does, the Asian woman acts upon her root belief that in softness and in silence there is enormous strength. Thus it follows that by opening up my life here, in America and in these pages, I feel somewhat like Samson being shorn, in this case shearing himself. It is a price worth paying, though, for the delight that lies not in self-revelation but in self-comprehension.

Today I live much more sedately in a fifth corner of the United States, sculpting, raising a son, and (to be candid) still making diary entries every now and then.

But only in my head.

1

STREET SCENE

Bangkok 1976

When I first see the gun, there is, of course, panic and shock. It appears slyly and sorcerously as if in a dream, the serpent revealed in the long grass, the forbidden made real, as real as its silver three-inch barrel glistening in the night.

There is also protest, a scream jumping out of my throat. Even as it does, I am dimly aware that this is to be one of those events that transforms the lives of its participants for worse, forever.

They have argued about families—my muscular, aggressive brother Sumwong and my cultured, cynical fiancé Suwad —and too much has been drunk, too much said to be called back and forgiven in the fading hours of this outing to see Suwad's relatives in Pak Nam. It started so brightly for the three of us. We had so much fun on the train and in the streets that even to guess, to *imagine*, that it could end like this was impossible.

They have always been rivals of sorts, friendly enemies, trading repartees, with a few scuffles in which my brother's skill at karate landed Suwad on his back or in tears. Now everything is venomous—deadly.

Without will, I let out another scream an eternal instant later, and in that instant the gun goes off. It fires one time, then, a second and a third. The topsy-turvyed world closes down around me as I cry out, shouting for help and for salvation, screaming until, like some broken machine, I am hoarse and voiceless.

My brother has fallen to the sidewalk; his assailant, my fiancé, has dropped the gun nearby. A crowd has gathered in a semi-circle around the three of us outside the huge dragon-decorated portals of the Chinese restaurant in this northern exurb of Bangkok, buzzing and gawking and not daring to come any closer. Their faces still rim the memory's image like some grotesque, ill-conceived border.

I plead with someone in the crowd to step forward and help. I bend over my brother, holding his hand, as he winces in agony, his features scrunched tightly together. His breathing is labored, tortured. Blood oozes from his wound, staining his clothing and inching along the sidewalk. It is obscenely slick in the light of the streetlamps.

I glance over at my fiancé, but he sits dazed on the curb, as if in another world.

Four or five minutes pass. No one in the crowd of forty or fifty persons comes one inch closer to us.

It is next-to-useless to hope for police or EMS, for at this time in Thailand, in the exurb of Bangkok, they are, like forests in the distant Himalayan north, simply an undeveloped resource.

STREET SCENE

"Tanom," someone finally shouts above the hushed buzz. "Tanom comes!"

A moment later, the crowd parts and through it pushes a huge, heavy man without shirt or shoes who is later identified to me as a taxi-owner well known in this area of the city. He stands for a long moment looking at my brother while I ask him over and over again, in as even a voice as I can master, to drive Sumwong to the nearest hospital.

Finally, he says in a guttural voice that perfectly complements his looks, "It will do no good."

"Why?" I ask, losing control, "Why? *Why?*"

"This man is dying."

"But no, he is not, please, plea—"

"No, Miss, he is dying. I cannot take him in my cab."

Suddenly I understand, and I grow paradoxically calm and incensed at once. If my brother were to die in the taxicab, his soul would remain there forever. This is Thai belief. No one would ride any more, and Tanom would lose his livelihood.

As simple as that.

Tanom walks away, the fat jiggling around his hips, and with him seems to go any hope for my brother. I watch his naked hugeness get swallowed up by the crowd, and at the back of my mind he registers as the very image of what is backward in my native land—the dark superstitions, the stubborn ignorance, the strange quasi-religious "rationale" that is able to justify the most inhumane of human actions.

In him though, I am myself reflected, for I am Thai to the core. I am Wanwadee, but I am also Tanom. All that he knows, I know; all that he fears, I fear.

But could he not just shut his eyes and help, in the name of mercy, in the eyes of Buddha? Not a chance.

For all that is good in my country, I am thinking, *there is much that I would change or, failing that, much that I could bid fare-well to easily enough.*

What an odd, prophetic thought to have . . . to bid farewell, and at a moment such as this one. Yet, at the back of my mind, it registers as certainly as the toll of a *rakong* cymbal in a Thai temple.

And I have had the thought before.

I start sobbing in total despair, and perhaps it is this noise alone that brings an elderly man forward at last. Quietly, he volunteers to carry Sumwong to the hospital in his *rod samlor*, a two-passenger rickshaw-like tricycle. I protest, still sobbing, that it will take too long, but he assures me that there is a small public hospital less than a mile away.

Three or four other men materialize out of the reluctant crowd and together they lift my brother, who groans sharply in pain. They carry him into the middle of the street. There he is placed very gently into the tricycle, sprawled across both seats, while I stand on the entry step and cling to the metal rail.

As we pull away to the old man's huffing and puffing I pray that Sumwong does not die. A police siren fills up the night, growing louder, closer. It seems irrelevant, like some vague and inappropriate afterthought.

The old man grinds along among the cars and trucks crawling by in the late hours, some of the drivers honking, others staring at this garish sight in the late-night traffic of exurban Bangkok, this apparition—although not so very un-usual—of a blood-covered youth paraded through the narrow, noisy, clogged streets. I am right: despite the short distance, the trip takes too long.

Too long, too long. I curse all Bangkok and its never ending traffic. With gasoline at forty *baht* (over two dollars) a gallon, people still find reasons to drive about at ten in-the-evening, grinding their engines in every gear. Absurd, laughable under almost any other circumstances, now it only adds to the hellish effect.

As we draw within sight of Pak Nam's small public hospital, I look down at my brother and see that his eyes are closed, his face colorless. Assuming that he is already dead, I begin crying once more, but in the din of the traffic there is no one to hear or to care. I do not know that almost twelve hours of agony remain for him, hours during which I cannot contact my family on the chronically fouled-up long-distance system, and am afraid to leave my brother alone for more time than it takes to make the telephone attempt. I wish to be with him both to comfort him and to be present should he pass away.

In my heart I know for all those hours that he is a marked man, one labored breath away from death.

In America, death carries on its work behind closed doors. It is rarely encountered outside the confines of ghetto streets and funeral homes. When it does penetrate the havens of the middle class, it is either acted out, as in soap operas and cinema, or neatly compartmentalized, as in "segments" of television news. Americans, generally, come no closer to real, unsanitized death than they do to the dead dog or mangled possum on the shoulder of a highway.

That's the way they want it. Probably, that's the way it ought to be.

But it is not so in the Third World. Death is one of life's daily constants in most parts of Africa, South America, and Asia. We see it first at our mother's apronstrings in backyards and butcher shops; then on the mean streets of domestic violence and vehicle accidents; often, too, in the never ending factional countryside skirmishes, communist vs. conservative, death squad vs. democrat, *ad infinitum*. The old in our families die in front of us, groaning away their last breaths on beds we have slept in.

The death rattle of my father's mother is as clear in my

ears today as it was when she passed away of liver failure in the next room. I was five.

For all that, nothing really serves as preparation for the death of a close loved one. Then, despite one's profoundest religious convictions, those hallowed beliefs meant to spite death and dying, death itself cuts like a razored guillotine. It is so final, after all. No, you will not see that face again. Nor hear that voice. Nor ever touch that flesh.

Doctors and nurses come and go in the night, and Sumwong lolls under three suspended bottles, two of them empty; he has a helpless air about him. His eyes, when they open, are as glazed and sightless as a fish's.

My brother and I were close. Up until the time that he was eight and I six, we slept on side-by-side pallets. We ate the same food, played the same games, held the same passions for karate and chess, swam and boated together in a muddy Chao Phraya tributary. Before the slight but swaggering figure of our father, a typical Thai household tyrant (whom we—being typical Thai kids—both feared and worshipped), we were alternately craven and dutiful. To the schoolteachers who had me in their classes a year or two after him, Sumwong and I were peas from the same pod.

Growing up against a background of war to our east in Vietnam and civil turmoil in the west in Burma, we harbored ourselves in one another.

Of course there was the usual teasing, the petty fights over the few toys that passed from child to child in our extended family. But the daily evidence of real violence virtually in our own backyard brought out the best in us much more often than the worst. We had only to watch its images on the screen of our tiny black-and-white TV set to know that people

STREET SCENE

out there were doing obscenely cruel and unjust things to one another.

Sibling love, even if we could not name it, seemed a precious jewel to have in one's hand.

Against that wartime background, we caught together, early on, our first glimpse of a real, live American: a soldier in fact, one of that superhuman breed that had conquered the world and driven the hated Japanese back to their distant island. This sighting was in 1969, in our hometown of Nakhon Narai, a few hours' train ride north of Bangkok.

An American!

We practically worshipped anything American. The United States was like Shangri-La to us.

To be sure, we had seen Westerners before, such as the French Catholic missionaries left over from the long and useless efforts of France first to conquer, then merely to dominate Siam. But this was an American, conqueror and hero from that fabled distant land. And a soldier, too! (Actually, he was a military tactician of some sort, there to advise a local unit of the Thai army, which was on continual alert.)

Yet, following him around with the other kids and the barking dogs, the most memorable thing we did was to giggle to ourselves at his appearance; we did that with most of the Europeans we saw in life or at the cinema. Their noses—so big, like some sort of weapon! And this one was so eerily white, a scary cartoon ghost! No wonder they were such formidable soldiers—they were *born* with essential parts of their equipment!

To think of going to American and living with all those *jamuk yai*—those heavy-duty schnozzes.

But we had no *real* second thoughts, only the absurdly comical ones of youth.

Of such moments was growing up made, long episodes of fishing and boating and laughing in the tropical heat, star-gazing on clearer, cooler "winter" (there is no real winter in the Thai Rice Belt) nights with few electric lights to dim the sky, being allowed to watch Father (a construction engineer) pore over building blueprints, getting "switched" by Mother with a banana leaf stem.

My brother, despite his aggressive style of playing and arguing, was what is called a "good boy." The middle child and the only male, he was the apple of Father's eye. Like Father, he was to study building design and construction—full-time in the fall—and eventually take over the small construction consulting business that has been providing so well for us. He was brash like Father, but also quiet and determined like him, full of confidence and possessed of skills in woodwork, mathematics and electronics.

It would be neither overstatement nor family chauvinism to say that he was a model for what was best in young Thailand, an image of its hope for a brighter future.

But it was Sumwong's poor fortune to have inherited my father's volatile temperament as well. Short male fuses are not uncommon in Thailand, nor are they commonly deplored. An old Thai saying can be roughly translated, "Slow to boil, last to eat."

As Thai women cultivate a gentle dancelike grace, Thai men pursue the aggressive quickness of a boxer. To it, they attribute their success as individuals and the success of the country as a whole, on the international scene—an arguable point, since some people see Thai volatility as more a hindrance than a help.

It was my brother's double misfortune finally to come to blows with Suwad, who for so long had been his friend. Scion of the wealthiest family in town, Suwad, at twenty-five, was used to having his way in everything.

Our marriage had been arranged by three or four families, our own included, and, although I regarded him as good-looking in a soft sort of way, I did not love him. I had, in fact, been wondering for months how I would go about getting along with him, except by total surrender of will.

Even back then, at barely twenty-one, there was something in me that balked at that idea of absolute submission—lifelong material ease be damned.

It is not that I would have done anything rash, anything to displease any of the families involved. I am too Thai for that. It is, rather, that I would have found a way—within tradition, the unwritten rules of Thai matrimony—to let him know that he was not truly my boss. Despite their image of submissiveness, virtually all Thai women exploit the principle "You catch more flies with honey" to shift the balance of power in their favor. Granted, their spouses can guess what they are up to, but men, generally, do not like the taste of gall any more than flies do.

Beside flies, there are tigers to consider. Thai women carry them around inside, and although they are extremely reluctant to let them out, they can hardly keep them in when they encounter foolishness or incompetence or infidelity in males. The tiger roars little but has extremely sharp claws.

Suwad and I would have had our troubles.

But there will be none of that now: there will be no marriage, good or bad, for Suwad and me.

The morning comes.

I watch my brother sink slowly into oblivion before me, ultimately sighing, shutting his eyes, and passing quietly without, by the grace of Buddha, the slightest semblance of a death rattle. All that night I had known that he would go; the nurses in attendance had gravely told me so. It was just a matter of time; too much blood had been lost, initially; nothing more to be done.

"He is so young; it is too bad," the nurse's words echo down though all my mornings and all my nights.

"Too bad, too bad."

Outrage, impotence, pain fill me.

All my twenty-one years are circumscribed by these three related but distinct and separable emotions, occurring over and over again, minute by minute, in that precise order: outrage, impotence, and pain.

There seems nothing else in life, now or ever. A past there was, one of joy and innocence and even rapture; what future there is now does not seem worth having.

"If only you had gotten him here sooner," one of the nurses says sympathetically.

I want to say, *if only you had done more to save him.* But I hold my tongue. It is not her fault that in Thailand blood is in short supply.

At the moment my brother dies I feel his soul pass beside me, and I am glad to have remained at his side.

No, I will never again see him in this world; but in that other, in which Thais universally believe, he now resides in peace. Something inside of me seems to seal up at last, to become final, and I smile as well as I can at the kind words of the nurses as they disconnect the suspended bottles (all three of them empty now) and pull the rough muslin cover over his eyes. They ask if I wish to come with the body to the adjacent morgue, but I decline.

I tell a staff person that my father will send temple aides to retrieve the body for cremation in Nakhon Narai.

The clock on the wall says nearly ten a.m. I am surprised; I would have thought it afternoon at least. It comes to me that I am tired, exhausted actually, and after trying long-distance one more time without luck I leave the hospital to find a bus to the train station. It is a Sunday. The outing is over.

STREET SCENE

Now I must go home as quickly as I can and tell my family how badly it has all turned out.

This will be as hard as having seen my brother die.

On the way out, I stop in a restroom. Looking at myself in the mirror, I am dismayed at how suddenly old I look. There are rings under the eyes and a sour little twist to the mouth.

But then, what do I expect? The same fresh oval face that attracted Suwad in the first place, drove him to request an arrangement by the families (as I was later to discover)? No, that Wanwadee seems gone forever now; the "classical Thai" look, as it has been called, is already in decline.

And in its place . . . what?

Choosing not to consider the matter further, I brush my hair back with my fingers without looking up and leave.

Outside it is dizzyingly sunny and hot. The sounds of the city well up over me like a tidal wave. My legs feel inert, like tree trunks, and my brain holds many painful and distracting images of Sumwong dying.

Entering a busy main street where the busses run, I pass a newsstand on the corner. The headlines of both major Bangkok papers have the same large-type banner, something about Gulf pirates decimating a boatload of Vietnamese refugees: slaughter and rape.

I have seen the story before, a dozen times or more: outrage, impotence, and pain. The refugees are apparently as defenseless as chicks before a duckhawk. Here, though, perhaps because I am so weary and defenseless myself, the story strikes straight through the heart. These people, the murdered, the violated, are somebody's parents, children, sisters, brothers.

Now they lie without life in the brackish Gulf of Siam or, if female, enslaved under the weight of some foul and worthless bandit. It is with that morbid and insistent thought that the idea of flight, an insane inkling of escape, escape from everything my life has suddenly become, flashes through me again as if I have been struck internally by lightning. The flame goes out as quickly as it came, but an ember remains alive inside me.

Who knows in what unforeseen way it will flare again?

With my beloved brother dead and my prospects for marriage and fortune defunct, what is left for me here?

Scared, confused, groping for enlightenment—hopeful as a schoolgirl and utterly without hope—I cross the crowded street, nearly getting run over by a speeding lorry, and flag down a bus for the train station.

2

THE FLOW OF THE CHAO PHRAYA

Nakhon Narai 1976

Before a few pivotal events, my family home in Nakhon Narai was set to a routine that varied little from day to day. Father would get up before everyone else, drink coffee mixed with tinned condensed milk, and go to work, just as Mother was rising to fix the first meal of the day. Then we three kids would emerge from our small, separate sleeping areas to eat and be off to school or work.

In the afternoons there was laughter and play among us while Mother sewed clothing and cleaned house; this done, she would turn her attention to the long preparation of the evening meal, her daily crowning achievement. Father would be home to eat this large, elaborate meal sometime after seven. In the evenings Mom worked her garden while we kids played or performed chores, and Dad prepared his figures, drawings, and blueprints for the next day.

Not so very different from an American day.

But, as in America, nothing stays the same: eventually the routine altered. One pivotal event was the marriage of my sister. Veena became a member of another household, and the space under our roof turned quieter with her departure.

Another was my father's completion of the studies and apprenticeships that qualified him to become a master construction engineer. He started traveling now and then to Bangkok and elsewhere on projects, and within a year or so we had some of the material goods that Thais desired at that time: a television set, a new Japanese truck for Dad (to replace his battered old Japanese one), a few additions to our house, and the continuation of Sumwong's schooling, which had been interrupted from time-to-time by lack of finances.

The event that altered the routine the most was the death of Sumwong. It was the bitterest pill our family ever had to swallow, and it sticks to this day in all our throats. He left a space in our house and hearts nothing on earth could fill.

After his death, a cloud came over us and stayed; laughter vanished practically overnight. For many despondent families, there is a core event before which they are all together and happy, and after which they split apart, like spores, and become distant, sad, or discontent.

For us, it was the death of my brother Sumwong.

For a few years before the shooting, part of the kids' afternoon routine was canoeing, the three of us at first, then, after Veena got married, with my eventual fiancé Suwad. We would go at sunset usually, when it had cooled off a bit, along one of the small tributaries of the Chao Phraya that ran near our house and served to irrigate the rice fields.

THE FLOW OF THE CHAO PHRAYA

On the river, our small but mythical Mississippi, it was a time for laughter and talk. We felt free, balanced so neatly on the turgid water, to say whatever came to our heads. I spoke little in the presence of these two older and revered males, but I enjoyed listening to them. They talked a lot of America, of the big cars and the beautiful women there—especially of the women.

One time Suwad brought along with him a copy of *Playboy* magazine—not impossible to get outside Bangkok—that had several pictures of blonde women with large, white breasts as bared to the world as papayas at a stall. We could read hardly a word of what accompanied the photos, but all three of us stared at them and stared at them, in curiosity rather than lust (I, anyway), almost until we burned a hole through the slick chromatic paper.

But Sumwong and Suwad argued over the magazine, and eventually it wound up at the bottom of the river.

Most days they would talk of the opportunities people had in the United States—the chance to get rich and drive fast cars. They would talk and talk until they got tired, then I would talk and they would pretend to listen while they daydreamed in the shadows of the bank. Finally we would all grow silent, and brush away the bugs, and watch fish jump free of the water, their scales flashing in the twilight like elusive dreams.

On the few times Veena was along with us, she too spoke of the United States, telling of her friend Marree who lived now in someplace called New Mexico where it was supposed to be hot and dry and rocky, as full of mountains and deserts as Thailand is of jungles and savannahs. She would tell us how Marree got there, and I could hardly believe my ears: she had exchanged letters with an American, an artist, and they had agreed by mail to marry.

It is not at all unusual for marriages in the Orient to be

arranged by contract, usually between neighboring families. It is of course more unusual for those marriages to be between complete strangers who live thousands of miles apart and are from totally different cultures. But the idea of interracial, Oriental "mail order brides"—they are never referred to as such in the Orient—dates back at least to the end of World War II and probably much further, with the chief participants being Filipino and Southeast Asian females, and Northern European and North American males. Although some stigma is attached to the practice in the West, in the East it is one of several acceptable means by which a young lady may find an appropriate mate.

It becomes even more acceptable when the prospects of the lady either run out or are cut short for one or another reason.

Still, Marree's story seemed to me like a romantic fantasy, yet the story was corroborated whenever it came up by her family, who for a while had been feeling embarrassed over it—their daughter going off like that! To marry a stranger, a foreigner! But now they proudly showed photographs of her and her American baby.

Their revitalized pride also had something to do with the service in Bangkok that made the arrangements—the fact that it was reputed to be excellent. To be listed, I found out gradually from Veena, all Thai and foreign parties had to meet strict criteria of income and character; likewise to obtain a listing of eligible partners and the right to correspond with them was expensive and therefore exclusively for foreign suitors.

Marree now lived in a distant place called Santa Fe. No one knew exactly how to pronounce either *New Mexico* or *Santa Fe,* but they had the ring of mystery about them, of the faraway and the exotic—the same aura, I was to learn much later in life, that *Thailand* and *Siam* have to New Mexicans.

THE FLOW OF THE CHAO PHRAYA

"I want to go to America!" I blurted out one day at home.

"Poosh!" Veena said. "What do you know of it?"

"I want a college education, like Marree." With Sumwong in college and my sister's wedding expenses, there was no chance of my going to anything more than a one-year business training program—if I did not get married off first, as was planned.

Yet there was Marree in college in America, thanks to her American husband.

"Dad will never allow any of us to do something like that," Veena said. It was easy for her to say—her marriage was only a few months away.

"I know," I said, "but I would like to think about it."

"Sure. And I would like to think about a million *baht.*"

I understood that to my father such a move might be a form of defeat for the family, a source of shame. People would say that he could not take care of his own children. Yet I knew also that Marree's folks were well off—they owned a cinema theater in town—and had ultimately approved of the marriage.

But how could I have known then, even *guess*, how real the idea was to become to my own family and to me?

My family had known that I did not want to marry Suwad. They knew I felt I could never love him. He had always seemed more like what he actually was—one of my brother's friends, somewhat of an ass but a well-educated one—than anyone I could spend my life with. The idea of living with him *conjugally* twisted my stomach into knots.

But it was not as if I had the right to agree or not agree with anything. The families making the arrangement believed the match to be a good one, regardless of the two individuals involved. Feelings played only a minimal role in the process. It was enough that Suwad thought I was beautiful; no need to make any further commitment on his part—and none whatsoever *required* on mine.

None of this struck me as strange, of course; it was the way things had been done for centuries. Any protest I might raise would be either ignored or reasoned away. Protesting too loudly would be breaking every rule in the book—and that was simply unthinkable.

My father was a straightforward, conservative man, very hard-headed when he believed he had made the right decision—which occurred every time he made a decision as far as I could tell. He also possessed a violent temper when set off, so I have no doubt that this combination of factors negated my options entirely.

I would be married to Suwad some day, regardless; get used to the thought, Wanwadee.

How nice it was to get away on the river to dream, even with Suwad at the opposite end of the boat. Perhaps, seated between us, dreaming also, my brother could sense how unsatisfactory it was for me to consider the reality of my future. Perhaps it was this unvoiced conflict in me that, in ways I can only guess at, would lead to gunfire and death in north Bangkok.

Surely my brother was able to read me as clearly as I could read him. Or was such intuition, I wonder, a gift of biology or the gods to the growing woman in me—to offset some of the things not generally granted to females?

I put my hand in the water and dreamed, now and then, that I was drifting toward an ocean, as wide and blue and limitless as the sky.

My brother had almost finished his *reurbod*—his canoe. Modeled after my father's, it was somewhat shorter and noticeably less well-made. The lapboards, in drying, had come apart slightly, making it unseaworthy. Now he had to chink them with a compound Dad made for him, a laborious process.

It would be another few weeks before a test run on the river could be made—"It needs drying time," Dad said, "then we may go."

In one week Sumwong would be dead.

Sumwong said to me after Dad left, "Just think, Wanwadee. We will have our own canoe."

Even though we were no longer teenagers, we still lived at home under parental dominance, and the mere thought, like a canoe being *all our own,* excited us both. Unlike Bangkok or Pattaya (Thai Riviera) street kids, who tend to grow up faster than their American counterparts, middle-class Thai kids grow more slowly, probably because, like a keel, family ties and obligations run deep and slow the process down.

You were expected, for one thing, never to leave your family. For another, you remained a child until you had children of your own. Even after that, you still respected, and abided by, the wishes of your parents.

On the river that evening, Sumwong spoke once more of American cars and girls and those wonderful opportunities. I had my own corresponding thoughts of Marree far away under the bright staring eye of the New Mexico sun.

Almost every evening, for a month after Sumwong's death, I walked out into the yard to look at his canoe. I saw the compound dry a tiny bit more each day, then become harder and harder as it set for good into the cracks and slits between the wood.

Neither Father nor I wished to move the boat, much less try it out on the water. To do so, of course, would be to disturb something precious to Sumwong and to us. It may be that it will have to sit out here for good, a sort of monument to his life; or until it rots, a mute reflection of his dreams.

When I was alone with the boat, I said over and over to it, with tears in my eyes, "You are so beautiful, you are so beautiful." As a boat, it was not beautiful at all; as what was left of Sumwong, the vessel of his soul, so to speak, it was surpassingly so.

Sometimes Father would come up behind me and say, "Your supper is ready, Wanwadee."

And: "Please don't cry."

Then I would see the tears in his own eyes, before he was able to turn away. It was the only time I would ever see him cry—near Sumwong's canoe, so imperfect a copy of his own.

Blowing his nose, he would say something like "Dreamers, both of you," and I would follow his slow steps into the house. It was frightening to see how old and bent he had become just since the death of his only son.

It surprised me and shocked my family to find out how soon I was to resurrect my own dream, the very one that had preoccupied me from time to time over the past few years.

The same one as Sumwong's: going to America.

At first I was afraid to mention it aloud to anyone but Buddha. Alone on my pallet, I prayed each night for the strength to do something with my life. I thought of Sumwong, naturally; and of Suwad and the not-unwanted ruination of our wedding plans; and of Marree, educated Marree, American Marree of the mountains and the desert.

One evening I was called to supper. The days were slightly longer now, and hotter, so that the evening was purple with steamy savannah warmth.

Mom looked at me. To her I had become somewhat of a problem—what to do with a daughter of twenty-two, good-looking but without current prospects. I was not certain, but around town I might have picked up the aura of a jinx; Sumwong died, after all, practically in my arms—and shot by my intended!

"Look, Wanwadee, I have made *gang gai.*"

It was a hot spice-and-chicken dish, my favorite; yet I picked away at it but could not finish.

"Eat," she admonished. "You are losing too much weight. No man wants a bag of bones."

"I don't care about that."

"What do you care about, girl?" my father asked.

Opportunity dropped upon my plate. After a long moment's consideration, I spoke: "I want to go to America. Like Marree."

Dad choked on his chicken, cleared his throat, and asked whether I knew what I was talking about. Mom looked scared and confused. This was more of a bombshell than I thought, but I was glad to have gotten it out, at last.

"What is left for me here? In America I could be educated."

"I have no money for that. I have money for your wedding and your needs, but not enough to send you to the United States for an education. Do you think I am a prince?"

Mom chimed in: "I hope you are not serious about this."

"I am, Mom. I want to go as Marree went."

"Which is . . . ?" Mom asked, voice quavering.

"For you to make arrangements for me to marry an American."

"Never!" Dad said. "We have had enough trouble. Do you want to bring disgrace upon bad fortune?"

"That is not what I want at all. I want a future."

"It is out of the question. Everyone knows me here. Where am I going to hide my face?"

"Where can I hide my own, now?"

CONFESSIONS OF A MAIL ORDER BRIDE

"It is not the same for a girl."

"But, Dad," I pleaded through his blind side, "it is not so different from my marrying Suwad. I never loved him at all. This is at least a chance for—for something better."

"It was different with Suwad. At least we know his family."

"Yes, and look what they have done to me and *my* family."

They said nothing, so I put down my napkin and left the room. I had barely touched the *gang gai.*

Weeks of silence went by before the subject came up again. During that time, while my former fiancé was temporarily incarcerated, the charge of murder was reduced to manslaughter. Then, with another hefty payment to the authorities, it is dropped altogether under plea of self-defense (even though my brother was unarmed). Now my only reservation over getting out of Thailand by becoming a mail order bride was having to leave my family. For with Sumwong dead and my hometown tainted, the decision was easier to make. My departure would also help heal a very serious wound between prominent small-town families, so in a sense I would be a sacrificial lamb as well.

Then one night just before Dad got home, Mom told me that she had spoken with Veena and had found out the good side of such marital arrangements—that they can and do work out. American men, America itself—the unknown variables—are not as formidable as they might seem.

The bad side of such arrangements is primarily logistical: the right ones cost a lot of money. Father would see it this way.

"But not any more than he would pay for my wedding here," I insisted. "Not a whole lot more, anyway."

"Maybe not. But there is another bad thing."

THE FLOW OF THE CHAO PHRAYA

"What is that?"

"Why, that you will be so far away. Haven't you considered that, daughter?"

"Of course I have. My answer is that . . . maybe I want to be far away. Not from you, but from—from everything else."

Her brow wrinkled, and I noticed again how much older she too seemed now that Sumwong was dead. "I understand what you mean. You have thought about this a lot? It is not something foolish that comes from being young?"

"I have thought of it for many nights."

"I will speak to your father. We will at least look into it." She put both arms around me and held me very tight. "Please give it much thought, my dear."

From my pallet that night I heard them talking it over. Although I didn't catch everything, I made out enough to understand that Dad was having a hard time accepting it, of course, but Mom, sweet Mom, always on her kids' side, was emphasizing the good points. Luckily, her voice rose just a bit when she pointed out that there was not much left for me in Nakhon Narai, and there was much that Marree had found in America.

I heard *that* clearly.

Less clearly, I thought I heard my father eventually agree to look into it. It was hard to make out exactly what he said because his voice lowered in what he must be interpreting as a defeat for him.

For that and a dozen other reasons, it was a victory for me—a victory of sorts, at least.

A week later I asked Mom whether Dad had checked into the marital service. She said that he had been very busy with work, including a three-day stay in Bangkok to supervise the pouring of the foundation of a major construction, the largest new hotel in Thailand. But he knew what my wishes were.

She managed to add—and it was not the first time I had heard it—"I still do not think it is a good idea for you to go to America. It is too dangerous. We may never hear from you again—and then what?"

"Please, Mom," I answered as usual, speaking to her as well as to my own fears. "It will be okay."

"You know I want you to be happy, but this is not the way to go about it. There are still many fine young men in—"

"Please!"

If I made any kind of strong protest like this, she grew quiet. I did not want to hurt her feelings, but I did not wish to see anyone else—not here, not until Dad let me know one way or another.

I was aware that mistakes could be made—serious ones. Yet no potential mistake seemed as serious as remaining here without prospects, without love.

Mom retreated to the kitchen to peel mangoes. I wanted badly to tell her how much I loved her, but nothing must soften my resolve to leave if the opportunity came, especially her pleading. To ease her mind I sang a little Thai country song, her favorite, just loud enough for it to carry into the kitchen.

Walking to where I could see her back, bent over the table as she was, I thought of the type of wife she had been to my father, sweet and responsive, while he had been relatively cold and brusque. Although I had never given the matter much thought in my brief term as an adult, it struck me suddenly, here and now, as unfair.

She was a woman, and in Thailand the lesser for it. How common and yet how outrageous that seemed!

Vexed by my thoughts I almost went into the kitchen to voice my displeasure, but then I recalled how she had somehow gotten her way virtually every time there had been a split in the family, as in Veena's choice of a husband (a teacher with little money) and the addition of a special room for fine furniture and family photographs—an American-style living room.

All this, without ever visibly pushing hard or fighting him.

Not too long ago, I asked Mom about this paradox, and she gave me a proverb—*Nam ron plah pen nam yen plah tai* (Fish will survive if the water changes slowly). At the time, I did not quite understand how it related.

Now I did, as I also grasped what she had meant when she said that you do not have to lead a man or even let him know who is boss, in order to be boss. Men are like cats on their feet. Push down on them, and see how their backs tense and their stance rigidifies. If instead you stroke, the entire back "gives" and the cat feels your love. When it comes time to be petted, the cat will want more of the stroking, not the pushing.

Flies and honey, flies and gall.

Mom was like that: when she wanted you to truly understand something, she phrased it as an anecdote or proverb. And you understood it, if not literally, then even more profoundly—in the blood, so to speak.

It was difficult for me to say that I was a typical Thai woman—perhaps I am still too young to be typical anything—but my mother certainly was. To her, a liberated female in the Western sense makes a dozen mistakes and creates a dozen hardships to correct one perceived injustice; and the atmosphere thus created is unhealthy.

They score their points but they lose the game.

But then, she had never lived in the United States, never had to adjust to *that* drastically changed water.

In the evening Dad came home an hour early; we heard the huge gate unlock and his new truck ascend the driveway.

Then the footsteps went back down and the massive lock clanged. My two pet chickens squawked and scattered.

"Wanwadee, get your father a glass of cold water."

I ran to the kitchen and filled a glass with water and six ice cubes from the new refrigerator.

When he entered the main room, my heart sank: a scowl was locked onto his face like an iron mask.

He sat across the room from Mom and me without a word, staring at his briefcase. He did not touch the water. Finally he opened the briefcase and said, more to himself than to either of us, "It is a mistake, in my opinion—a terrible mistake."

"What is, Dad?" I asked, my voice shaking. I knew what.

He reached for the glass and took a long drink.

Clearing his throat, he took a sheaf of papers out of the briefcase and spoke in a voice hardly any stronger than mine:

"This is what I could find out from and about Mr. Phat of Bangkok. It is all here in these papers."

He handed them to me. Quickly I scanned their contents.

Mr. Phat's (pronounced *fot*) credentials seemed impugnable. He was said to allow no riffraff whatsoever—on either side of the ocean. His agent Wu, for Nakhon Narai and surrounding regions, was a remote friend of the family, a professional investor with fingers in ten dozen pies. Both men are part Chinese.

The total cost, including transportation, is over 100,000 baht ($5,000) for a Westerner, American, Canadian, or European. Asian families—and the entire family of the prospective bride was expected to be consulted—also had to make a commitment of many hundreds of dollars. With it came the guarantee to both parties that they would be corresponding with potential partners of some substance.

THE FLOW OF THE CHAO PHRAYA

"Oh, Dad, you spoke with him and told him I want to do it?" I looked at Mom but her eyes were down.

"Yes, I did, and he seems an honest man. All the families that he deals with are of the better class. There are not many who use his service because it is so selective and expensive. But the ones who do are satisfied. I know this because I spoke also with business people and even the Prefect of Police."

"Thank you, Father," I said, and I knelt before him.

He patted my head and sent me back to my chair. My mother still had said nothing.

"I have also spoken with Wu, his agent here in town. He vouches equally well for the Americans and Canadians on his list—these are all first-class gentlemen. The matter can be arranged fairly smoothly after you study these papers and make a few decisions. We will have to see Wu first and go to Bangkok next week or the week after."

He paused: "Understand, daughter, that all of this does not have my approval. I think it is a mistake for you to go to America to meet and marry a stranger—I don't care what kind of guarantee there is."

"It will not be a mis—"

"Be still and listen! That's the trouble with kids, they never listen. The money to pay Phat is your ungiven gift to Suwad's family—as if they ever needed it. All your other expenses will be covered by Phat through the contract. When you get to America, you will be virtually on your own. Do you understand, my child?"

My mother spoke: "Oh, but she can come home when she wants. Of course you can, my dear. For whatever reason."

Ignoring her, Dad repeated, "Do you understand?"

"Yes, Father, I understand."

He took another long drink of water and leaned forward to look at me directly. "Wanwadee, I do this only because I love you. I know you are at the lowest point in your life, and I must help to bring you back up. I know also that, on all the days I was not here for you, your beloved brother helped to raise you, almost since you were a baby. I am not surprised to see how his death has devastated you."

At the mention of Sumwong, his eyes grew watery again. "It has hurt all of us," Mom said.

"Just one thing more, my girl."

I listened.

"I am sorry that your life is not satisfactory here any-more. But your mother is right. You are welcome back at any time, for any reason."

How it touched my heart to see how much they will miss me! And yet I knew without the shadow of a doubt that I must go, and that I might not ever be back. I was twenty-two years old, and time was no more likely to stand still for me than for anyone else. I took a deep breath and refused absolutely to cry, at least not until I was on the plane out of Bangkok.

It had to be that way for me—and for them.

"Thank you both," I said. I kissed them both, then left the room and did not look back, thinking *all will be well.*

All will be well, echoed an unfamiliar, tiny, yet ever changing, ever-stronger voice within me.

A month later I went to Bangkok with my father to meet with Mr. Phat. He turned out to be a thin, old, shifty-eyed man; so I was glad my father and others, including the respected Prefect had reassured me that he was a known and a reliable quantity.

In his office, I was allowed to browse the neatly-bound folders of six or seven recommended applicants and to see pass-port-type photographs of them sent to Mr. Phat by various American contacts.

I chose the best looking of the group. His name is Rich-ard.

THE FLOW OF THE CHAO PHRAYA

The papers gave no physical facts except height (6'2"—I am exactly a foot shorter) and weight (190 lbs.—I am eighty pounds lighter). I felt slight misgivings at that moment, basically a fear of being smothered, but it passed as I studied the picture of an intelligent, handsome face with a smile that in its genuineness seemed enchanting. The eyes were as clear as pools and, according to the information, green in color; I tried to imagine green eyes, never before having seen anything other than brown and blue (very few at that) Western eyes.

I continued to read the curt but (to me) engrossing translations of comments and biography: an active, accomplished man, I was assured; a voracious reader; exercise advocate; computer hobbyist; steady wage-earner—words to that effect. And those years of study and planning resulted in a Master of Science degree. Looked at in retrospect, the packet of papers before me fairly crackled with *can-do.*

There was more: middle child in a family of three, he had been raised by a mother widowed since 1945, the year his decorated father, a Navy pilot and gunnery officer, was killed in action (shot down, I would learn later, over the South China Sea—the very sea the Chao Phraya empties into). His older brother George was a physician, younger sister Barbara (born after the death of her father) married to one.

Among the "official" reasons Richard listed himself as seeking an Oriental bride was that he desired a more traditional marriage than he might be able to have with an American female. Not that he resented or could not cope with American women. He simply had not been able to find what he was looking for.

I was told by Mr. Phat, moreover, that this reason was offered by virtually 100% of his American and Canadian candidates. The percentage of single American men who at least *think* about arranged marriages—brides by mail, in particular—

by responding to an ad was estimated in 1986 at one eligible male in 20,000.

Of that number, according to Phat's documents, less than 10% ever bring a contract to serious negotiating stages, as has Richard. Select, misinformed, or desperate—which word characterized the majority of that number? Which word characterized *him?*

Several times Phat assured us that Richard was the cream of a mediocre crop. He was more "like they used to be" —handsome, still reasonably young, employed in the professions. But perhaps that was just his sales pitch, I thought, and then discarded the negative thought.

I did have something going for me at the moment; a quiet sort of resolve. It had always seemed to me to be a prime characteristic of Thai women entering a relationship. Thais prefer never to contest their partners, or vie in the slightest for dominance, or engage in any battles of the ego. To them, that approach is as much a mistake as trying to physically out-muscle a man. Either you or the relationship loses, ultimately.

They accept, rather, a subdued and subordinate role, but one with very stringent conditions. Their major resolution is that the man to whom they give their deepest love and loyalty must prove himself worthy of it: he must be strong, kind, decisive—in general, right-headed. If they—we—choose wrong, or cannot *eventually* (we are nothing if not patient) elicit that desired response, we give up and bide our time, divorcing usually, defecting at any rate, waiting for the opportunity to offer the best we have to someone able to reciprocate in kind.

If we do find the right (or lucky) combination, we give that love and loyalty with everything we have in order to make the bond a good and lasting one. Usually it works. Patience-born, the relationship endures, flourishes. Surviving those rigorous conditions, like a desert perennial, a Century plant, the love can last—well, a century, if life would permit.

THE FLOW OF THE CHAO PHRAYA

So Thai women believe, and so they carry forth on that belief. Perhaps it is not so very different from what Americans believe, deep down.

I continued to read the brief, cleanly-typed comments and biography—excellent Phat with his excellent documents—in English and Thai.

This is why they can pay Phat so much, I thought.

So ambitious, these American and Canadians; so well-rounded. Most Thai men tend to do or to be one thing only in life: fishermen, rice middlemen, engineers, kickboxers, bar owners, whatever. They don't expand with time—the opposite, in fact. They shrink, more or less, into the roles that life offers them, rather than stretching themselves, reaching out for more.

Or perhaps it was opportunity, in so crowded an custom-bound a land, that shrunk before them.

Conversely, this packet of papers about Richard fairly crackled with American *can-do.*

The folder went on to say that, although he was a native New Yorker, he lived now in the city of Atlanta, in the "Southern Sunbelt" (those words were in English) where he was an instructor at an urban university. His specialty was "applications software and technical communication"—English phrases again which at the time meant as little to me if they had been in Thai.

On our second visit to Bangkok before signing the final papers, but *after* my father had paid the $250 (by bank-certified check, *if you please*), I was allowed to read the full dossier of my intended and to see three photographs of him supplied by the American contact. The papers revealed one new fact, somewhat disconcerting at this late stage: that Richard had been married previously, for eight years to an American woman. At this point there was nothing I could do, no protest I could raise, except to be grateful that the marriage had been childless.

CONFESSIONS OF A MAIL ORDER BRIDE

I sighed. Later that night, I wrote in my diary: "It will work out, by the grace of the Lord Buddha."

A month afterward Mr. Phat phoned my Nakhon Narai home from Bangkok and told my parents first, then me, that I had been selected; now precise arrangements would need to be made.

Thus it was that I was to wed an American teacher ten years my senior, a man reasonably well-off and highly recommended both as a provider and a person by Phat's American contact.

Prepaid trip tickets and an accommodation voucher through to New York were waiting for us in Bangkok. We must come as soon as possible—and don't forget the additional $250 due by contract, in certified check if you please. Phat was a shrewd businessman, manipulative and insistent. Later I was to learn that he had already collected his $1500 fee from the American side—$2000 altogether for the mail-handled matchmaking.

My father went to the bank that afternoon, and I retired to my room to cry again for my brother Sumwong, whose death had initiated the chain of events leading me to depart my family and homeland.

In the intervening weeks, I corresponded with the man whose folder I had picked out, a man by the given name of Richard, a teacher (*oh, no, not another,* Father groaned) and a resident of the Southern U.S. city of Atlanta. By airmail we exchanged six letters, three from each side. With my second letter I sent photos of myself, and the return letter came in only five days, also with photos.

This was not the first time I had seen him—a passport-type photo was in his folder—but they showed a youngish, handsome man with pure Western features. In one he was wearing eyeglasses and seated at a computer terminal. In another, he had a baseball bat in his hands; although he was fairly slender, his shoulders were broad and his arms, like Sumwong's, sinewed with muscle.

With the help of my old preparatory school English teacher, Mr. Tong Shai, I described myself and my family to Richard, and told him some of the dreams and goals that I had. Mr. Shai also helped me translate the return letters and agreed to give me two hours' conversation instruction each weekday afternoon.

There was also one short telephone call from Richard that did not go particularly well, ending up with Mr. Shai doing most of the asking and answering for me. At least I got to hear his voice—and I liked it. It was smooth and friendly-sounding.

To judge from his carefully worded letters about himself and his life in America, Richard seemed to be exactly the type of person I would like to meet: professional, accomplished, and, of course, good-looking.

But to *marry?*

That was an entirely different question. The more I thought about it, now that my dream of America took on the name and face of a future *husband,* the more scared and doubt-ridden I became. So I decided to do an about-face and not think about it at all any more, except for the many logistical details of completing the arrangements. Like jumping off a diving board into an unknown lake, it was a chance that I would simply have to take when the time came.

Yet I knew, too, that when the time came I would have prepared myself to take it. I had done and would do my best at everything. And, all along, I had been prepared as well by fate, doing very nearly its worst at everything.

I kept very busy, and the weeks passed so quickly that I wound up with precious little time to think about anything. Once my father signed the papers and paid the money, it was a *fait accompli* anyway, and there was little else I could do. To turn tail, back out, and waste 6,000 up-front *baht* was out of the question.

I would not permit myself even a passing thought of that potential disgrace. It is on to America . . . or *nothing*.

It would be totally unwise, however, if I did not arrange for a way out just in case the whole thing turned out to be a disaster. With the not entirely unselfish help of my mother (I knew that she pictured me coming back, Buddha bless her), I sewed into the lining of my carry-on suitcase—it was never to leave my sight—a thin little packet of jewelry and cash. It was just enough with which to bail myself out—to buy a return-flight ticket.

Somehow I had a feeling that I would not need it—the spirit of Sumwong seemed to be telling me so—but it was nice to have it there just in case.

On the day before the flight, July 2, the temperature was still close to one hundred degrees at seven o'clock. Every fan in the house was on. Mom was in the kitchen washing dishes while Dad and Veena and some other relatives (who had come over to bid me farewell) were watching "The Beverly Hillbillies" dubbed in Thai. They were laughing a lot, which made me feel good. It made me feel good to thank Veena, earlier in the day, for setting up this option for me to begin with.

The closer the time came, too, the more optimistic I became. For that I thank Sumwong. Even in death he continued to be what he was in life for me, a guiding spirit.

Thinking of him, I left the house and walked out in the yard in the shimmering twilight haze. The aroma of *banyan* and savannah filled the air, as thick, almost, as smoke. Trucks ground by beyond the thick ferro-concrete wall Dad designed and had built several years ago, and little tan *nokrajog* birds traced the air over the garden.

I walked to the end of the yard to the two canoes propped up on frames, clear of the ground. Dad's was so sleek and perfect it commanded the sense of sight. Yet I could not help but look past it to Sumwong's boat, flawed, uneven, the chink-compound split by dry-spell summer heat into dozens, hundreds of interconnected hairline cracks like the zigzag trail of some tiny creature crazed by heat and thirst.

All of a sudden I was overtaken by an impulse to try the boat out, to set myself in it in the main flow of the Chao Phraya River and let the current carry me where it wanted. How sweet it would be to trail my hand in the water as I was swept downstream toward some place I had never heard of or even imagined existed.

Foolish thought, fit more for a romantic novel than for real life. There was no time, no reason, no *excuse* for such a dream—not even as a daydream.

But I allowed myself the luxury of keeping it for another few minutes, picturing new and unknown waters coming up ever wider and ever more placid than any I have known, an Indian Ocean of the mind that opens out onto broad blue swells as we leave the land far behind, I and my miraculously fine and sturdy canoe.

I allowed myself to have the thought, the dream, because I might never have such a one again.

And so, quickly, for time is short: tawny islands, all beach and soaring palms . . . sunlight and shadow and sunlight again . . . long azure waves beyond the reefs . . . and always my infallible *reurbod*, chinked and flawed but uncannily seaworthy, buoying me up as I drift on the swells and rise and fall and drift some more . . .

"Wanwaaaadee," my mother called, the same voice and intonation that she had used for as far back as memory goes. "Wanwaaaadee."

Just as I thought: hardly time to complete the trip before I had to go in and finish packing for another.

I took the time to run my fingers over the varnished

boards of the canoe, surprisingly rough to the touch because, in contrast to Dad's, they had been incompletely sanded. Then I stood back to take a final look at it.

Would I ever see it again?

I looked around the yard—the papaya tree, the small coop for my pet chickens, the battered old truck, and our beautifully matured bamboo stands—and beyond the yard to the fields and the fruit orchards and the water buffalos standing as still as statues in the gathering dark. Would it all still be here if —if I ever came back?

"Wanwaaaadee!" Same call, only somewhat more urgent, full of worry, as always, as if I might disappear into one of my childhood games, never to be seen again.

The next day I left for *Don Meung*, Bangkok's International Airport.

3

IN TRANSIT

July 1976

The flight from Bangkok to Tokyo to Honolulu to Dallas is a draining one: sixteen hours not counting stopovers. I begin to think of the seat as a permanent part of my derrière.

At Honolulu, I present the ultimate document procured from Phat's service: my signed marriage contract, airmailed to Richard and countersigned and returned by him, sanctioning (and, in fact, *legalizing*) our inter-country marriage agreement. Exhibited and explained in my halting English, this piece of paper somewhat miraculously obtains for me a Green Card, after a long wait, and permits my residence in the United States as the spouse of an American.

To have this done boosts my spirits, but so much of the trip remains that the relief is momentary.

During much of the rest of the flight to Dallas I am

41

wrapped in the sheltering cocoon of myself. I am remotely aware of the chattering Japanese salesmen beside me as I scan the mostly desert landscape below. After 200 years, it is as featureless and undeveloped as my future in this new country is, with a new life and a new husband waiting for me beyond the cusp of the mountainous horizons.

Dozing on and off during that flight as I read, I dream of and remember Sumwong and family and friends in a small Thai city half a world away: tears, smiles, the carefully woven bouquet of mixed flowers, symbol of enduring ties, that had already wilted by the time of our touchdown on United States soil in Hawaii—dreams and memories, memories and dreams, braided together like the flowers in my hand until at long last I hear a voice finishing in English almost as accented as my own ". . . landing in Dallas in ten minutes. Happy July 4th."

I lean over and look out the window to see that the gray stone mountains and red desert have given way to a vast and darkening plain that seems, from 10,000 feet as the plane descends, already infinitely larger than Thailand would ever be to me again. The plane swings round and Dallas comes into view, jeweled with evening lights, a miracle of concrete and power, steel and vertigo, threaded by sleek streams of late holiday traffic.

We circle a few more times as fireworks erupt over a bright stadium, color out of light, and finally land in the dark at 9:45 p.m. I bid farewell silently to the last Thais I would see for many days and go out into the bustling airport, searching for ground transportation to the Holiday Inn, at which I have been provided a voucher for one night's accommodation (and food, of course) by Phat's service.

The sight of all those Americans in one place at one time is overwhelming. Of course, by then I had seen my share of Western missionaries, tourists and U.S. Army personnel on leave, but in the past it had always been a case of one at a time, or in small groups at most.

Now here in the wide airport halls I feel nearly drowned in a sea of large, multicolored—the hair, the eyes—hurrying people to whom I am probably just a tiny tawny blur. Americans! So many! So different! Why, they even *smell* different—not at all like sweat and Burmese-tobacco smoke. A crowd whirls around me, using that tongue that I could read now but had been trying *so hard* to speak and understand that . . .

My head spins. The thought that Richard might not be waiting for me at my final destination gnaws at me. Pausing by a newsstand, I take a deep breath and scan the slickly colored magazines.

In one of the magazines I find, coincidentally, an article about arranged marriages. There was much I knew and much I did not. I simply could not figure out the English. But the article is interesting—striking close to home—and eats up a couple of otherwise dead hours.

Steadier, I find myself growing hungry in the Dallas airport.

On more than one occasion, when I will eventually recount to American friends this portion of "how I bowed my head and came to America as a mail order bride," I will get sympathy on the one hand, of course; on the other, I will be told what a great plot for a novel the story would make. But another lesson I will have reinforced in America is that life and romance are two entirely different things. They meet only at points where the profoundest love and the wackiest luck intersect.

A rare (but not impossible) occurrence.

I rise and lift my carry-on bag back over my shoulder.

Quite hungry now, I pause at an airport snack stand in

Dallas, Texas, USA, and buy a reasonable facsimile of an Oriental spring roll. Eating it quickly so as to move along to the courtesy vans, I drop the waxed paper wrapper into a trash can. Along with the wrapper go what is left of the flowers.

4

TOUCHDOWN

New York 1976

At eight-thirty the next morning, July 5, I shrug away a dream of rice fields and temple gold to find a steaming cup of coffee before me and the sunlit Mississippi River far below, a thick brown belt of water looping along between irregular sets of farms that are to Thai plots, in size, what my 727 is to a duck hawk. The dark brown and green rectangles of earth grow I can't imagine what, since it would take an army of laborers to tend them properly. The river itself is properly majestic.

I recall reading in a classroom many years ago of the mechanized means of agriculture that is the rule in America rather than the exception that it is in Thailand. Looking more carefully, I do indeed see what must be immense farm vehicles crawling slowly over the dry summer earth like shiny, slow leviathans. Dust billows behind them, barely visible.

Recalling more of that tenth-level prep class (preparatory to a local business school I hoped to attend) where we read often of America, I remember how the States were settled westward, generally, from the Atlantic Ocean to mountainous West. It occurs to me that I am moving through a paradox at 30,000 feet, drifting eastward, rather than west, toward an America at 500 m.p.h. which is gradually becoming mine. It is a pleasant thought, flowing through my drowsiness like the American Chao Phraya below.

The land grows denser, thicker with cities, as we fly over what I imagine is eastern Ohio or western Pennsylvania. On my lap I have an airline-magazine map of the United States, criss-crossed with air routes that look like the package cabling of a gift for me, a present whose value is implicit in its well-known shape but whose price I have no way yet of fully gauging. Backward we proceed over the American landscape, forward into my as yet unimaginable American life.

I read, doze off, wake up and read, doze off and wake up to glance at the wristwatch of the American man seated next to me: well past ten o'clock.

Richard, are you on your way to JFK?

The man tries several times to start a conversation about "these damn early-bird flights," as I try to cooperate over a sprawling, hilly city that perhaps is Pittsburgh. He has a pleasant enough voice, but he has (to me) an unidentifiable accent, and I can make out only every other word or so, not enough to sustain rational conversation. He probably gets even less than that from *my* accented speech, so we settle for exchanges of smiles as Cokes, then croissant sandwiches, are served.

We are already in descent through a crowded metropolitan sky. The plane turns left hard and over my shoulder New York appears, looking exactly like so many of the photographs of it that I have seen. Few Americans can guess that New York is usually pictured at great distances in foreign travel and textbooks, and almost always the Manhattan part—many times from the same general angles, such as the angle I am seeing now: from the Hudson River side, with the twin towers on the right, the Empire State Building in the middle, and the George Washington Bridge on the left.

So I remember it from one or two of my prep-school books.

The only thing "out of place" are the dozen tall ships, sails reeled in, distinct, bizarre even, as they sit along the dull green row of docks like thoroughbreds in a dingy and demeaning stable. The plane stays in that attitude for a remarkably long time as it descends, engines whining, and I wonder in my naivete whether every approach to New York is done in this manner so as to satisfy the tourists from Tokyo, Timbuktu, and Thailand.

The people glued to their windows as I am must surely think so.

We swing back right again and when next I see the buildings we are directly over them, their alternating blockish and spired tops thrusting at us like the hump of some beast whose size is exceeded only by its strength in the world's imagination.

New York.

I will learn much about it in the first two months I spend in America. But first there is the immediate future to confront—a landing, a meeting, a wedding (a wedding!), a life to begin again.

Off and on I remember, among other things, the American movie *High Noon*. Gary Cooper and John Wayne were popular for many years in Thailand. I picture myself in it, not as the bride, but as Cooper himself facing the "showdown" at high noon. Maybe that is why I am so curious about exactly what time it is. Confrontation coming up . . . dusty streets, no one around to help.

CONFESSIONS OF A MAIL ORDER BRIDE

Silly. I shut my eyes and listen instead to the hushed roar of the engines.

I pick up my *Newsweek* magazine to distract myself from the trauma of landing. The whole idea of jet flight is still a fathomless mystery, and on this transatlantic flight I am alternately thrilled and scared. Right now I am *scared*. I concentrate on an article about Presidential candidates for the upcoming U.S. elections.

Mondale and Carter are identified as leaders in the polls, and I cannot help but be struck by the frank honesty of their faces. They have none of the guile or world-weariness that one sees on the faces of people like the Filipino Marcos, for instance, or almost any local Thai politician. These seem like two men who care about more than just the power and the access to wealth that goes with high office.

In a darkly curious twist of thought it seems to me, then, that Americans evidently refuse to admit to themselves, in their lack of cultural maturity (being only so far along in the cycle of civilization), that corruption, that evil itself in all its ugly variations, actually exists; or, if it does, that it cannot be mocked with a healthy Howdy-Doody smile, like Carter's, or a frank, open-eyed, Middle-American stare, like Mondale's.

Moreover, evil may actually be only a temporary state that one enters in order to get something done—like making love or earning money, for example. When one re-emerges with pockets full or ego gratified, all is forgiven, forgotten, sane again in the Land of the Founding Fathers.

You can shake hands with demons in the U.S.A., but you need never call them friends, not where the sun always shines and success comes to all those who can do. In ancient, sullied Thailand, there are no precise analogues to this situation.

So it seems to me in Bicentennial 1976.

Stewardesses walk the aisle. People hush and grow still.

TOUCHDOWN

Landing coming up. 11:15 a.m. I close my eyes. Spirit of Gary Cooper, be with me.

The plane descends eastward over the Hudson River. I see a dozen or so of the tall ships visiting for the Holiday, furled and resting at anchor in their slips like proud, tired ladies after a ball. As with much in my native Thailand, they are at once anachronistic and symbolic, and therefore fit for occasions so grand and so inexplicable to the rational mind. On major holidays, the Thai royal family glides down the Bangkok portion of Chao Phraya River in a gilded barge so antiquated and ornate it looks as if it materialized at a stroke from thirteenth-century Siam.

Even though I have missed the world's largest birthday party, the spirit of the 200th Fourth of July is with me. I am quietly celebrating a birth too—a re-birth to be exact—my own as an American.

The plane touches down with the sharp rubbery thump that is becoming familiar if no less frightening to me, and the equally familiar roar of reversed jet engines as we slow to a crawl in the Bangkok-like haze of a noontide July 5 in New York.

5

HIGH NOON

New York 1976

As I descend the ramp into the airport my legs begin trembling. I tell myself that the cause is muscle fatigue from all those hours cramped aboard the plane, but my nerves do not believe a word of it.

Tum jai yen-yen, I tell myself: be calm.

The line in front of me disperses into the huge terminal. Emerging, I am tempted to glance around for a wall clock to confirm my suspicion that it is only minutes before high noon.

But I search the crowd instead, the sea of faces for one face that will be familiar or at least searching for *me*. Seconds pass, each one squeezing my breaths a little tighter. Is there *anyone* for me in this noisy, crowded place? Perhaps there is a mistake somewhere, a missed connection along the line?

Perhaps the whole thing has been a mistake from the start, and like a scared and confused child I have fled my family and homeland to a country full of strangers who no more care what happens to me here half a world away than if I were a stuffed doll in shipment. I think of the bag on the floor beside me, the money and jewels hidden there—the woeful process of buying return tickets . . .

At the very moment that my despair peaks and I am beginning to plan my inglorious retreat, the long road back to Nakhon Narai, a hand grasps my elbow gently from behind. "Wanwadee?"

I turn and look up into calm but penetrating green eyes set in a handsome Occidental face, familiar from the photographs, not young but not old either: mature, half-smiling, curious, above all concerned. He has pronounced my name right, accent in the middle.

"Yes," I say, repeating my rehearsed words, "I am Wanwadee. You are Lichard—I'm sorry, Richard?"

"I am Richard," he says, and smiles down at me for one long and magical moment of relief.

Then, in a whirlwind of incomprehensible words he asks me what sounds like *how I am, how the flight has been, am I hungry,* and a lot more that I don't catch, as he bends down to take my carry-on bag, the existence of which I have now totally forgotten. His voice is firm and clear, each word enunciated as only a teacher could; somehow that is as I have been imagining or hoping.

He is dressed casually but neatly, tan slacks and an olive-green striped shirt; his cordovan shoes are shined to a gloss. He has straight Western features of the "All-American" type Orientals admire in movies—John Wayne, Clint Eastwood— and a head full of brown hair, wavy but absolutely in place as if each strand has been individually attended to. The neck revealed by his open collar is sinewy, strong-looking, like that of an athlete.

HIGH NOON

He seems, in other words, the very image of America—youthful but maturing, clear-eyed, self-assured, fit.

Behind him, watching us closely, is a thickset Korean-looking gentleman in a dark suit. He steps forward, greets me with a stilted "Sawasdi" as he bows with his hands lotus-clasped before him. In basic English, he instructs me to follow him to the baggage claim area. As polite as he tries to be, I notice he is fidgety, anxious, clearly in a hurry. He is Phat's remote New York connection, and this event, so momentous to Richard and me, is for him purely business.

Glancing up at Richard, I smile, and he smiles back his genuine, ingenuous American smile, and we take off after rapid Mr. Lee-Lee through the crosscurrents of a noontime Monday crowd.

When we arrive at the baggage claim there are more than a few minutes to pause and reconnoiter, so Richard and I exchange sidelong glances and a few more smiles. Lee-Lee stands discreetly to one side, still distractedly fidgeting.

"I'm so glad you are here," Richard repeats to fill the void and take the edge off the silence. He looks directly into my eyes, searching me as I suppose I am searching him for some clue to the Greater Meaning of what is happening here, this long-awaited meeting of two total strangers destined for marriage.

Everything seems unreal, dreamlike, and vaguely threatening.

"I am grad to here—uh, glad to be here."

For several reasons, the greatest of which is my fear of further abusing the English language, I do not wish to say much. If there is to be conversation, he will have to carry it for now—this regrettable decision from one who as a schoolgirl was nicknamed Little Pepper and could hardly be shut up.

"Are you very tired?" he asks gently and then, almost as if he has read my thoughts, hurries on without waiting for me to answer. "These past couple of days must have been exhausting for you. We'll get out of here—out of the hot city, that is—as soon as we can. Are you hungry, no? I guess they fed you well on the flights. Boy, it's hot outside. Doesn't feel too bad in here, though. Lee-Lee's got an air-conditioned car. We do need to sign a few papers for him—right here in the airport if that'll be okay. Then we'll be finished with him. We'll get a cab—they're air-conditioned, too. It's very hot outside."

My eyes widen as I try to keep up. I have been nodding and smiling as he speaks, but my expression must have registered alarm. His face softens a bit, abandoning the cool "rational" mode that I will learn he can enter into like a car shifting into overdrive. I have understood enough to know that something is amiss.

"I do have to show him your Green Card and the signed contract for the prospective wedding before he can countersign and leave. The ceremony is scheduled for July 7, Wednesday—just two days away. My mother wanted it at her church, St. Anthony's, Catholic, but for several reasons I disagreed. I got her to understand that you are, ah, not Christian—Buddhist, right?"

I nod.

"Anyway, the wedding will be at her home, performed by a sort of official called a Justice. His office will handle everything from a simple blood test to the last bit of paperwork. All perfectly legal, all quite commonly done. That will be okay?"

"Yes," I say, "it okay. But I already take blood test. Paper is here." He takes it and shows it to Lee-Lee.

"Of course, the immigrant health tests."

"Yes, I have all paper."

"You are sure?"

"I am possible."

"You mean *positive.*"

I nod, slightly ruffled.

HIGH NOON

He smiles, and we lapse into a less comfortable silence, watching the people waiting for their bags but keeping an eye on each other as well.

It is beginning to dawn irrefutably upon me that in forty-eight hours I will actually be married to this tall, Western man beside me—almost a total stranger—and that we will be man and wife.

A mild wave of panic, half-fear, half-excitement, makes my knees buckles. Is this real? Or a dream I am having, in a sleep, on my pallet, in Thailand?

Among middle-to-upper class Thai females pre-marital sex is (or at least has been, through my youth) the exception rather that the rule. One explanation for this pattern of abstinence is logistical: there are simply too few places or opportunities to "fool around" given the omnipresence of relatives and the lack of motels and drive-ins.

A sturdier explanation, though, is tradition; chastity has been the norm among unmarried young ladies for centuries, perhaps millennia, and even in modern Thailand the situation seems unlikely to change very radically. In my own case, as the youngest of three siblings, I was conscientiously overseen by an entire family; furthermore, my father spent some portion of his income on "fortifying" our house with a ferro-concrete fence that he had built as his first daughter was entering her teen years.

At seven o'clock each night, returning from work, he promptly closed and locked the gate to it. (I can still hear its heavy clang, signaling the time like some gigantic, extremely faithful alarm clock.) "Communists," he would mutter, but we knew that he was protecting us from threats more personal and immediate than a political coup.

If thoughts of sexual adventuring had entered my head

at age sixteen or nineteen or even twenty-one (and engaged), in other words, I would have quickly expelled them. I had no real alternative.

Mr. Lee-Lee fusses through his pockets extracting a lone, bent cigarette. He lights it with elaborate care. His hands shake. Perhaps he fears that the deal will fall through at the last minute, that he will not collect his cut? He looks away without speaking, blowing a smoke ring, and I return to my thoughts.

To most Thais, sexual intercourse is a species of sacrament, an experience to be savored as well as to cement relationships, especially (if not exclusively) marital ones. Pornographic materials are thus virtually unheard of in town and village life, not because of legal restrictions but rather the power of tradition. Those who have visited the red-light districts of Bangkok or Pattaya (on the Thai Riviera) might think that I am just "whistling Dixie" for Thailand, but even to prostitutes a client is one for whom the bonding power of sex works as well; thus the special "caring" treatment of those clients, for which Thai callgirls are internationally famous.

Richard speaks: "Wanwadee, you will be staying at my mom's house until the wedding. In fact, we will be there for a couple of months. The city will be our honeymoon until I return to work in early September. I hope you don't mind. It's a big house. Lots of room, and only three people. You'll like it, don't worry, and you'll have your privacy until we are married —you may do as you wish."

He pauses and adds: "I am in the habit of doing as I wish."

It is an odd thing to say, and I will not fully understand what it means until later. At the time I turn the phrase over in my head like fruit at the market to see whether I have understood the simple English or am missing something.

As he has spoken, I have studied his gestures, his face, the earnest, thoughtful way in which he lets each word out,

HIGH NOON

watchful that it comes out the way he wants it to. Later on, when I point the habit out to him, he relates it to the exacting work he does with computers and communication.

It also strikes me as a male-American manner of speaking, one that, again, I will find to be fairly typical. American men wish to hide far more than they reveal when they speak, differing from Thais who rarely hold anything back, whether out of anger, curiosity, joy, whatever; everything seems more intense to them, apparently, and thus is more intensely expressed.

He speaks with an accent that I will come to identify as *New York*, although not really a heavy one. "You'll love Manhattan," he says. "There's so much to see and do—and we have a lot of time. But tell me about your trip. You must be absolutely worn out. How long did it take altogether?"

"Twenty-four hours from Bangkok. One day but seem rike forever."

"Have you slept?" He feigns sleeping, eyes closed, head on shoulder.

"On prane. In airport hotel, some. I am so afraid miss sik-thirty flight this morning."

"So you haven't slept well. I'm so sorry."

"It okay. I how-you-say doze well."

"You speak so well, too."

"Sank you. Could be better."

"That will come, with time. I was worried because Mr. Lee-Lee had nothing on your ability with English."

"I study four year. But it not easy."

"Only one year? The education in Thailand must be excellent."

No one has forewarned him that, like most Asians speaking English, I have an incorrigible tendency to drop the pluralizing *s*. I actually studied English in school for four *years*, not counting tutoring—but I have never conversed with a native English-speaker until this moment.

"And you have completed a college prep course, no? Lee-Lee says that it is the equivalent of a couple of years of college in the States."

"I'm sorry—repeat, prease . . . ?"

He gestures, moving his cupped hands back and forth between us. "Equal to our colleges—your high school, that is."

It is the first of literally thousands of times that he will correct or instruct me, patiently, warmly, in an attitude of caring that I will be happy to return to him in ways, that, from this moment on, I hope the future will open up for me.

The future will.

"Your diploma is equal to, say, a two-year college here."

"That nice. I am grad to know."

"Smart," he says. "And beautiful."

I study him, the half-smile lingering occasionally below his neatly trimmed moustache. He studies back.

"You *are* very pretty."

"Sank you."

I look away; he does not.

"Classic."

"Sank you very much." I am not sure what it means but it sounds complimentary. *Classic.* Hmmm . . .

"Extraordinary, in fact. Perfect."

"Sank you, but—is this game 'Merican play?"

"No, not at all. It's the truth, coming out."

"Ah. We have name for truth come out like that, boy to girl."

"Really? What is it?"

"Translate as *sweet talk.*"

Two tiny red dots appear on his cheeks like sudden daubs of paint. "Funny," he says, shrugging, "we have the same phrase in English."

End of conversation for a while.

In the days to come I will learn that Richard is indeed a practitioner of sweet talk, a mode of inter-sexual speech common in Thailand and intended to keep both speaker and hearer in a loving, "mellow" mood.

Sweet talk is also somehow congruent with his personality, or at least an interesting sort of complement to it, as a piquant fish sauce is to most meat-and-rice dishes. In this respect and in several others, I am to discover, he is a paradox, and luckily, Thais love encountering the paradoxical.

Moreover, it will eventually seem to me typically American to have hidden facets to one's personality; this, as a natural consequence of a lack of enduring communities in the United States. When no one truly belongs to a place, to its streets and people, where there may not even be a "place" for more than a handful of years as neighborhoods are destroyed and rebuilt *ad infinitum,* neither need nor opportunity exists for full disclosure of the self. There is no way, in fact, in which self *can* become fully known or revealed—perhaps even to its owner.

In my home town, a city of perhaps 40,000, with a surrounding-area population three times that, families have been living together for years, decades, centuries even. While relationships are not exactly casual, they are at the very least cordial and out in the open. To some, this condition might seem objectionable, but in the Orient we do not have a strong concept of the ego and of the individual's inalienable right to it.

Rather, we are more like the individual cells in a series of successively larger organisms, the smallest of which is the family and the most comprehensive the nation. We prefer to distinguish ourselves not by being—but by belonging. And we belong not by joining, as is done in the United States, but by simply being. Being in the family, the community—being Siamese.

These broad cultural differences may be one explanation of why we have few, if any, Beethovens in the arts or Einsteins in the sciences, even as they explain why we have no heroic John Waynes at the national level or lowlife John Wayne Gacys (the Chicago boy-killer) at the local.

We wait mostly in silence as we watch the trunks and suitcases glide by on the conveyor belt one after another, some new and fancy, others battered and worn, like accidental and often inaccurate extensions of the people who claim them.

At last mine come through, and Richard grabs them in his strong hands, two large suitcases containing all that I currently possess in the world—mostly clothes, including a simple off-white Western-style wedding dress that my mother and I made from photographs, but also an assortment of gifts given to me in departing. These include the cash and pieces of jewelry given me by my mother to use if things do not work out. By then she was no longer crying because she did not wish to adversely affect my prospect of taking a husband at the superannuated age of 22. She had begun to worry I would never marry.

Like Americans, Thais are essentially a practical people, a similarity which might explain why our political agreements and strategic alliances, from early 19th-century missionary *mob* (combination medical-Christian) activities to today's broad SEATO concordances, have been successful.

Richard walks over to Mr. Lee-Lee, and they speak for a minute; then he returns and we seat ourselves on the nearest vacant bench, side by side by side, and sign a few more papers. I sign first, thinking of the worlds of paper that men put up between themselves and simple good will. Richard signs, then Lee-Lee, both very carefully, as if they are pledging away the world.

In a sense, though, they are. I am, too.

Both rise and shake hands stiffly, like adversaries at a truce, at last; Lee-Lee bows again to me and is gone. That is the last I will ever see of him or hear directly of Phat's service, Buddha bless them well.

When Richard looks my way again, the momentarily dead-serious demeanor drops away like a mask and he broadly smiles. Business is done. His rational self can be shelved for a while. It is easy to see, even then, that he has two distinct and separable sides to his personality—a Dr. Jekyll and Mr. Hide-a-few-things.

Outside in the warm city breeze we hail a taxicab and ride over traffic-clogged highways and across an antiquated cabled bridge toward Manhattan, its many tall buildings spiking a hazed-over sky. It is a fascinating sight, at which a Thai might think, *man squeezed tight and stretching toward the heavens in a most commercial and secular way*—I know my father would. No Emerald Temples here. Commerce, trade, business, finance, money—these hold sway here as nowhere else on earth.

"Chrysler Building," Richard says, nodding toward the largest tower visible at that point, its tapered top lavishly ornamented in stone.

"Handsome," I respond, wondering if I have the right word.

Then we enter the city, hemmed in by the endless buildings, traffic darting everywhere, taxis, trucks, motorbikes, pedestrians, a mad rush of people who all seem to know exactly where they are going in such a breakneck hurry. In one or two parts of Bangkok the streets are hardly less choked with vehicles and people, but on most the pace is more relaxed. People amble and talk, most of them unaware of the exact hour.

Despite their enormous material success, Americans seem not to have found yet the secret of *sanouk*—the Thai word for *joie de vivre*. It may be significant that there is no easy English word for it. This is a thought that I will dwell on for a few moments almost every day of my new life, shopping at a busy, impersonal supermarket; hurtling down a characterless

Interstate highway; eating bland food in a fancy, immaculate restaurant recommended for its "decor."

"Saks Fifth Avenue." Richard nods toward a building with elaborate displays of glitz and clothing behind its enormous ground-floor plate glass windows.

"Expensive, no?"

"Expensive, yes. Some day we'll go in there—and look."

"Even look be nice."

He laughs and takes my hand in his warm hand, and I feel some long-term residual ice in my heart, source indefinable, melt away. Other than my father or brother doing it when I crossed a busy street as a child, it is the first time in my life a male has held my hand. Moreover, it is the first time I have wanted one to.

At last we arrive at an imposing but nondescript brick building, the world's largest bus terminal, and, struggling with luggage, leave the taxi and mount a long escalator for an orange air-conditioned bus to New Jersey. It fumes and crawls through more crowded, steeply-lined streets, then down, down, down and through a tunnel that seems to go on forever.

"Lincoln Tunnel. Very difficult to build," Richard offers—like any good teacher, always willing to instruct. "Goes under the Hudson River for 3.2 miles."

He has taken my hand again and is squeezing it occasionally, betraying a quasi-paternal attitude that I will at times find comforting, and at other times restricting—even though he will rarely try to rein or train me, preferring instead to resort to reason when we have one of our infrequent arguments.

Sometimes I find that tactic more maddening than if he indeed reined, trained, and ranted all at the same time. That is the Thai tiger in me: reluctant to get out but prepared to do so at the drop of an insult. Thai women will do almost anything to avoid an argument; but, once in it, they will stop at almost nothing to win.

Richard seems able to sense that untamable element from the start and will do his best to avoid arousing it, which, appropriately, makes me all the more reluctant to let it out.

"Two billion tons of water over our heads."

"Hope not leak," I joke.

He laughs again. "Hey, you're fun."

I want to tell him that I try to be, that *that* is also the Thai in me: the acceptance of a woman's duty—no, not duty—*birthright*, actually—to be everything to her husband, from laughbringer to loving comforter to restrained source of guidance. We strive to remain sweet but not ineffectually so. It's a complex equation involving flies, honey, gall, and tigers.

But for two reasons I say nothing: one, I honestly do not yet know whether I want to or even *can* be all things to this American man, to *any* man in fact; after all, I have yet to try it out.

Two, I am already testing what it is like to be less Thai and more American, having in a sense crossed my Rubicon, the Mississippi River, and been on American soil for all of thirty hours, counting from touch-down in Honolulu. Although it will never feel quite right to me, it is an interesting option for me to consider, as, for instance, my mother never would have— or could have.

Hearing no response, he squeezes my hand once more and lets it go. As we emerge from the long grimy tunnel, the bus shifts gears and picks up speed, and we roll onto a highway wider than any I have seen—eight lanes, ten, as wide across as a soccer field. The swaggering buildings are gone, there are trees to be seen, and the air seems somewhat brighter.

"Joisey," he says.

"I'm sorry?"

CONFESSIONS OF A MAIL ORDER BRIDE

"This is the New Jersey side. Where we will live for a while."

"At your Mom house. She is nice, yes."

I mean it as an affirmation, not a question, but he looks at me a little strangely. "The best."

"Of course," I hurry to say. "Have to be."

"How is that?"

"Like mother, like son."

"Now who's the sweet-talker? But you know American proverbs?"

"We study some in book. And we have same thing in Thai. Very . . . similar?"

"Yes, similar. Say it for me."

"In Thai?"

"Please."

"Okay . . . it go *meun mah, meun luk.*"

"Beautiful language from a beautiful lady." He is smiling, a twinkle in his eye.

"Sweet talk, *you.*"

His smile broadens. He has good teeth, evenly rowed and as white as polished rice. The bus speeds down the highway, which seems to broaden out even further, like some Lower Chao Phraya of concrete.

My watch says one o'clock: long past high noon.

6

WEDDING PRESENT

New Jersey 1976

Richard's mother is a quiet yet still vivacious woman after thirty years of widowhood—open and generous as well. With no apparent hesitation, she accepts me and the entire unusual situation. For that I am grateful, given some of the forms of racial awareness that I will encounter later on, and I remain faithful to her memory by continuing to light candles for her at Catholic churches wherever I happen to be.

Her spirit is a genuine "old-fashioned" American one, as I perceive that term, and, as with Sumwong's, I wish it never to depart.

Although in later conversations she will claim to be a New Englander, with forebears reaching back to the *Mayflower* (I have no reason to doubt her), when I first see her she is dressed very *New York*, as I will come to understand that term: stiletto heels, tight gray toreador pants and a flamingo red blouse, both of which she wears, amazingly, to the advantage of a sixty-plus-year-old body. Unlike my idea of "widow" derived from the third-world model of bent women in perpetual black, she is a devotee of Frederick's of Hollywood, the *National Enquirer,* and dancing at Roseland, all of which cause her children some discomfort.

I come to see no harm in any of them, as they too will strike me as typically American—for a female of her age, *Mayflower* lineage or not.

At times her behavior borders on the cinematic and comical, as when she puts tango music on an old phonograph and dances, most dramatically, with an imaginary partner whom she calls Raoul. She claims he is from Argentina, which fits the movies that I can recall from Nakhon Narai theaters and our old black-and-white TV.

In any case, she makes me feel welcome to both her country and her home, and she seems delighted that her son is about to be married—remarried—to a woman as petite as herself. She permits me to try on much of her fancy clothing and, when a proper fit is found with pants or blouse, insists that I keep it. For my part, I present her with several rare-wood and jade *objects d'art* which my family has given me specifically for Richard's family.

The largest of these I have myself carved from teakwood. It is a ten-inch Buddha head, which as my first sculpture happens to be an unconscious precursor of my future in art.

She is delighted with them. Seeing the gifts, Richard says to me, "So that's what made the suitcases so heavy!"

"Oh, mush more in there. It all of me."

"I can believe that. Together they weigh as much as you."

"A little more, I think," Richard's mother chimes in.

The house is a big two-story model, well-built, typical (it seems to me) of these particular suburbs, with four bedrooms upstairs and one downstairs. Richard especially loves the big old house, because the one he rents in Atlanta—a woodsy cottage—is about half its size.

I feel ever-so-slightly intimidated by it, because it is the sort of place that Thais consider inhabitable by spirits of the Thai version of Theravada Buddhism. Any large, relatively empty structure is ripe for otherworldly habitation—although I never detect signs of any spirit other than Sumwong's.

None of my countrymen, including myself, doubt the essential reality of the spirit world as a concept of the Beyond; nor do they doubt the essential correctness of Buddhist doctrine as a behavioral guide. There is little conflict between the two as there is in (to draw an extreme comparison) a hitman who kills on a Saturday afternoon, confesses that evening, and is in church the following Sunday morning.

What is religion, after all, but a sort of all-inclusive "packaging" of life and afterlife, the natural and the supernatural, for its adherents? It answers all questions, assigns symbolic values to every physical thing from mountains to whirlwinds, and lets people live in peace with their mortality. What works for any given people is simply what has *come* to work, what has evolved over time to suit their tastes, intellect, and, most importantly, their temperament.

Thus Thailand's religion comes out of the lore of India and the jungles of Indochina.

I am assigned the bedroom next to the vacant one, to maximize my privacy as I adjust to my strange new world. When left alone in it, though, I actually have too much privacy, having spent most of the other twenty-two years of my life in the midst of relatives and friends. Americans surround themselves with extravagant space, probably both to accent their status

CONFESSIONS OF A MAIL ORDER BRIDE

and to emphasize their individuality, but the result to almost any Thai is, simply, loneliness.

At times I am painfully lonely in the big empty house, spending most of my time in the room singing old Thai songs called up from memories already remote and wistful. I also continue reading my collection of American magazines. Thus pass the long hours before the wedding.

I see Richard at meals mostly since he, too, is reading a lot, as he develops materials for his fall courses, and otherwise "taking care of business" in his rational *can-do* mode. He seems intent on giving me my space and, loneliness aside, that is okay with me. In Thailand it is considered bad luck for prospective brides and grooms to see one another shortly before the wedding.

Our wedding ceremony is to be held at four in the afternoon of July 7, a Wednesday. On Tuesday evening I unpack my simple wedding dress from the larger of the two suitcases. That night I dream of boating on the Chao Phraya with Sumwong. The water is miraculously clear but strangely salty, and saltier, and I wake up suddenly with tears in my eyes as I realize that I am not with Sumwong but entirely by myself, and not on a river but in some vast, unknown ocean named America.

Now, it is Wednesday morning, five hours before the ceremony. Richard has gone off to pick up a suit custom-altered for the occasion. I unpack my last few items, including a sewing kit. As I make some last-minute adjustments to the dress, including lace trim at the sleeve ends, I try to imagine what this moment in my life would be like if the argument between a hot-headed, protective older brother and a willful, spoiled fiancé had not resulted in disaster.

But I cannot, my thoughts running headlong once again into lingering sorrow over the loss first of my brother through death, and then of my entire family through dislocation. I have no earthly idea if I will ever see them again—Mother, Father,

WEDDING PRESENT

Veena, all the aunts, uncles, nephews, nieces, cousins, friends. They are as far from me now as the stars in the sky.

Not good thoughts for a wedding day. I lay them quietly to rest, and sew, and sing. Before I know it the clock says 3:30. I hear some rustling around below, then piano music. (Richard has hired someone to play soft music for the event.) The hour is nearly at hand.

At 3:50, as I finish putting on the dress, a muffled knock at the door.

"Yes, prease," I say.

"Are you okay, honey?" Richard's mother whispers through the door.

"Yes, sank you."

"Ready to descend in a few minutes?"

"I'm sorry?" *Descend?*

"Will you come down when the Wedding March starts?" There is a note of apprehension in her voice. She wants everything to go off without a hitch, like all mothers in this situation—her house, her son and daughter-in-law, her prospective grandchildren. The wedding itself is as much hers as it is ours.

"Yes, sank you. I will."

Her footsteps click away down the hall.

The day before, on the piano, Richard's mother played a few notes of that tune, which is to be my cue, as well as rehearsing me on what to say and do. I am at first surprised, then disappointed, then finally relieved (this is America, after all) that there is to be no tying of a sacramental white cord, common to most Thai marriages. It is to be a very simple ceremony: words spoken by an official, our mutual agreement on their content, the slipping of a ring on my finger. There seems no reason for it to be any fancier, given that it is Richard's second marriage and that the circumstances themselves are extraordinary.

With no blood re-test necessary, Richard has seen that the proper papers have been filled out and filed. Everything, at this penultimate moment, is in place except . . . except my heart, which still vacillates uselessly. I tell it to be still, under pain of eternal spinsterhood.

Still uncomfortable with the strangeness of the situation—there has been so little time to adjust to it—I take comfort in the simplicity of the planned ceremony. Marriage for love only occurs infrequently in my native country, so *that* apparent obstacle is of no special concern. It is probably not for Richard either, given that he initiated and has accepted the terms of this arranged marriage.

Yet love seems to have in fact stirred incipiently, a mutual attraction even this early on; fruition will take time, of course, but something is definitely there to build upon.

That is another good reason for a simple ceremony—to symbolize the tentative beginning of what we both hope will be a loving and lasting relationship.

Long eleventh-hour thoughts.

I hold my breath until I hear the opening strains of the March. Then I take a deep one and turn the bedroom doorknob.

Panic! It's *locked!*

But no—no low comedy. No soap opera, no fatuous romantic novel. This is real life.

I recall what in my concern I momentarily forgot: that it was I who locked it, a couple of hours ago, to eliminate the chance of jinx. That is a good sign too—my continual maneuvering for the blessings of the beneficent spirits. Yes, I want this to work out—with the fervor of those who in drought pray for rain. What, after all, are the alternatives?

Taking the brass key from the dresser top, I carefully unlock the door and descend the stairs, legs trembling even more than they did when I deplaned three days ago. When I reach the bottom, I glance around and smile, and, with absolutely no other options at the moment, walk directly to Richard's side, picking my way deliberately through each separate note of the music.

The ensuing wedding, a hushed blur of gestures and words, is over in fifteen minutes. The only people present are the two of us plus Richard's mother, the Justice, the pianist, and several not-so-close relatives who happen to live nearby. Richard has decided not to impose on his brother to come from Florida, nor his sister from Chicago, especially since family reunions are (as they tend to be in America) so difficult to arrange. Everybody's busy.

Piano music has started again; a ring is on my finger; I am actually married (*at last!,* a hovering messenger-spirit of my mother whispers). Splendid in his tailored summer suit, Richard bends over to kiss me, the first time in my life that I have been kissed on the lips. It is short, wet—nice, in fact. But at that moment I start sobbing, not really sure why; to cry also is nice, and similarly wet, and I understand it as an emotional extension of the kiss, a release, like the welcome breaking of a small internal dam.

It has been slowly dawning on me that this moment is, to date, the climax of my life—the *positive* one, at least.

People swirl around wishing us well, and someone brings me a big silver knife to cut the cake, which I do, serving Richard first bite as flashbulbs pop.

Champagne is sipped, jokes made, presents opened as the music swells and the afternoon fades slowly and talkatively into evening. More than one person asks me about Thailand, and Oriental customs, and, of course, the details of this "arranged" marriage. I respond as well as I can, hampered by my English and the limits of propriety. A few of the questions—

including one I do not fully understand about bridal chastity—seem to overstep the line.

But it is all in good humor. And they soothe my ego, whatever there is of it at this point in my life, by calling me the most beautiful bride they have ever seen. I surprise myself with my own gullibility. But perhaps it is the champagne that makes me ready to believe—one cup for me is one too many.

At last, well after seven o'clock, the last guest, an aunt, makes ready to leave, and Richard's mother appears from upstairs with a small suitcase in her hand. It is a surprise to Richard and me.

"Mom?" he says.

"I've been planning to spend a few days with Aunt Rae anyway. This is the perfect time to do it."

"But you don't have to . . ."

"Of course not. I just want to. And Dee wants it too, no?"

I shake my head an American *no* but she winks, and kissing us both, is gone—for what turns out to be a week.

And so we are suddenly alone in the big house, my *husband* and I, with the hall clock ticking loudly through the rooms. Richard smiles and takes me in his arms, kissing me a little longer and with slightly more passion—still careful, considerate of me, always alert to the complexities of the situation. He has accepted unquestioningly that I am a virgin—perhaps all mail order brides are advertised as such—and handles me a bit like jewelry or fine china.

He kisses me again, softly.

Releasing me, he says that he is going to wash up; why don't I switch on the television after I get out of my dress?

I go up to my room, change to a brocaded *kimono* Mom made and, descending again, turn on the TV. I watch the final portion of a program called "Cosmos" as the sound of running water periodically punctuates the silence beyond the screen.

WEDDING PRESENT

Although I can understand only parts of it, the program is more engrossing than anything I can recall seeing on Thai TV, which has been increasingly given over to dubbed movies, many of them of the "choppy-sock" type, and variety shows that are at best amateurish, at worst unintentionally farcical. My father used to complain bitterly about it all—a "vast wasteland," in so many Thai words.

What I see of "Cosmos" lives up to Richard's later description of it as "one of the best things on American television." In Thailand it would win my father's approval—he would watch.

At the moment as the show fades off, a strange but somehow familiar aroma, smoky and sweet, like a faded memory, drifts to my nostrils. At first I do not recognize it, but after a few moments it gets stronger, the room smokier, and the proper associations are made in my brain. I know what it is: marijuana.

Marijuana?

The thought registers in force, my mind doing a double-take, and I rise from the sofa, sniffing more deeply, trying to discern its origin. What can it be? Some neighborhood children outside? I go to several windows and peer out each one in turn: nothing but a man walking his dog in the night.

As I return to my seat I see that a haze of smoke has nearly smothered the room, and the next thing I know Richard is coming downstairs, slowly, carefully, proceeding with a strangely fixed hit of a smile, as though savoring each delicate centimeter of his motion through space.

When he gets close enough, I see that his eyes are no longer green, now, but predominantly red. His face seems florid and puffy, like a large, bizarre *dim sum.*

"Mind if I put out the lamp?"

I say nothing, but can't help shivering. How abrupt!

How different! He does not look the same at all. Suddenly nothing seems the same.

I can do nothing but return his gaze. Stunned silent, I feel shock first, then disorientation, then a smothering sense of disappointment tinged with deep fear, while for the ninth or tenth time—albeit now for a different reason—I ask myself what have I gotten myself into.

What indeed? Halfway around the world for this . . . this deplorable spectacle of a grown man drugged out of his senses?

I try not to let my rising emotions show, but I know that they do. There is no help for that.

I look away from his watery red eyes. This—my American hero? Sour, sour, sour in the mouth, to the eye.

The part of me remaining rational remembers that, *knows* that, in Thailand smoking marijuana is associated with the dirty drug trade, a "business" at least as lowdown as it is in the States. It is severely frowned upon in most areas, and by all classes; moreover, the weight of tradition in a country where high-THC *cannabis* grows everywhere untended has come down heavily against it as, ultimately, a destroyer of lives.

My rational mind is chewing that over as he speaks again.

"I hurt my back in school. The doctor prescribed this and some pills for the pain."

"You have to take much?"

He laughs, a short, unfamiliar bark of a laugh. "Only when I play sports or need to move around a lot."

"And make love?"

He says nothing, shifting uncomfortably, while his eyes refuse to meet mine with any consistency. Perhaps he senses how badly red compares to green as an eye color. The room is charged with both the smoky haze and a silence so loud it blanks out the dialogue on television.

WEDDING PRESENT

After three or four very long minutes, during which my thoughts stretch back into the tunnels of the past and forward into the branching future, I manage to make a decision that works for my head, for now, but not for the rest of me.

This is no longer the wonderful "paper" Richard in front of me; he is smeared now, smudged, almost unrecognizable. But his is still the name on the contract. On *two* contracts, including the one I assented to orally earlier on this very day.

For better or for worse.

Richard has been fumbling with the lamp switch.

Reaching over, I switch it off for him. I have no real choice but to make the best of a bad situation and work afterwards on making it better.

Once more, it is something that *has to be done.*

Richard turns the TV off and gently, almost apologetically, takes my hand. We sit that way for another very long moment. Then I lay my head softly against his chest, and he softly lifts my chin and kisses my lips, lightly at first, then with increasing passion.

This is to be it, then. Strange circumstance upon strange circumstance, an ever-spiraling ascension. Or descent?

The question gets lost, at that moment, in a rising wave of heat. We kiss again, and he begins to unbutton my kimono.

My head swims at the thought of making love, but thought melts away into pure sensation, and sensation becomes everything that I am at that moment.

The next thing I know we are on the carpet, which seems perfectly natural; yet it also seems strange that I have neither time nor *breath* to do anything but cooperate as willingly as I am able, aware that he is being extremely gentle with me, almost as if I am a rare and delicate piece of jewelry, newly discovered. It is dizzying, flattering, supremely pleasurable to the woman in me, the emerging female, the Thai wife I am about to become to this tall, muscular, flawed American male.

CONFESSIONS OF A MAIL ORDER BRIDE

Despite his "high" condition, he is able to ease me through the sexual experience with much gratification and a minimum of discomfort. For that I am very thankful, as I try to show him wordlessly by curling up in his arms afterwards and remaining that way for many, many minutes.

Later that night, upstairs, he smokes another "joint" and we make love again, just as gently and nicely, if also as breathlessly. I begin to wonder if, with experience, one gets better at respirating during the act. He is as considerate and loving as I have hoped he would be. I have no right to complain on that score.

But I silently make, and as silently resolve to keep, a solemn vow—allowing myself weeks or months (it turns out to be *years*) to do it: I will break or coax or otherwise free him of what I consider to be a stupid and self-destructive habit, inexplicable and unforgivable on any terms.

When at length he offers me a "hit" on the cigarette and I refuse in a tone of disdain, he seems not the least bit offended. They say that marijuana is a relaxant, a mood-mellower, and this perhaps explains why my attitude does not easily seep through to him.

Another thing might be the music he seems to be engrossed in when he is not being attentive to me, a mixture of jazz, rock, and rhythm & blues (as I will come to understand these terms) emanating from an FM station in Manhattan that identifies itself several times as "the home of sophisticated funk for the city." Even without the dubious advantage of being high, I am enjoying it too, unsure whether *funk* is not the dreaded F-word naughty Thai boys pick up from GI's.

It is American music and I like it.

And in truth I find myself enjoying him. Flawed yes, but easy to talk to, mindful of my needs, totally "laid back," tapping his foot softly to the rhythms. He seems an almost archetypal Western lover, suave, manly, a type familiar to Thais from imported movies and TV programs.

But that thought only makes his drug use worse. Richard fits the American mold but he also has the "American disease," as Thai media call it.

Yet, knowing the habits of GI's on leave, as depicted by these media, should I have expected any different?

At 2:30 a.m. he wakes me by rising and going downstairs to satisfy a craving for food, "munchies" (I would eventually learn all the terms), and returning with a glass of ice water for me. Reaching down, he draws the cover over me as carefully as if I am indeed that priceless jewelry or china, to be secreted once again.

And I continue to be flattered. This is new, and, as with the music, I like it.

"Little Thai gal," he whispers, more a sigh than a statement.

"Big 'Merican guy," I whisper back.

"We'll make it, Wanwadee."

"I'm sorry?"

"You say that so sweetly. I mean, this is an—an unusual marriage we have begun, but that won't count against us."

"I am hope not."

"I *hope not.*"

"Yes, it what I say."

"I mean, I was correcting."

"Oh. Sank you. I *hope not.*"

"So don't worry." His tone is reassuring in its confidence. "It's in the bag."

I can guess what that means.

"Good night. Tomorrow we hit the city."

"You sink you be able?"

He holds up the ashtray. "Stuff never gives a hangover." Then he leans over, turns (fumbles) off the radio, and puts out the light.

Hangover or no hangover, it will have to go. That much I have decided. This could be a long campaign, but glove down, challenge accepted. Thais love paradox, but they love challenge equally as well.

And Richard is both.

For a long time I lie awake listening to the tick of the hall clock through the open bedroom door as Richard drifts slowly to sleep. Along with the rhythm of his heavy breathing, it seems to bring a sort of final leaven to the long day.

Pressed not uncomfortably to the pillow by the weight of his arm across my shoulder, I try to relax and settle toward sleep myself. But it will prove a different sleep, as different as monsoons are from summer rains. In my half-conscious state I realize this could be a very long campaign indeed.

7

SAVING GRACES

New York 1976

I awaken at eight to find Richard gone. This puzzles me, but I am sure nothing is wrong. After the activities and revelations of the previous night, not to mention the reassuring confidence about us that he has expressed, what could possibly go wrong? This is America, and I am not about to wake up to find that the sky has fallen or that the Communists have taken over.

He will be back, I assure myself.

But perhaps I have expressed too *much* concern over what appeared to be occasional use of a so-called "mild" drug?

No, I did not think so—not at all. None of my Thai friends ever do more than drink a few bottles of Singha beer at a sitting. About drugs and alcohol, all I know is that they are trouble for most people precisely because most people can not handle them well. In Bangkok I have seen Thais in the gutter with booze and GI's as high as kites on God only knows what. Neither cut a very admirable figure.

Totally awake now, I sit up in bed. Switching on the radio to occupy my mind, I find Richard's music still there, at 103 on the dial. It will do for distraction.

An interesting thread in the fabric of America: so unlike the music of Thailand with its seven-tone scale and lack of systematic harmony, and like (but somehow sharper than) the American rock-and-roll found on Bangkok and even Nakhon Narai radio. "Sophisticated" is the proper word, for it often seems that four or five different things at once are happening in the sound—rhythms blend, melodies interchange.

I think with contentment of last night. Even though parts of me are sore, I feel an expansive sense of possibilities, as if I have climbed a mountain and seen beyond to the next ridge, and the next, all difficult, yes, but not as seemingly out of reach as this, the first, has been. Everything looks rugged but serene and potentially conquerable in the long run.

At 8:30, Richard comes back.

In singlet and shorts, he is covered with sweat. His body is muscled but not heavily so—chest broad, legs slim but sturdy. At 32, because he works at it, he has the physique of someone my age. Sun-weathered, his face looks his age, but nicely so, with those steady green eyes and chiseled lines that signal what in the West is known as "character." It relieves me to see in broad daylight that Richard has it, and that there is definitely something there for a Thai wife to work with.

"Rough out there."

"I'm sorry?"

"Hot already. Hard to put in the miles."

"You enjoy run?"

"Very much."

I weigh an option, studying the relaxed, satisfied expression on his face—Thai women are taught to go softly for the jugular in worthwhile causes—and decide *yes*. "You are not, what it is, contra . . . contradicting. I have right word?"

He studies me. "Depends on what you want to say."

"I mean, smoke and run. Not go together."

"Can't argue with that. Yet they both give me pleasure. If I could do neither one again, it would make me sad—very sad." And I couldn't, not with my bad back.

"Does not make sense."

He rummages in a drawer. "What in life does?"

No. I change my mind, deciding not to pursue it so soon; at least I have made him aware again of my concern. "You want shower first?"

"No, go ahead. I'll use the one downstairs. Can you be ready in, say, thirty-forty minutes?"

"Thirty." In Thai time, as opposed to American, that comes out to forty anyway—maybe fifty.

"Good," he says as he goes toward the door, and, as he walks through it, back over his shoulder in a most casual and friendly way, "Hey, don't worry 'bout me. I'm a big boy now."

Big challenge, I think, as I disrobe and head for the shower. *But I am absolutely sure there is something to work with*.

At 10:00 we are half way into Manhattan on another orange bus. The bus is on a different route to the city, over a big bridge from which one can see all the way south to the end of Manhattan Island, her tall buildings glistening, a glorious sight in the morning sun. We are on the Washington Bridge, Richard tells me, built in the 1930s, named after the first President of the United States, and known to me since my first glimpse of a textbook photograph of New York.

"George Washington," I tell him.

"Right you are. You learn a lot about the United States in Thai schools?"

CONFESSIONS OF A MAIL ORDER BRIDE

"Yes." I nodded enthusiastically. "The President—presidents. And Constitution. Thai Constitution copy American."

"Is that right? Well, I'm not surprised. It's one of mankind's greatest achievements."

"I'm sorry?"

"Great for all mankind, the Constitution."

"Sank you. Thais very proud of it. Copy your, though."

He looks at me curiously.

I glance past him down the great sweep of the river for a glimpse of the tall ships, but they are lost in the complexity of the scene. From almost any angle and distance, Manhattan is one of the Wonders of the World, a dream of *can-do* sculpted of stone and steel on a vast scale.

During the period in which it was conceived and erected, that drive to *do* was strongest in the Americans, peaking in the decades around the Second World War. In contrast, Thailand during that time, lulled into weakness by years of peace, was coerced into being an ally of Japan—through a puppet government set up by the Japanese after they had overrun our flimsy pre-industrial defenses. Thais like to claim that they have never been subjugated to a European power, as have all our Asian neighbors, but for nearly five years we were under the thumb of Nippon.

I remember my grandfather, a sailor of the globe, telling me how joyful he was when the United States was drawn into the war at Pearl Harbor. Even half a world away, legend of American might was such that few people in a position to know doubted the eventual outcome once the United States became a combatant.

So I reflect, as we change busses to a green one and roll through the streets of upper Manhattan, exchanging words only randomly.

My grandfather told us also of several retreating Japanese units in 1945 becoming trapped near an airfield in Northeast Thailand. Hill tribes to this day will demonstrate, to anyone willing to look, their collection of artifacts handmade from the bones and teeth of the Japanese who did not make it out.

America became, around the world, synonymous with *winner*, and civilizations emulated and eventually caught up with its standard of industrial production and technological expertise. If Thais wish nowadays to drill for gas, or build computers, or erect a 60-story skyscraper, they do it mostly by themselves, as I am sure Ecuadorians and Mongolians do as well.

Driven by new experiences, the mind shifts into a sort of overdrive. Each turn of a corner brings a fresh idea. In Thailand, I was never really encouraged to think. Whether it was because I am female, I cannot say for certain, even though that is in fact an age-old pattern; at this moment, nevertheless, it feels nice to reassure myself that I am able to and actually enjoy thinking. It is like rediscovering a room in a house long inhabited but not fully *lived in.*

We get off the bus at a huge building which Richard identifies as the Metropolitan, one of the great art museums in the world. It is larger than any temple in my homeland, this monument to the monuments of Western art. I say *Western* because it holds only a very desultory selection of Eastern art, mostly old Chinese and Japanese artifacts.

Once inside I search in vain for pieces from Thailand.

Thailand is a lot like France—it can be thought of as the France of Asia, in fact, with Japan being the island equivalent of the politically influential British, and America roughly equal to the vast, sprawling, multi-ethnic Chinese mainland. The likenesses are approximate but worth considering. It is of course immodest for a Thai to say so, but Thailand has probably the richest culture in Asia, just as France has the richest in Europe.

For instance, Thai cuisine—either *haute cuisine* or people's cuisine—can be compared to France's; in Thailand a great deal of time and effort is spent on the preparation of daily meals, with results amazingly similar, if not in style then in creativity, variety, and consistency of excellence. Like the French, Thais believe that a meal must be a sort of multi-media event, with appeals to all the senses. Cooking is as much an art as poetry or sculpture.

Ask my Mom, who cooks—or my Dad, who eats.

To put it another way: my Dad would never settle for *mediocre* at supper. Nor would my mother.

What can be said of Thai cuisine can also be said of its arts in general. A centuries-old tradition of sculpture and architecture is on display at sites and in museums around our country, and, like the French, Thais try to keep most if not all of it at home. It is not just a matter of laws restricting the export of national treasures; every country has these. It is more the *pride* of the typical Thai, as fierce in defending the art and culture (if not the politics) of his or her country as the Frenchman is. Just as the French scoff at Neuschwanstein, say, and hold up the example of Versailles, Thais scorn Angkor Wat and point to Ayuddhya.

That few non-Thais have heard of these magnificent ruins suggests that Thais, like experienced duennas, prefer to keep their rich and varied past to themselves, an attitude that may have roots in the centuries-long desecration of theft of third-world treasures by European colonizing powers. Almost everyone has his price, of course, and artifacts have left and will leave—for a price. But let each family tend its fences first, *then* its fields, an old Thai saying goes.

We stroll for hours through the great museum halls on this, our honeymoon excursion through art.

SAVING GRACES

I am overwhelmed by the size and richness of the collections, even as I regret the tenacity by which my countrymen hold onto their native art. How proud I and other Thais would be for *our* achievements to be on display in a "Thai Room." But we want to keep our cultural cake and eat it too. It may be that very afternoon, anyway, in that very place—awestruck beneath the soaring female figure of the Winged Victory—that the seed is planted for the growth and direction of my own American education.

I stand mesmerized by the statue for many minutes; it is an epiphany in the midst of swirling crowds. Years later, many miles away, I will declare art as my college major, and beyond that, portrait sculpture as my calling—all this, perhaps as a way of establishing for myself and Thailand a small-scale cultural presence in America.

People will say that all my works, even the portraits of Americans, come out somehow looking *Thai*. And I will be quite proud of that.

Laying chauvinism aside, I catch up with Richard, and we exit to the honking, hurrying presence of New York.

Given the flood of people that will be departing work for the suburbs over the next two or three hours, we decide to eat at a deli and take in a classic movie.

"That will put us home before dark, around eight p.m.," Richard says, reminding me that the city can be a dangerous place at night.

As we board a southbound green bus, Richard says to me, "Can you believe I haven't been to the Metropolitan since I was about seventeen. Ridiculous, isn't it?"

"Ridiclus also my family go to Bangkok one a year. It only few hour on train."

"That's *ridiculous*."

"Yes, I know. I say so."

"I mean the word. Ree-dick-you-luss."

"Oh. *Ridiculous.*"

"Good."

We will go on like that hundreds, maybe thousands of times, a sort of Abbott and Costello routine of mini-language lessons. And Richard will never lose patience.

"What do you, or *did* you, do in Bangkok?" he asks.

"Shopping. Or see 'Merican movie. Once we go to Thai National Museum. Another time to classical dance."

"Do they have opera in Thailand?"

"You mean sing—loud sing, Western style."

"Yep, that's opera—loud sing, Western style."

"So sorry. Not mean insult."

"That's okay. Most operas fit that description. You ought to hear a Mozart, though. Might change your mind."

"I would like."

And in fact I do hear and like Mozart, from the concert that Richard plays for me on his stereo to the opera that he finally finds, at a festival, just before we leave for Atlanta in late August. So smooth and melodious—everything touched with genius. And he died so young, buried in a potter's field—as if the man were nothing more on earth than a vessel for his own divine works. In Thailand we have nothing at all like him or his music.

I ask Richard how it is he can like both opera and rock-and-roll, and he corrects me.

"I don't like opera and rock-and-roll. I like Mozart operas and sophisticated urban music, the best of both worlds."

I smile and put my head on his shoulder. This is the sharp-minded, well-educated, Apollonian Richard, the dominant side of the complex American man I am getting to know. I avoid, for the moment, consideration of anything else.

We get off the bus near mid-town, and Richard buys a

New Yorker magazine at a newsstand. We enter a crowded Jewish delicatessen and eat pastrami sandwiches five inches high and cheesecake so dense and moist it melts before you can chew. New sensations for someone from the Rice Belt.

Seeing how much I am enjoying it, Richard laughingly says, "Welcome to Manhattan. Don't expect to eat like this anyplace else in the States."

"It okay. I cook instead. You like."

"I'm absolutely certain I will. Looks good, cooks good—hey, I lucked out."

"I'm sorry?"

"I am a lucky man."

"Sweet talk."

He leans forward and searches my eyes. "Seriously, I'm glad you are what you are."

"What I are?"

"Beautiful, talented, and as nice as pie. As nice as cheesecake. Jewish cheesecake."

"More sweet talk?"

"Okay. From this point on, since I can't stop, I declare that all sweet talk is truth. No exceptions."

Seeing that I decline to answer, he squeezes my hand, and I smile at him. He is as nice as pastrami sandwiches.

Studying the magazine, he sips at his iced tea. "Look at this. There's a great old movie playing at the Empire, on 76th Street. We can walk there."

"What movie is it?"

"*The Thief of Baghdad.* The 1940 version, with Sabu. It's a classic."

"I would like to see."

"Agreed then."

And so we start to walk ten or twelve blocks uptown and over—the "over" being much longer—to the Empire theater. On the way Richard explains that on any given day one can find at least three dozen things of real interest to do in New York.

Even walking on the streets is, for the unhabituated, one of the pleasures of Manhattan. The air seems to vibrate with action and excitement. A constant level of sound, origin in part indeterminate, hovers all around, like the white noise of progress, business, humanity. There is always something happening, or about to happen, and one moves as if in the center of the place where the universe is recharged.

Richard's tastes prove remarkably akin to mine. Not only in food and art, but by the time the movie has run five minutes I know that I have seen it before, two or three times in fact, in another time and place, in another world—my childhood. In its expertly edited and dubbed Thai version, it has been one of my very favorite films too. Moment by moment, we seem to be breathing new life into the cliche "made for each other."

Somewhere, though, Fate tries to snicker at that pretty thought. Life is hardly ever as patly played out as a Harlequin Romance. Lesson Two—remember, Wanwadee?

At the time, though—those long afternoons in New York—to discover such affinities so early in our relationship makes the very atmosphere glow.

He insists that I look exactly like the princess of Basra, whom the prince rescues from Jaffar's foul clutches and eventually marries. To me he is Ahmad, my prince, saving me from—from whatever my life would have become in that Thai town half a world, half a lifetime, away.

"Sank you," I say as we emerge into the fading daylight.

"Thank me for what? The movie? I enjoyed it too." He has held my hand throughout.

"For be here."

He shows he knows what I mean by thanking me for being there for him, for being his Princess.

"Somebody hear, think we crazy."

"Well, we are," he says, "for trying to pull this deal off —and getting away with it, apparently."

"What means, appalently?"

"Well," he says, measuring the words in his manner, "in this case I think it means 'What you see is what you get.' "

"That is good, no?"

"That is good *yes*."

All around us Manhattan pulsates with life in the warm evening. It seems as if we are on the crest of a lovely wave sweeping us along, giddy and almost out of control. Off in the distance at the end of our magical ride is a sunny beach, the shining Future, where we will be able to harbor securely. Can he see it too, beyond the drugs and whatever other reefs lie ahead?

I am certain that he can. I am sure, too, that the reefs are illusory, there just to add a little extra thrill. How can *anything* deny us, this transcendent honeymoon evening in New York?

The answer to my question is, of course, nearly *everything*: everything that we do not know or can only dimly foresee. That is what Fate is able to snicker at—the reality that lies beyond the "mail order bride arrives from the Far East and lives happily ever after with handsome American" part—*that* part looks so good outlined against the tall towers of Eighth Avenue that it seems as durable as they.

Given the precariousness of our situation, though, and given the knocks we have already separately taken and are sure we will take together, we still are able to ride and enjoy the wave, to cling the more tenaciously to what we are delighting in. Regardless of what ensues, for better or for worse we will always have this much to remember, this ecstatic time together in New York. For now, it's all that really counts.

And who knows: it could actually last.

CONFESSIONS OF A MAIL ORDER BRIDE

Life is no soap opera, no romance—the idea that it is dies off very quickly for everybody who doesn't live in fiction. But, on the other hand, pulp pages and afternoon television aren't the only places to find love that crosses barriers and lasts beyond infatuation.

As Richard steps off the curb into the darkening street, I see a Yellow Cab heading toward him with its headlights not yet on. Almost as if out for prey, it veers directly for him. He does not see it. Desperately, I grab at his arm, get a hold, and jerk him back as firmly as I can.

He stumbles toward me, nearly tumbling into the gutter. The cab rattles by, its horn sounding much too late, less a warning than a final braying insult.

Ruffled but composing himself, Richard takes a deep breath and looks at me. "Dee, you saved my life."

"It okay. You save mine too. We save each other now."

He puts his arms around me, and we stand there hanging on to one another as people hurry by in the twilight, as oblivious to us as if we were statues in Central Park.

8

FALL APPROACHES

New York 1976

It is a Thursday morning in late August. The weather is sunny and cool, with a "tang of autumn" in it—or so I hear. I really wouldn't know because there are no autumns in Thailand: no dramatic falling off in temperature, because it is so near the equator; and, because there are no deciduous trees, no colorful leaf changes. Other than days like this, I am not certain what to expect of the season coming up—and even less certain what to expect of winter. I am glad that we will be spending it in the South.

We are chugging along on an orange bus again for the tenth or twelfth time, heading into Manhattan via the George Washington Bridge. Far below us the Hudson River sweeps grandly toward the sea, transformed by sunlight into a million glittering water-borne jewels. It has been a heady honeymoon, but now it is coming to an end. Richard has to be back in his office early the following week, and his classes begin the Monday after that.

Recently he has told me that this is a crucial year for him, since he does not know whether his year-to-year contract with the college will be renewed. With only a master's degree —all the new people coming in have Ph.D.'s—he is beginning to feel like low man on a top-heavy totem pole.

I am to learn, in time, that he is an excellent teacher, but also that he is correct about his credentials being inferior.

In any case, this is to be our last trip to the city. We have already done almost everything once, it seems, from catching a Broadway show (a revival of *The King and I!)* to sailing the Circle Line around Manhattan to downing soft drinks in a Soho bar. This time we plan just to "wing it," as he says, to stroll around a little, mostly down at the south end of the island —Battery park, the World Trade Center, whatever else we can find.

Serendipity is the name of the honeymoon game for today.

As the bus proceeds over the bridge, Richard takes my hand and lays his head back on the seat, eyes closed. He has been putting in longer hours on his work, trying to put together a journal article on the new microcomputer industry. Except at meals and in bed, I do not see much of him at all on Tuesdays and Wednesdays, his heavy workdays. But, then, mealtime and bedtime are the best parts of the day when we stay home.

Richard's mother cooks most of the meals for the three of us. She serves a variety of ethnic dishes that, living in the New York area, one picks up almost by osmosis. Whether it is Italian lasagna or Hungarian goulash or Cuban sandwiches for lunch (when son and daughter-in-law are home), she fills us up with food wonderfully varied and completely new to me. I copy down a new recipe almost every day.

FALL APPROACHES

Also, helping in the kitchen, I learn how to operate a trash masher and an automatic dishwasher—amazing Western devices. I cook an occasional Thai or Chinese meal, about which they both rave for days afterward. Like most Americans, they especially appreciate the Oriental standbys—Shrimp Toast, Sweet-and-Sour Pork, Spring Rolls, the ones I can do blindfolded. But, they also like Thai Steamed Fish in Coconut-Pepper Sauce and even the Thai version of Kim Chee, which I "ferment" under the kitchen sink.

After a while the days simply meld into one another, as the best of times do, so that they seem to be a continuum of "highs" (to borrow Richard's terms), at the peaks of which we are all intensely satisfying one or another of our appetites, like voracious birds of paradise. Bedtime is neither a slowdown nor a let-down: Richard and I make love almost every night.

But there is a serpent in our paradise: dope.

It annoys me somewhat that he indulges himself in marijuana each time we make love—I say only "somewhat" because he is the most considerate, careful, and sensual of lovers. Because I want to maximize both our pleasures in order to enhance the bond between us, I hold my tongue again and again—even knowing reticence can itself become a habit—and say hardly a disparaging word about the smoking, not wanting to ruin any part of our honeymoon Manhattan summer.

In between the pleasurable activities, moreover, he has been not only working hard but worrying hard, too. Although he refuses to say much about it, at work he is between the proverbial rock and hard place—or, as Thais say, either chased to death by dogs or bitten.

Thus I am reluctant to provoke him.

One night after we have made love, a soft, full-moon night, in response to unintentionally leading questions from me, he mentions his ex-wife. Jokingly, I have asked him if he likes me better than his other girls.

CONFESSIONS OF A MAIL ORDER BRIDE

He answers me seriously: "There haven't been that many. The only one I spent any real time with was my former wife." When he is high he is more intimately talkative than usual. I see a chance to learn more about him—knowledge of spouse being a typical Thai wife's tool—and push it further.

"How many year you know her?"

"Oh, let's see . . . ten altogether."

"You think of her now and now?"

"Now and then? Yeah, now and then. But only to—to feel sorry for her."

"She has marry again?"

He shakes his head up and down, and I have to think again because this familiar American *yes* happens to be rude in Thailand.

"If she marry, why feel bad?"

"Because her husband, whom she apparently loves, has had two children and a vasectomy."

"I'm sorry?"

"An operation. He can't have any more kids. And therefore she cannot have her first one."

"Oh, too bad, too bad. You think all woman should have kid?"

"Sure, don't you?"

It seems a point impossible to argue. "And man too," I say instead.

"It's less important for a man, I think. They do not actually carry the child, give birth to it. They never get quite as close to it. Actually, they never get that close to anyone— they're more likely to get close to ideas, or things. To be obsessive about fitness, money, whatever. You understand?"

"I sink so. But not agree." It is difficult to say that. Thai women are taught to agree with their husbands about almost everything unless, of course, he is an incompetent fool.

And Richard is far from foolish in anything but his recreational habits, and he seems incompetent in nothing. I disagree however to make him know that should we ever have a baby, it will be as much his as mine.

Before he has a chance to respond, though, I go back to his ex-wife: "She is American, Julie?"

"Yes. Southern girl. My brother introduced us. He was attending college in Atlanta at the time, and his first wife knew her. It was a decent marriage."

"And so why . . . ?"

"Why divorce? We had come to the end of our road. She was heading one way and I another. That can happen when you marry too young."

"We are not young?" I probe.

"You are, of course. You're young in years and looks but seem old in wisdom—ancient Thai wisdom, you know?"

"I hope true. Sank you."

"And I am just . . . old."

"Thirty-two not old."

"Well . . . thank you for coming from far across the sea for this—this retread."

"Do not sank. I have no choice."

"By that you mean . . ."

He is probing *me* now, and he is so easy to talk to, to open up with, that over the next half hour I unfold, like a dark lily, my most haunting memory. I tell him of my brother's murder and the surrounding circumstances. It is hard to get it all out, and get it into English, but by the time I finish I feel such a sense of relief that tears come.

Richard holds me in his arms tightly, stroking my hair, until we both grow drowsy and fall asleep.

Reaching out fervently that night, under a full moon in this unlikely (to me) place called New Jersey, two souls thus join together more securely as one.

9

THE GIFT OF LIFE

Atlanta 1976

Atlanta used to have all the elements of the perfect American city: Sunbelt climate; clean, pine-scented air; low crime rate; friendly, efficient "Southern Heart, Northern Mind" spirit; genuine cultural amenities (including annual visits by the New York Metropolitan Opera Company, for which Richard would always cadge tickets); gleaming new construction all over the place; and a sort of aura that you had to be there to truly appreciate.

Or so Richard, and others, tell me.

He had been there. *They* had experienced it. By the time *I* arrived, apparently, it is no longer available to be experienced. What I get to know instead, at first, is a large American city much like any *world* city—monstrous traffic jams, acres and acres of slums for the poor, ubiquitous air and noise pollution, daily murders and rapes in the news—except for one thing: the attitude people have about the way the city *used* to be back in those past golden days.

The city does prove to have, the more I get to know it, some uniquely American charms. It has, for example, a combination of rolling, pine-covered suburbs and exurbs, and a relatively clean, safe downtown, plus a pleasantly relaxed atmosphere that in my growing awareness of Americana I am able to identify as residual Old South.

It certainly contrasts favorably with those few Thai cities with which I am familiar. As cities go, it is an 8, perhaps a 9. In my opinion all the 10's are either Celestial or, what might amount to the same thing, figments of some collective imagination.

Among Thais, however, it is hardly ever a particular place with which we associate good times, and usually not a special group of friends, either; rather, it is our *families*. They are the axis around which Thai wheels spin.

Robert, Richard's best friend from the college, is a bearded, cantankerous lawyer who has been in Atlanta for well over a decade. Like Richard, he is a reborn Sunbelter, a latter-day Carpetbagger from Massachusetts or Minnesota (I haven't learned to distinguish yet) who, like many of his kind, curses the sultry, slow-moving South with one breath and, with the next, swears they will never go back North again. The syndrome is common also to some Americans in Thailand.

For Robert and others, nevertheless, it has been downhill for "The Big A" ever since the encircling Beltway was finally completed in 1975. Atlanta was then both literally and figuratively trapped into the twenty-first century, a victim of its own concrete-and-steel progress, and therefore doomed to suffer the fate of all American cities: internal suffocation. Now the entire city, they just knew, would be nothing but concrete and steel, crime and statistics, gays, freak-o's, bag people, ersatz gentrification, the whole sorry modern urban works.

THE GIFT OF LIFE

At times Richard betrays this strange attitude but only when he seems to fall under the spell of "back-then-ers" like Robert. Mostly he makes up his own mind about things, a sensible, rational opinion reached after many hours of mulling— for Richard is nothing if not a tireless muller. The advice and the pronouncements of others have no noticeable impact on him, although it is all grist for his perpetual mill.

Robert loves to cite the example of the Peachtree Road Race, an annual 10K footrace that he and Richard have run for several years beginning with its inception in 1971. Together, over late summer beers in the backyard of one or another of our friends, they reminisce, again and again, about the way it used to be.

"Remember the weather in '72?" Robert says over the loud rattle of a neighbor's power mower. "God, it was brutal."

"God, yes," Richard responds. "84 degrees at race time." And, to me, sitting nearby, "Race time is 8 a.m."

I smile.

"Beat that in Thailand if you can," Robert jokes.

"We can," I say. By this time I am feeling more comfortable with English, able to catch some of its nuances—which, in its turns of phrase and clever linguistic shortcuts, if in nothing else, is akin to Thai.

"Sure. Sure, sure, sure. Hey, Ricky, what'd you finish in that year?"

I get a kick out of people calling Richard *Ricky;* he will not let me do it because, he says, it invariably comes out *Reeky.*

"Seventy-two? Let's see . . . that was before they changed the course, right?"

"Yeah, long before. The buggers. *Everything* has gone downhill since then. Eighteen thousand runners this year. I hear it takes 90 seconds of running in place just to get to the *starting* line."

"That sucks."

CONFESSIONS OF A MAIL ORDER BRIDE

Neither of them ran in the race anymore.

"And the ten dollar entry fee. The money grubbing buggers. Whole damn city now."

Silence, except for the persistent sputtering roar of the mower, filling every crack in the sunny afternoon like warm putty.

"42:05."

"Huh?"

"My time. In seventy-two."

"Oh."

This is American backyard conversation: casual, jocular, non-intellectual; no political agendas, nothing about strikes or riots or assassinations. Or art. Or literature.

As a woman and a foreigner, I like to think that I sit among these men and other women as an equal. I have been anticipating some overt signs of prejudice, but among these particular educated people there seems to be none—except for a slight tendency of the women to ignore me. Perhaps it is just that they cannot quite figure me out.

Robert's slender, busy wife Anne is like that. While I am almost certain that she holds no racial animosity against me, she seems to regard me with a certain amount of apprehension. It is as if I am unpredictable to her; as an unknown quantity—the Mysterious East—I am best avoided, more or less. It creates for me a certain amount of emotional isolation, but small talk is not on the prohibited list, and I am comfortable with that.

I try to regard the chit-chat as a *start* and, in fact, with a few women it leads on to genuine friendship. Most women remain wary, however, and chit-chat is as far as it ever gets. So it goes with Anne.

With a few women, snobbery factors set in when they discover the background of my marriage. It will always seem to

me, however, to be less racial than social—i.e., class-based—
although I would be naive to think race played no role.

Part of the penalty of relocating from a very different
culture like Thailand's is a degree of isolation and alienation. It
goes with the territory of one's new land. What one tries to do
is accept it as best as one can, minimize it as often as one can,
and carry on.

And so the afternoons pass on into a long cool dry fall,
marked by football on the television and, when no one else is
around, a haze of marijuana smoke and that sophisticated funk
—now the background music of my life—on the stereo. Richard seems agonizingly content to let his life drift, even though
he is increasingly certain his teaching contract will not continue to be renewed, that he will lose his job either this year or
the next.

Things will somehow turn out well, he insists when he
is straight; and, when he is high, he puts an unreasonably optimistic sort of trust in "the breaks," which seem to me to be
about as reliable as another American concoction, The Tooth
Fairy.

Still, in the mornings-after, more than a few times, he
says to me, "My dreams, Dee—they're all terrifying now. Or
crazy. Like I go to Hell, literally, when I fall asleep."

"What are they about?" I ask. Thais have an intricate
and comprehensive system of dream symbology; I think I can
help, in a kind of folk-psychiatry way.

But he will always respond, "I can't say precisely. Regardless of how bizarre and authentic they seem, they disappear when I awake. Getting one back into reality is as impossible as . . . I don't know, like passing fire through water."

For me it is frustrating. I need those dreams to work on,
as a weaver needs thread, or I can no more help him than a
doctor can a patient who claims something hurts but can't say

what or where. Still, I cannot resist getting in a word each time: "You smoke each night before dream?"

"Well, yeah. So?" It is always a tender area.

But I press: "Now draw conclusion, please."

"No, that's not it. The dreams are there to be dreamt anyway."

"That not make sense. You invite."

"Let's not get into this again."

I shut up, as I usually do, still counting on the medicinal aid of time, foreseeing victory somewhere down the long road of our future together. Lately, though, that road has grown even darker, primarily because he is smoking again with his friends and some of the younger, less "stable"—committed, professional, whatever—members of the academic community.

Although Richard's habits worry me, I understand now that within him there is an instinct to rebel, to turn his back on accepted "truths" and even to bury his head to others' attitudes and expectations.

In this respect and others he has come to remind me somewhat of my brother Sumwong.

Both Sumwong and Richard bear the imprint of being middle male children. Part of Richard's attitude is residue of his defiance against his straight, strict older brother, left over from their childhood conflicts. Perhaps it is also in the genes that drove his father to fly one last mission (at age 32, and with a pregnant wife at home halfway around the world) against the already defeated Japanese, and as a consequence to lose his life a month before the war was over. But, then, Thai people tend to see almost everything in terms of intra-family dynamics.

Perhaps Richard merely enjoys being high on THC, or discovering the "intricate alternative universe." He reminds me of what I have already observed about drug use in America, that there are the biker and the yahoo *abusers*, and the poet and the explorer *users*.

Granted he is in the latter class, but to me the whole category stinks.

When I ask him specifically what the attraction is of LSD—a substance which, being unfamiliar, frightens me more than marijuana—he says it would be like trying to explain mature sexual love to a fourteen-year-old who has gotten just to the masturbation stage.

"Or, to paraphrase Mark Twain, the difference between the 'real' universe and that special, limited-admission universe is like the difference between a lightning bug and lightning."

"I see," I say. But I don't.

To keep me from feeling left out of a good thing, he often invites me to try a joint with him, but I do not mind at all being left out. To him I know it must be like running into a brick wall over and over, but I have two brick-solid reasons for continuing to reject his offers: one, as a small-city, middle-class Thai, "doing dope" is as anathematic to me as painting parasols or watching elephant games would be to the average American; and two, with a recurrent shiver of fear, I see how the stuff makes one react to the realities of life—like not caring about losing your job, or not being able to do anything to prevent or overcome it.

I am in no position, and of no disposition, to put my foot down: it is not the Oriental way, nor is it *my* way. A hard line stance might bring an immediate foreswearing from him, and grant me a moment's satisfaction, but easily overturned short-term results are not what I am after, for both our sakes. It will have to be my way, the "patient Oriental" way, or no way at all.

Paradoxically, only by not pressing time into the issue will I eventually have time on my side. It is perhaps difficult for American women to see my point, to understand why in Thailand we nudge instead of push, especially when there is much at stake. It is equally difficult for me to explain. Some of it has to do with tradition, with "the way things are done." Some has to do with views of what, in the long run, makes for true marital stability. And some more has to do with our differing concepts of exactly what a woman is and how she is supposed to react to, to cope with, not only males but all the varying circumstances of life.

The net result: I determine that short-run sacrifice of ego, the surrender of my right to confront Richard and make my position harder, will bring the most desirable long-term result.

Ancient American saying: win some, lose some.

Win some, lose some.

The axe that we both see falling falls, ironically, over the Christmas holidays. Some present that year.

Before then, though, Atlanta holds out its greatest present, one that will, for us, far outdo the immediate pleasures of a genuine Chicago-style pizzeria opening in our nearest shopping plaza and the fact that the NFL franchise team (the Atlanta Falcons) has become a serious contender for an NFL title. Both these events are widely taken as signs, Richard claims, of the maturation of a city.

I take his word for it.

But, no, Atlanta has much more than pizza and playoffs for Richard and me: it has the gift of life, a new life, life that grants our union the most precious of sacraments.

I am pregnant.

It is an early fall day when I come to that realization. The leaves have just begun to change, an event that strikes me with wonder since the only such color changes that I have ever seen in plants signify death. Several times, especially during the ensuing winter, I have to ask Richard if he is absolutely certain they will all come back in the spring.

THE GIFT OF LIFE

"Of course," he says. "All but the ones that have actually died."

"A-ha!" I exclaim. "I know there was somesing."

"But that will amount to only a fraction."

"Nine-tenths is a fraction."

"Okay, a small fraction."

"All fraction small."

"You know, I think you ought to forget this art stuff and plan to go to law school. You've got that type of mind."

"So many will not come back? Yes or no, Reeky."

"See what I mean? And please: *Ricky.*"

"*Ricky.* We wait till spring to see."

At the moment I suspect my pregnancy, I am at a convenience store to buy beer for Richard. Parked in front, I fish around in my purse for my small calendar to see if my period is about to start so that I can buy tampons as well, if need be. Since onset, I have been as regular as clockwork—28 days *always*—and all it takes is a glance at my calendar to see when I am due.

Oh-oh. Make that *was* due. Five days ago.

Putting that fact together with Richard's reluctance to use condoms and even greater reluctance to put me on birth control pills, I arrive at the only conclusion possible.

Emotions rush through me like a flash flood: fear first, in the gut; then a growing sense of wonder, in the brain; then a deep and resonant elation, throughout my body.

But no disbelief: I am pregnant.

I sit there for many minutes thinking the matter through—from *whether* it will be a boy or a girl and *when* I will tell Richard to *which* doctor we will go to and *what* will he/she be when he/she grows up. Back to the calendar—what will the birth date be? Will he/she have *my* black hair, *his* green eyes? And what if it's *twins?*

I might have sat there speculating the entire afternoon

if a pickup truck had not pulled up beside me. In it are two white men with unshaven faces and baseball-style caps that say *Caterpillar* and *Red Man*. This distracts me—what in the world could these words actually signify?—as does the fact that the one who remains in the cab, the passenger, keeps staring at me.

As I get out, he says in that thick, slow accent I now recognize to be Southern, "Excuse me, miss."

His tone and manner are polite, so I walk over. It is then that I see the big brown bulk in the bed of the truck—the garish antlers, the open, mooning eye. It is deer season, and these two men are hunters in this, the hunting season.

All this registers in the two seconds it takes me to come around the fender. "Yes?"

"I hope you don't mind. Are you from Vietnam?" He is thin and fairly young, with flecks of gray throughout his hunting-season whiskers. His blue eyes study me intently.

"No, I am from Thailand."

"I knew it was somewhere there. Not China"—it comes out *Chahna*—"or Japan. You are very pretty."

"Sank you," I say, accent to accent, and back away a little.

"Me and my buddy here was wondering whether you—you work around here."

"No, I live with my husband two mile away."

"Oh—is that right? You married, then."

"Yes."

"Coulda guessed it. All the good-looking ones are. I was in 'Nam for eighteen months—you know, back then. Used to go with a gal name of Lily. Claimed she was half French. Boy, she was a looker too."

"Yes," I say, and back away a little more.

He notices the move, and my ring now, and says, even more polite and soft spoken, "She died. Her house took a hit

THE GIFT OF LIFE

outside Saigon." He pauses and adds, more to himself than me, "Seventeen years old . . ."

"I'm sorry."

He is looking at the ground. "It don't matter now."

"No," I say. Traffic noise rushes in to fill the void of a momentary silence.

"For a minute there, you reminded me of her."

I say nothing.

"Well, look, you have a nice day now, hear."

His friend, about the same age, emerges from the store, and as we pass each other he tips his hat. I smile.

He gets in the cab, and they both stare through the plate glass window at me for another half a minute; then the truck backs out. As it pulls away, I catch another glimpse of the deer. Its eye is large and round and moist, and as lifeless as stone.

It takes me a moment to remember that I came for beer, and another moment after that to realize I won't be needing tampons for a while.

10

SOUTHERN WINTER

Atlanta 1977

At the start of my second trimester of pregnancy, I know more by instinct than by science that it will be a boy—although a routine ultra-sound test will confirm my suspicion. If statistics don't lie, many people in America want males; in Thailand, it is *most* people—it had *better* be a boy, in fact. Alliances have been lost, even small wars started, because of that very issue.

Sad, but true; sadder, in fact, just for being undeniable true. In the Third World, the earth is still mainly a male domain, and women in many countries are fearful of not being able to bear their husbands male children. Veiling their faces, covering their womanly curves, bowing their heads as well as their wills, they serve the meals, bind the wounds and hold their households together from kitchen and hearth.

But it had better be a boy.

These are facts, not opinions. I do not celebrate them.

CONFESSIONS OF A MAIL ORDER BRIDE

It is a fact too, however ironical, that Richard happens to want a girl. He has always, he says, wanted a daughter. I do not raise the question of why, for I suspect that it is part and parcel of his urge to be different. Whatever the reason, the desire is real. For this man, it had better be a *girl*.

Although I first missed a period at the turn of the seasons, late September, I withheld telling Richard until I had missed my second period at the end of October. With Richard's future at the university so uncertain, I simply did not wish to add another variable to an already unstable equation until I was sure. Then it was merely a question of *exactly* when to tell him.

I chose the last day of the month, Halloween, when I had been told to answer every ring of the doorbell, for kids would be coming around dressed as anything and everything under the sun. "You and Ricky will laugh yourselves silly," one of the distant but friendly faculty wives told me. "The kids are so cute."

So at ten o'clock that night, after a dozen or so visits by goblins, witches, and Nixons, I told him my news. It did not surprise me that he accepted it with a whoop and a hug and, round about midnight, a joint. I could have predicted as much, knowing the mixed joy and worry of the situation.

Now, in late fall, I certainly do not expect the announcement of the gender of his forthcoming child to evoke any different response. But with Richard, unpredictability is the rule rather than the exception.

I choose a late afternoon to tell him it is a boy. I will catch him as he returns from work—before he can light up a joint. His marijuana-smoking has now become more frequent. He lights up on almost all those evenings when he knows we won't be going out or he will likely not have to field a phone call from someone like his supervisor, or a student, or a "straight" friend.

SOUTHERN WINTER

(More than once, I have to play "husband not home" for him when he is in his home office, stoned, with the stereo headphones on.)

As usual, on what is to prove a doubly-momentous afternoon, I run down the stoop of our house as he drives up the driveway in our creaking, six-year-old Ford Maverick. He gets out and puts his arms around me, as usual, and we stand entwined for a long time, enjoying our reunion after a day apart. Despite the difficulties, our love for one another is like a song that is reaching, and remarkably holding, a sweet crescendo. It is one of the few constants among these precarious variables.

To have that is to have—well, almost everything.

"How's my favorite mother-to-be?"

"Fine, sank you."

"Something sure smells good. Is it my favorite?"

"Which favorite?"

"Dunno. They're all my favorites when Wanwadee cooks 'em."

"Sweet talk. And it is won-ton. Two way. Won-ton soup and then fried won-ton with cucumber salad."

"Great. I'm starving."

Hand in hand we walk inside, and, after he has washed up and taken his place at the dinner table, I spring the news upon him. "Richard," I say simply, "I think, I *know*, it is a boy."

His entire body goes flaccid—limp, just like that. Head down. Lips loose. Eyes closed. As though he has died.

In a sense, he has, or something inside him has. I hold my breath, hardly aware of the irony of promising a male scion to my husband—I, an Oriental woman—and having him react like this.

But, after a moment, he smiles, simply, and holds me again, and thanks me for bringing happiness into his life from the moment we met at the airport—no, he insists, from before that, from the moment he had the idea to seek out the reality behind this woman in the mailbox named Wanwadee.

So far, our life has been like this: we can ride it out, whatever it is, the big and the small. He attributes that ability to me, to the patient and enduring Oriental love he says I give him; I attribute it to his American strength. Regardless of the cause, it is there, and I will do what I can to keep it that way—including trying to stay off his back about certain things.

He stays off mine, after all, about whatever problems I present to him—even if he assures me there aren't any.

He sits down in a living room chair, the smile on his face as indecipherable as the one on the Mona Lisa or a Chinese Buddha. We speak once more of the problems of pregnancy and the question of birth dates. Everything seems to be in a reasonably calm holding pattern.

Later on as he eats, though, his face gradually darkens again and he grows silent, a strangely grave silence, as when a heavy cloud passes over the sun on an otherwise clear summer day. When he retires to the den to watch the news without saying another word, I decide to confront him—why like *this* after news like *that*?

"You do not welcome son into world?" I am not angry, just puzzled. "It has to be girl?"

"That's not it."

"What it is then, prease?"

"Oh . . . nothing. Not a thing."

That is where the conversation usually ends. He does a Silent American Male routine on me, and I can now expect no more than a Gary Cooper *yep* or *nope* out of him.

Again, I resist pressuring him—despite the fact that at times like this I would love to emit a high-pitched scream.

I concentrate instead on the television.

Walter Cronkite is saying something about Dr. Jeffrey McDonald, the All-American boy with the All-American name and the All-American profession, who has murdered his wife and children. Now it looks as if Jeffrey will actually have to pay for the crime, and for the betrayal of his image, with a life circumscribed and totally wasted by prison. Justice, yes, but justice as only the merest final commentary, like a tinny echo, on a series of despicable perversions.

But in a moment that story will seem irrelevant, that and yet another Mid-East crisis, and an airplane disaster in which lives have been lost, souls departed, on some remote mountain range in old Mexico.

"They're getting rid of all their instructor-level people," Richard says in an expressionless voice. "Anyone without a Ph.D. will go this year or next."

Shock, followed quickly by numbness: "It is certain?"

"As certain as anything that comes out in the *Faculty Insider*. Who says lightning doesn't strike twice in the same place."

Even though we have been anticipating news exactly like this, I feel sick, woozy all of a sudden, small and scared. What will happen now, with the baby on the way? Speaking of perversions, what kind of twisted dream is this that I have come so far to live? To have a husband with no job—in America?

"It is certain you must go?" I only want to confirm my worst fear—perhaps I have missed some implication in the English.

"Does the sun come up in the morning?"

I have missed no implication.

"It will be this year, too," he adds, "since it's the end of a five-year run. In academics, things tend to go in cycles of five. I'll get an official letter soon. It will say very simply that my yearly contracts cannot be renewed beyond the summer because I have made no progress with my Ph.D."

CONFESSIONS OF A MAIL ORDER BRIDE

"They do not know baby come?" The question is worse than naive, and Richard chooses not to respond.

Although I try to prevent it, my tears start to come, hot as spice down both my cheeks.

"Baby come, job go."

He laughs, and puts his arm around me. "You know how to slice through to the bone of it, Doll. Like a Chinese cleaver."

"Thai cleaver better."

That breaks him up. He laughs harder, so hard that I cannot resist laughing with him at last, right through my tears.

"Somehow you make it good, Wanwadee. In spite of . . . everything."

I am flattered, and respond the way flattered Thais often do, by turning the compliment around: "You do same for me. Sank you."

"No, my love. Thank *you*."

I do not draw the point out. We have both thanked each other again for being each other, and that is good enough. It beats arguing, especially when there is much to argue about. We have found this cross-cultural secret-of-success together: that consistent mutual respect for one another's differences leads to an even deeper respect for feelings as well.

The realization of our continuing love takes some of the sting out of Richard's announcement, at least for a moment.

"Hey," he says, taking my hand, "let's talk about the baby. What do you think is a good name for a boy?"

"Thai name or 'Merican name?"

"That's up to you."

"I do not really know 'Merican name."

"How about from the movies?"

"Well, then, there is Gary. No, wait minute, we do not want a kid who say nothing but *yep*, who keep it all inside."

"Why not? It's the Great American Way."

"I mean like his Dad."

"I *know* what you mean, Doll."

We both laugh.

"Okay, we'll decide on a name later," Richard says. "Whatever it is, we're going to love it to death anyway, don't you know?"

"To death?"

"It's an expression—means all the way, one hundred percent."

"I am not sure I like."

To death.

I think fleetingly of Sumwong, of his actual ashes ten thousand miles away in a decorated urn—and then of my family, of Thailand, of no work and the prospect of no money in America—and the sobs begin again.

"Now, look, don't go morose on me. It's not the end of the world. The opposite, in fact. A beginning."

"Can't help. I feel like I do when I know I must leave home. Like scared kid. It made worse by be pregnant."

"Listen, it's not like I can't get another job. With my knowledge of computers and tech editing, it'll be easy. The only adjustment I'll have to make is working nine to five. That will be harder but way short of impossible."

"You are possible?"

"*Positive.* Yes."

"Baby be okay, then?"

"Hey, what did you think, that I'd tell you to have an abortion? Of course it'll be okay. All miracles are okay."

He pauses. "Even those that happen when they're not supposed to."

After supper he disappears into his office, the second bedroom of our two-bedroom cottage on three suburban Atlanta acres that have not fallen yet to developers' powersaws, the bedroom that is to become the baby's room in a few months. In it he has his notes and books, and a small computer he has borrowed from a colleague.

But I know he is not going in there to work this evening, not after a day such as this. I sit at the window of the small wooden-floored dining room watching the sunset and listening to the plaintive warble of a woodthrush, so like the song of a small Thai jungle bird that a wave of nostalgia sweeps through me.

A Southern January chill is settling into the twirling air, seeping through the loosefitting windows and gathering around my bare feet like the incoming swirl of a tide. A pale pink sun glows through the trees, accenting their winter nakedness. Before too long I smell marijuana smoke in the chilled air, and I shiver down to my bones.

Despite the bad things that happen, my images of the South's number-one city, Atlanta, are basically warm and satisfying ones. It is here that I moved fully into the United States.

In Atlanta, first and foremost, of course, I become pregnant.

In Atlanta, I learn to cook collard greens with fatback.

In Atlanta, I take my first college course, Math 101. Make my first B in it, too.

In Atlanta I learn about another matter: patterns of American racial discrimination.

It is a curiosity to me that white Americans almost unhesitatingly accept Orientals as "intelligent" and "ambitious," while at the same time denying black Americans decent and consistent opportunities to display those same characteristics. Old-line Southerners in particular, likeable people, some of whom are guests in our home, seem to begrudge blacks credit for any of their accomplishments, even in arenas (such as sports and music) where they clearly excel. If a black happens to achieve ascendancy in a *profession,* he or she is said to be either a fluke or to have mostly white blood.

In the same vein, on TV boy-girl dating shows, it seems perfectly acceptable for white youths to vie for the hand of an attractive lady of, say, Japanese descent. But it is totally out of the question for the female (or, in vice-versa situations, the male—*especially* the male) to have even the slightest visible strain of black blood.

Similarly, some of the hottest-selling pornographic videotapes, I am to learn from a friend of Richard's who works part-time in a video store, involve black-white interracial copulation. The fruit is not only forbidden but, to some, absolutely rotten, yet it apparently has as much fascination for a small number of whites as did the notorious Apple of Eden for Eve.

Richard's selection of a second wife does not seem to draw even the faintest whiff of condemnation from acquaintances or friends. Our marriage is, to judge from all evidence, not only accepted but even, in a sense, wholesomely stereotypical—"brainy" American prof marries "cute" Oriental gal. No matter that, in the summer after gardening or a trip to the beach, my skin is as dark as that of the average mixed-race black.

"Suppose I am black?" I ask Richard one day out of curiosity. He hardly ever speaks on the matter and, when he has in the past, it has been basically indecipherable, coming from a professed liberal.

"Instead of that beautiful rose-beige? You know, your skin actually glows."

"No, for serious. Would we be marry if I am black?"

He pauses. "That's an awfully tough question to answer, you understand—so many variables—racial permutations and social combinations."

"Answer like husband, not computer, prease."

"Okay: no."

"I was not think so."

"*Did* not think so."

"*Did* not."

"It's not me, particularly. It's the system. I had a close black friend for a while when I lived in Europe—a Kenyan. Funny, over there it seemed okay. I suppose, in a way, with her beside me, I was showing how liberal I was. We drew a few stares, but no more than you or I do walking downtown on Peachtree Street."

He pauses thoughtfully and adds, "My thoughts have changed over the years, however."

"How?"

"We'll talk about that some other time."

One of his typical put-offs. Okay, I think instead of Richard and the Kenyan. "Then Thailand must be like Europe. Black GI have no special trouble, except from white GI. Some Thai girl prefer go with them, in fact. Marry them also."

"I suspect it's like that in a variety of places. But not, in general, in the good old U.S. of A."

"It too bad. Black seem all right to me."

"Would you have married one? No, wait a minute, let me rephrase that: would you have married *me* if I had turned out to be black when we met at the airport?"

"I see your picture first."

"That doesn't really answer my question."

I decided to try out one of my ever-growing collection of new English words and phrases: "It is moot point."

"Moot, schmoot. If it's a point, I just won it."

The truth is, I do not have a certain answer to the question.

But I suspect that, all else being equal, I would not have hesitated a moment to marry a black Richard. But—paradox again—that is something I do not want to tell this living, breathing, culture-conditioned Richard who is my white

SOUTHERN WINTER

American husband, especially since it has become difficult to read his real thoughts on this topic.

Instead I go to the utility room to do a load of laundry while he retires to his study. *Touche*—both of us.

I regret having brought the topic up; yet I continue to wonder what it would be like for Richard and me if *I* were black, even foreign black—another Kenyan, say, or a Jamaican. There is an unfathomable, disturbing quality to the hypothesis, and for the moment I prefer not to pursue it although I am certain that race will be a continuing issue of discussion for us, especially with a mixed-race child on the way.

I abandon the train of thought by concluding that, while I am of course grateful not to be the object of scorn and prejudice, at the same time I would like a better explanation than that blacks are inferior by nature of their former slave status, especially when they have generally proven able to do the job—any job—when offered an opportunity.

Rumors and news of another sort of racial conflict reach me now and then—as in the personally affecting case of brutalization of Cambodian-Americans by, ironically, black youths in parts of Los Angeles. "Dog-eaters," the blacks call them, and worse names, as they rob them in the streets and beat their children in the schoolyards. Explicable, in terms of oppressor and oppressed, but nonetheless sad: sad for me, caught in a place in-between with more questions than answers; sad for the future of my "rose beige" son, perhaps, as he grows into a society polarized by the pettiest of things.

It worries me, being pregnant, watching the evening news with stories from refugee camps, Honduran jungles, and Angolan deserts. It worries me, with my family back home in Thailand smack in the path of the Asian Communist juggernaut.

But it catches my breath to remember that Thailand is

CONFESSIONS OF A MAIL ORDER BRIDE

not really "home," at least not for me, not any more, not for my immediate family of husband and eventual son.

Native-born Americans probably tire of hearing how good they have it, yet, except for the destitute, there is no truth more important for them. At virtually any other time, in virtually any other place, the conditions of their lives would be far less comfortable and secure.

Nowhere is that fact more apparent than in the daily lives of Richard and me—despite the troubles beginning to pile up like a trash heap at our door. We are still relatively secure and comfortable, with acceptable prospects; our lives are still filled with daily pleasures and, just as significantly, the absence of any unendurable pain. Like most, if not all other Americans, we may still find, over the hump, that we "have it made."

And in the shade, too—the pine-needle shade.

Still-life of a transplanted Thai woman, heavy with child, lolling at home beneath a White Pine tree on a pleasant Southern winter afternoon in Atlanta, Georgia, U.S.A.

11

GETTING AWAY

Florida 1977

To a foreigner, there is something unique about the landscape of the Southern United States. It floats serenely past the glass of the train or car window, acres and acres and *acres* of virtually featureless New World, spreading ever outward like an unblemished alternate universe of forests and fields, neatly demarked by America's Great Wall of China, the Interstate highway's fence.

For me and, I suspect, any visitor from a densely populated country, some of the initial interest in this scenery comes from the miles upon miles of vast and relatively underdeveloped, underpopulated land. It is not that the landscape is empty; it is just empty of people and (except for farmland and billboards) of the artifacts of people as well.

There are no crowds afoot, no ubiquitous villages, hardly any farming complexes. While such is not the case in

121

and around urban areas, probably 90% or better of the surface of the South is, by the standards that foreigners bring with them, non-urban and *empty*.

Between Atlanta and the billboards that welcome visitors to The Sunshine State, there are approximately 225 miles of high-speed Interstate highway—no traffic lights, no stop signs, no detours. Although one does pass (or by-pass) cities and towns, there are also few clear signs of densely settled populations—hardly a church steeple, in fact. Essentially, all one really sees are other cars.

Here, unfortunately, boredom begins to set in. There are so few points of *reference*. It is as if one were indeed plunked down in a separate universe, and, after an initial overwhelming arousal of curiosity, finds that it is exactly like the universe left behind, only with less of everything.

What one does see are woods and fields, fields and woods, and, at the interchanges, woods and fields and motels.

(Later in my American life, I will learn that the Far West has its variation on this theme of the achingly vacuous landscape; it goes "rocks and sagebrush, sagebrush and rocks." Because the West can be stunning in its beauty, however, travelers tend to have more patience with it. And it changes more often, with mountain ranges and squared-off buttes and astonishingly vast deserts looming into view at irregular but aesthetically pleasing intervals.)

Hihira, Waycross, Valdosta, Unadilla, Tift—names on exit signs, identities without faces; cities unseen are, therefore, as non-existent as the breeze, as substanceless as clouds.

Occasionally, at the busiest crossroads of this endless trek on the concrete slabs of I-75, there drift into view fast-food outlets and gas stations *cum* convenience stores. As pleasant as these are to encounter, and as clean and efficient as they may turn out to be, they have the same basic flavor of the landscape: vanilla. They are bland to the point nearly of lunacy, as if some great unseen hand designed them at a single stroke with little attention to texture and no eye whatsoever for detail.

Perhaps it is just this route. Perhaps it is just the Interstates. One way or another, foreign visitors should be forewarned.

Still, the closer Florida draws, the more excited at the prospect of change I become. That is one of the purposes of this trip: to let me see more of America. Another is for Richard to get away for the first time, including weekends (he has Saturday classes) this year.

Perhaps entering Florida will surprise me—perhaps it will be like traveling up to Chiengmai from Nakhon Narai, with the land growing ever greener and hillier, quasi-Himalayan, while the houses become teak-constructed rather than *maimakha* wood; the rice fields change to tobacco and soybeans, livestock from water buffalo to cattle; and the people themselves, seen in droves along the roadside, are perceptibly lighter-toned than in the Rice Belt.

I do, in fact, get my surprise when we pass those welcome signs into Florida. It is, like most states will prove to be as I travel through them, slightly but noticeably different from it's neighbors—*physically* different, not just conceptually. In this case, it has something to do with the trees, both natural and cultivated. While the landscape's long, cresting-sinking rolls remain the same, in Florida they became peppered with wild palm-family trees and cultivated orange groves.

The creeks and streams seem to change as well, becoming black on white, swamp water on fine sand, and comparing them absently with similar ones in my homeland, I begin to envision populations of pythons and crocodiles.

I mention my musings to Richard.

"Water moccasins and alligators, maybe—definitely not crocs."

"What is difference? Alligator and crocodile."

"To the former, you are a threat; to the latter, a potential meal."

"You mean alligator friendly?"

"Not exactly. But they don't cause the havoc that crocs do."

"Havoc mean like bite off arm or leg?"

"Yeah."

"Then I understand. Crocodile in the Thai jungle very well-fed this way. I am glad to hear 'bout alligator."

"You won't be glad about sand sharks, though. Where we are going, they do some damage. And the man-o-wars."

"I'm sorry?"

"Man-o-wars. Sort of like jellyfish, but with a sting." He pauses for a moment. "One of them sent Julie to the hospital once." Another pause. "Poor girl."

He rarely mentions her, and even more rarely with any sort of emotion in his voice. The last time he did so was about a week after my announcement of my pregnancy. Somehow our conversation landed on her, and he expressed again, more to himself than to me, regret not that she had been unable to bear children for them but that she was barred now from bearing them at all.

Sitting there in the car, almost six months pregnant, I believe that somehow Julie had not really wanted children, that she was first and foremost a career woman.

The new thought leaves a funny taste in my mouth, regret tinged with a sourceless jealousy, and in my mind she takes on a different, "rounder" dimension. I would like some day to meet her, a wish that will never be fulfilled as she and her pianist-husband move lock, stock, and Grand Piano to a place called Seattle, which to my mind is as far away as you can get and still be in the contiguous United States. (I am not too far wrong, as it turns out.)

Swallowing back tears without fully knowing why, I

turn my attention to the late-afternoon Florida landscape floating by under a sky alternately sunny and gray. The topography is flatter now, more tropical, and not very different from the land around my family home—just emptier of everything but scrub trees and sawgrass.

In one of the streams we pass over, a snowy egret—*nog kayang* in Thai—stands balanced on one delicate leg, like an object placed for the momentary inspection of motorists hurtling by toward Tampa, Miami, and Daytona Beach, to remind them (if they do not blink and miss it) that before DeSoto and Disney came, a thing called Nature ruled completely here.

I blink and it is gone—as if I have imagined it.

Not too much farther down the road, Richard and I encounter what he terms "a genuine relic"—a prison road gang, picks, shovels, uniforms, and all—at work alongside I-75.

"Mostly black," I say.

He yawns. "Of course."

"Why 'of course'?"

"Who do you think commits most of the crime, from rape to armed robbery to Murder One."

"Not true. I see and read 'bout many white."

"Statistics don't lie," he says sternly.

"Well, maybe because they always on bottom, since slavery. Maybe whole world ride on their back."

"I'm sure it does. But I'm equally sure they can do more about it than they have so far."

So these are Richard's thoughts. Odd that they do not seem even remotely liberal. "Does not sound fair."

"I'm sorry, Dee, but it *is* fair. Blacks are being given their chance in this country, and they are blowing it. They just don't seem to have what it takes—and not only in this country. Of the ten poorest nations in this world, eight are predominantly black."

Surprised at the depth of his feelings, shocked even, I

refrain from answering. He seems to have no personal reason for speaking like this except for the fact that he is himself a white American. I wonder if these feelings are universal among whites, liberal or conservative, existing just below the surface of civility and Civil Rights. Perhaps he is, in a sense, merely the Voice of America on this subject—White America.

It is an unpleasant thought to pursue, apparently for both of us, for I cannot speak, I know, without turning the discussion into an argument.

Richard, too, prefers to drop the subject and fiddle with the radio dial.

He stops, paradox of paradoxes, when he locates a station playing his beloved "sophisticated funk."

After a night at an off-season, bargain-rate oceanfront motel, we are on the road again by 8:30 a.m. I would have preferred sleeping in the queen-sized bed or lolling on the beautiful, relatively empty beach spreading so grandly in the sun below our sixth-floor balcony.

I think my baby would prefer it, too.

But, Richard says, "If you don't get to Disney World before ten you can kiss the day goodbye. Unless you like standing in very long lines—and I wouldn't let you in your condition."

"It crowded in March also?"

"In any month you care to name. It's a circus."

"I'm sorry?"

"A madhouse. Crowded as Hell."

"Must be very crowd then."

He does a doubletake at me. "Why, you think Hell is any more crowded than Heaven? Wait, don't answer that."

I don't.

He says, a twinkle in his eye, "Whichever one I go to, I

ask only one thing." I can feel it coming; am I becoming jaded to his niceness? We have a phrase for such an irrepressible strain in men: *pak wan gon preu* (sweet mouth, sour bottom)— but the last part hasn't really applied to Richard so far.

And, knowing him as I do now, there's a chance that it never will. "That is," he says, "I want Wanwadee there with me."

"So I think. More sweet talk."

"Of course, but I told you it is truth—all of it, every word of sweet talk."

"So you want fry together?"

He laughs. A billboard with a gargantuan, grotesquely smiling Mickey Mouse floats by. "If that is where we are going —together—then yes, I do. Pan-fry, stir-fry, deep-fry, whatever. Besides, I don't think you'll be headed anywhere but up."

"Sank you. What 'bout you, though?"

He frowns. "Well, I do get visits from Satan when I'm in a bad part of a trip, if that's what you mean. They could very well be figments of my imagination, but wow! It's a trip to Hell."

"But why?" I am curious, for demon figures do not come just by whim in the Thai version of Buddhism.

He measures the words. Off to our left a huge thunderhead has billowed out. "I rarely do harm to anyone but myself, yet I see harm and hurt done all the time by others."

He pauses again, and a sparkling row of condominiums sweeps by, the near edge of Orlando. Texture, color, life.

"Sometimes I'm not sure it isn't someone or something called Satan running the whole show. There's just a little too much shit out there."

I have an inkling now of what needs working on once I get past the drug problem. This man needs to believe in a God; to put it as an American would, his *soul* needs saving.

CONFESSIONS OF A MAIL ORDER BRIDE

Tall order for a mail order bride, but a fresh horizon to set my sight upon when the time comes.

"Anyway, evil is just a part of a whole that is also harmonious and lovely. The whole is where I want to be—and for you to be, and the little one." He pats my tummy gently. *"Kun kaow jai mai?"*

"Yes, I understand." I appreciate his using one of his infrequent Thai phrases, but my mind is distracted. Instead I am wondering where it is he learns such things. From drugs?

Still, I love to listen to him. Just the idea of exchanging ideas with an intelligent and well-educated person, especially my own husband, gives me a good feeling. I want to be able to do it on a higher level, though; as it is, I miss a lot and my mind wanders and drifts.

Like now.

In the fall, I muse as he speaks, I will enroll in a college course, a philosophy class, a literature class, math, music, above all *art*.

I do not deliberately tune Richard out, but I am on my own thought track—college and classes and textbooks in English and bespectacled professors and, eventually, me, holding a degree from an American college in my hand. I could start in the fall, when the baby will be—no, no, better make that the following spring. He would be eight or nine months old by then, and I could easily manage one or two courses at a time. Maybe three.

It is a thrilling thought to have under the bright central Florida sky. Me, Wanwadee, mail order bride from Thailand— an American college student! There are many young Thais who would give up almost everything to be just that.

Off to the left a wide, lovely blue lake sails by, glittering in the sun, and it seems some sort of objective confirmation of the rightness of my idea: yes, of course! A college education. It is something I wanted in Thailand—though it would have been denied me—that, and to be a wife and mother. Now there is a chance. The place for doers, can-doers, is America.

I am becoming an American.

Can-do!

". . . the difference between the way it is and the way it ought to be, Orwell's boot in the face of the human race or true freedom in all aspects of life. See—it's a dilemma, no?"

"Dilemma—let's see. Some choice to make, all bad."

"Two choices, actually. Both bad."

"What you call when two thing, both good?"

"I don't know. Maybe nobody's ever been in that situation."

"I don't know. Always first time. You have to make like that."

"Sure, if you can."

"You can," I say, "and I can too." It seems for one stumbling moment that I am talking nonsense, but I bite my lower lip hard. "I promise I can."

"Promise what? Remember I told you don't make promises that you can't keep."

"It just promise to myself."

But now, fooling with the radio again, trying to tune in Orlando's funk, Richard isn't listening to me.

12

FIRST FIGHT

Florida & Georgia 1977

Theme Parks are totally *American* fun. Where else in the world can you see imagination played out on so large a scale and with such colorful cleverness? Where else can you ride a Screaming Monster Machine roller coaster or have your picture taken with one of the Singing Chipmunks? Nowhere in Thailand.

At Disney World, the sight of Snow White and one of her dwarfs sweeps me back to my childhood. I have seen the feature-length cartoon *Snow White and the Seven Dwarfs* three or four times, dubbed in Thai. In real life, with her American blue eyes, she is just as beautiful. Nearby, with his giant *papier-mache* scowl—that has to be Groucho.

(Or is it Grumpy? Do I have my dwarves and Marxes mixed up?)

In the warmth of the late afternoon sun, Richard and I

131

stroll around the big EPCOT lake. My pregnant paunch goes before us. Some of the international exhibits are as yet unopened, and most of the early spring crowds are in Disney World proper.

Arm in arm, we walk slowly; he is tired from waiting an hour in the long line for a half-hour jungle cruise and a twenty-minute Communication of Tomorrow audioanimatron show. The cruise idea was Richard's—I have seen enough jungles in my lifetime—but the show idea was mine.

Although I read recently of "audioanimatrons" in a magazine, I have to see for myself, of course. I am not disappointed. Introduced into some remote Indochinese hill villages, one of these technological marvels would stand a reasonable chance of, if not being worshipped, then at least being elected chief.

I am amused by Abraham Lincoln, whom every Thai schoolkid knows as the man who refused a gift of war elephants from our most famous King—King Mongkut, of *The King and I*. The present was to express admiration for Lincoln's freeing of the slaves, which Mongkut completed for Thailand just a few years after the Emancipation Proclamation was issued. Lincoln sent a message of thanks-but-no-thanks; he wanted not even an overture to an "entangling alliance," must less the alliance itself.

The descending sun gleams prettily off the lake, reminding me of the glitter of the Hudson River far below as we bussed into Manhattan on those honeymoon days of nearly a year ago. How long ago that seems now, and how much longer ago my days in Thailand.

Remembering my homeland, I have difficulty realizing that it was I who walked those narrow Nakhon Narai streets, swam with water snakes in the Chao Phraya river, recited the ludicrously misapprehended English phrases in preparatory school while boys outdoors in short-pants uniforms shouted after a soccer ball as if it had ears and could respond.

Long ago, far away. There's a wistful American song with those words, and an even more wistful Thai one, too. I start to sing the latter, softly as we complete our circuit of the lake.

"I love to hear you sing," Richard says.

I am hardly aware that he listens. "Sank you."

"You make the songs sound so—so *real*. They are all folk songs, no—most of them?"

"Some of them. Some of them popular. Some even Thai version of American song."

"Song*s*."

"Song*s*."

"Yes, I thought I recognized a few. When I listen, I can almost imagine what the words mean. Love, sorrow, joy—familiar stuff, you know."

"I not realize you listen."

"All the time."

"I sing that mush?"

"More than you are probably aware."

"It bother you?"

"Are you kidding?"

He pulls me closer as we start toward the huge, unfinished geodesic dome that looms over the entry gates like some metallic idol of technology.

"It has become," he whispers in my ear, "the beautiful background music of my life."

Not entirely sure what that means, I can nevertheless guess, and it makes me feel good all over. Okay, so it is sweet talk, but that isn't going to prevent me from enjoying it. I regard it as a privilege—just as long as it remains sincere. For both of us, in fact, it has become a sort of addiction.

CONFESSIONS OF A MAIL ORDER BRIDE

A positive addiction—unlike some other addictions I now know.

Back at the beach late in the day, we rest for an hour, watching the evening news with its usual assortment of local and international mayhem, relayed by an anchorman to whom dips in the Dow-Jones seem about on a par with a massacre of refugees in Palestine. Then we head out to eat and be entertained.

On the basis of its name and clever pitch ("a meal you'll remember for a price you'll soon forget"), we choose a place called Kokomo Joe's (we should have *known*) and are subsequently treated to a meal we easily forget at a price (considering the food) we have a tough time *not* forgetting.

It is typical American Bland, Richard's term for food prepared by a chef who apparently has never heard of seasoning. The phony continental dish-names (Scampi Fiortina, Fettucini del Buerro, etc.) and the tacky vinyl tablecloth ambiance match the food itself: a not untypical American dining-out experience, Richard assures me.

Skipping dessert (Cherises Flambeau, Tart de Fromage avec Frutti, etc.) at Kokomo Joe's, we opt for a small "Home-Made Ice Cream" stand that we passed on the way out. Although the ice cream is not, of course, home made, it is exceptionally good. Richard comments that his Pecan Praline double-dip would be enough to make his day if everything else had gone badly. I respond that, in Thailand, if one *good* thing happens, it is enough to make one's day; whereas in America it often seems that one *bad* thing is enough to ruin a day.

"I never thought of it that way," Richard says. "But that's probably accurate. We're a bunch of spoiled kids. Take away our candy and we scream blue murder."

"Give Thai same candy and he scream for happy."

"Just the same, most of us work for our candy. And it's not always that easy to come by."

"True. It pretty big 'Merican candy store, though."

He laughs. "Lots of expensive chocolates."

After the ice cream, we drive down the main street for a while, U.S. Highway One (I love the sound of it), then stop at a small bar advertising nightly jazz, just before driving out to the beach again. Richard has been looking forward to a beer.

At the front of the small barroom, an all-white trio is making pleasant-enough sounds, but Richard asserts that they would sound much better if they were all-black.

Strange attitude.

I am happy enough to be sitting in a dark American bar in the remote state of Florida listening to a native American art form, regardless of who is playing it.

Richard listens politely, tapping his toe, and, after an hour and another beer, calls for the bill.

"It was okay," he says as we leave, "but white people just tend to—well, to *sound white*."

I look at him.

"It's an expression."

One of many I take joy in learning, even memorizing, in this curious American culture where white is white and black is black, and in between are acres and acres of varying shades of gray.

Before going to our room, we decide to walk on the beach. The tide is in, and in the dark the breaking surf catches enough of the hotel lights to reflect isolated lines of creamy white as each wave topples over and gives way to the next. There is a salty tang in the air, clean as on the day of creation, and motionless gulls stand on the wet sand like random statuary. The hotels stretch in either direction, lit guardians of their little strips of sand and surf. Over the water a sliver of moon hangs nearly upside down. A few stars shine through the mist.

"Some American Indians had a myth," Richard says.

"Each star represented a soul, and they saw their ancestors in chosen stars."

"So each night they could visit a dear depart one." I nod. "That nice."

"Yes. It also explains why each star has so many names in Indian lore."

We both laugh. "Could be confusing."

"In modern times all the stars have one name each, but the names comes from different sources—Roman, Greek, Arabic, et cetera."

"Any Thai?"

"Could be. Just to be sure, though, let's name one now. In Thai, Dee, for one of your dear departed. Pick a star, any star."

"Okay," I say, studying the heavens for a good one, ". . . that one over there, just left of moon. Bright one, all alone."

"I think it's already called something, but name it anyway."

I pause for a moment, making a silent prayer. The surf whooshes rhythmically against the sand.

"Go ahead," he says gently watching me closely, as I brush away a tear.

I have finished my prayer. "*Sumwong*."

Back in the motel room, Richard shows no interest in making love. I am not surprised. I am pregnant, of course, but that is not it.

From our honeymoon night to this night, he exhibits interest only when he is stoned. With his marijuana nearly four hundred miles away, he prefers watching television.

I lie down beside him and nestle in his arms, pleased to be with him, sex or not—just as I know he is pleased to be with me, dope or not. Light, unspoken agreement; it can do no damage at all to our marriage, not this far into it and into love.

FIRST FIGHT

Jimmy Carter is on the screen—a documentary on his life in politics, keyed to the recent Inauguration. Presidential news is always news in America, even with no major elections on the horizon. In Thailand, such out-of-season political broadcasts would have to be a form of propaganda, not to be wasted on the potentially indifferent. When elections come, they come like a storm—and go like one, too, with bodies and debris in their wake.

Richard and I study him, commenting to one another briefly, desultorily, as one might speak of a specimen in a lab— Carter means little to us in the daily stream of our lives together. Essentially, he is just a remote force, one of many in the universe, however cute his Howdy Doody smile. Surely he will come into sharper focus for us once he assumes greater Presidential definition.

But, then, maybe not. We have problems of our own.

"Mr. Peanut comes to town," Richard says.

I can tell him what people in Thailand will think of Carter: a good man, a farmer, and, yes, a peanut farmer at that. His Presidency should go over quite well in a land where peanuts are harvested by the billion each year. It is Thailand's third most important crop.

"Thai sticks are number one, of course," he says.

I consider. "It makes much money, marijuana. But for bunch of bandit and crooked politician. No, not number one with Thai people, man on street. Number zero."

"Dee, Dee, Dee," he sighs. "There are two or three things you rate *zero* that are not that bad, not when viewed objectively."

I think for a moment. "What else?"

"Sunning on the beach," he grins.

Oops, Achilles heel: he remembers what I told him when we left for Florida, that my Thai skin turns a dusky brown under the sun. Since light skin, such as Thai Queen

Sirikit's, is so highly prized (a phenomenon attributable to our respect for European culture—and an inverse form of racism as well), my fear of exposure to the sun, and the thriving Thai parasol industry, are easily explained.

"Okay, what else?"

"Gotcha!"

Got me? On what? "Go ahead, Richard. What else you got?"

"I don't really need a *what else*. There's the dope, the tanning, and—and communism."

Okay. Now I am warming for a fight, one that we have never really settled in the past. Richard has only to have lived in Southeast Asia during the past couple of generations to understand what a real-life menace that particular political system is.

"You like be free?" I open. I am thinking of the millions of Thai people who awaken each dawn to the threat of communist takeover from east, north, and west like three sharp knives at their throats.

"Do I like to be free? Am I American? That's not the point."

"Of course it is point!" I feel my blood rising, blood of the tiger, for my people the Thais. "You live in communism state, you be like stuck pig."

"As an abstract way of life, though, it is noble and ideal. From each according to his ability, to each according to his need. What could be simpler—or better?"

"Foolish speech. You think that is way they live, you wrong. Look at Laos and Cambodia. Communist grab you and cut throat when you extend hand. All they want is takeover."

"You know, I think we are talking about two different things. You're speaking of communists, *people*, corrupt people, while I am talking about the system of communism itself. The idea."

FIRST FIGHT

There is a difference? I want to say—but, feeling my anger about to get out of control, I remember what my mother taught me about arguing with men, especially one's husband with whom one must co-exist forever, presumably; and I struggle to clamp the lid on. We believe there is really no such thing as an inconsequential or "shrugged-off" marital argument. They all count toward or against marital harmony and the longevity of love. Either find a way to make them count *for*, or avoid them altogether.

That, too, is the Thai way: put the tiger away, in "abstract" situations like this, before it breaks its leash.

I am glad to see that Richard seems to understand this principle as well as I; I am sorry, on the other hand, that I cannot keep the tiger from one final growl: "People and system are same. It mistake to unconnect one from other."

"*Dis*connect. And, look, I guess you're right. You've been there, I haven't."

"*Dis*connect. Sank you. But that is three of your thing you mention. Too bad is those three."

"It's not that important in the scheme of things. Political ideas are among those we can't really resolve—nobody can. And I understand your concern over your family as well."

"Of course I am concern."

"And pregnant, too. Let's not argue over anything, okay?"

"I don't want to."

"Good. Come lie by me, please."

"What for?" I am still peeved; hot blood remains in the system for a long time.

"So's I can attack you."

"Is suppose to be funny?"

"Would I kid about a thing like that?"

I consider. "Question is, can you *do* thing like that?"

He laughs; I do not. He stops laughing and sits up. "You mean—I mean—I don't know what you're talking about."

"Of course you do. And it shame."

"I mean, you're six months pregnant."

"That not stop you week ago—*when you high*."

"Yeah, okay," he sighs, "I do know exactly what you're talking about."

"So?" Is it time, finally, to confront? It doesn't really feel like it, but I make a stab. "You want to talk 'bout it?"

He lies back down, and a long quiet moment follows.

"I would like to share problem," I say softly.

He laughs, a bark—not nice. "I don't have any problems."

"You want talk, yes or no?"

"What for?" He mimics me.

Silence fills up the room and strangles off the inane nonsense of a hemorrhoid salve commercial. Difficult things are always harder than they appear to be before they must be done. No, this not—not *yet*—the time. "Okay. Some other day."

He gets up and changes the channel to a basketball game. "Yep," he sighs. "Some other day."

Am I afraid to deal with this problem I ask myself? In a way, yes. If confronting it, confronting him, will erode or destroy any part of the beauty of our love, of course I am afraid.

But, sooner or later, the day of confrontation must come.

Sooner or later.

On the beach the next morning, I stay with him for a few minutes in the warm and breezeless 80-degree weather. But I soon leave, fearful of the sun. He waves, and says something about finding a good Chinese restaurant that evening.

Maybe it is the pregnancy, but I feel immensely weary as I climb the wooden stairs from the beach to the motel pool area. The weight I carry seems concentrated not in my womb but across my tight and aching shoulders.

When I get to the room, I go to the window and look down the six stories to Richard on the beach. In his sunchair with the high-tide water lapping gently at his feet, he is virtually alone out there, this weekend before Spring Break, except for the strollers and an occasional car crawling by, a lone anomaly on the broad white strip of sand.

On the one hand, I have an immense pity for my American husband with the "American disease," for the circumstances in his life that have caused the miniscule character gaps, the hidden weaknesses through which drugs flow in.

On the other hand, I am exasperated that I cannot yet get through to him, become any closer with him.

Become one with husband, is a saying repeated over and over by parents and relatives to impressionable Thai teenagers.

They must have been thinking of platonically ideal husbands.

This American husband of mine has apparently embraced too strongly the American ideal of independence; so strongly, in fact, that the meaning has become warped in *defiance,* into *rebellion*—probably a fairly common occurrence in the United States, one that gives rise to the murderous aberrations about which one reads or hears daily in the news. People often invite their own phantoms and demons—bad enough the uninvited!

Although, by comparison, Richard's "cancer" is benign, the damage it causes will not only be to himself but to us, his wife and forthcoming child, as well. If only he could see that!

Looking down at him, then, I find myself full of worry not for him, or for me, but for our baby, for the ruinous world of a father in decline into which he may be born.

Unless something happens—or can be done.

Although we have planned on a four-day holiday, the March weather turns windy and cold, and we cut the mini-vacation short. The very next day, in fact, we are back on the Interstate, headed home.

It is a long four hundred miles. Neither one of us has much to say, and we sit in silence, without even the radio on, as the green-brown landscape floats by under a sky that is mostly gray. It rains off and on, alternately cleaning the windshield and spotting it with road dirt and dead bugs.

At a couple of points along the way, Richard inquires about my comfort, and I assure him that both the baby and I are doing fine. Just past Macon and a refill of gas and Coca-Cola, on the final run toward Atlanta, he asks sheepishly whether my feelings are hurt. We came awfully close to our first major argument last night, and in fact did have a fight; I am still smarting.

But I respond, "Feelings 'bout what?"

"Anything."

"What mean *anything*?"

"Sex, politics, God—anything."

"We talk 'bout all that last night?"

"Most of it. Especially politics."

"You talk politic. I talk family."

"Boy, that *has* got you worried."

Here we go again. "Of course it does. What you expect? Suppose it your family could die like dog."

"But with the U.S. Navy and Air Force all around, the chances of a takeover in Thailand are awfully slim. Miniscule, in fact. I think this communism argument we've been having is kind of a glossover for some deeper stuff."

I consider. "It possible."

It grows quiet again in the car, except for the hum of

FIRST FIGHT

the tires and the occasional swish of windshield wipers on intermittent. Richard has slowed some as we speak, and a huge semi-trailer sweeps past us, drafting along a mini-cyclone of swirling mist and rain. Two cars follow right behind, blind, speeding, like parasites who know only the host, its way, its destination.

At length Richard says, "I know I've said this before . . . but there's nothing in my life that I can't handle. It's a matter far more of time than of strength. Just give me some room—please, Dee. I can't hurt anyone but myself, and I'm not even doing that."

"I give lot of loom."

"*Room*."

"*Room*. Too much, in fact."

"The hell you do. You *haunt* me about it."

His voice becomes steely all of a sudden, and all of a sudden I feel bad—bad about everything. There are a thousand things that I want to say back, to shout back, in rising shock and anger. What would an American wife say now? What does a Thai wife say—a *real* one, not a pregnant, disenfranchised mail order bride?

I bite my tongue and look at a McDonalds floating by. *Yellow, yellow, yellow, yellow arches. YELLOW ARCHES!* There. It is better now.

Almost.

Whatever I can say I have already said, either to him or to myself, so I know what all his answers are or will be. And, such as they are, they are surely more of a frustration to me than my questions are to him.

Still, I cannot shrug it off—my tiger refuses to. "I wish it only yourself you hurt. But it not."

He hunches an icy shoulder up against me, and I cry softly to myself and my son until we reach the city limits of

Atlanta, where the gleaming highrises deflect my attention and the increased traffic his.

Gazing up at the many windows, lit against the gloom of the day at 3:30 on a Thursday afternoon, I think of the lives going on behind those concealing panes of glass.

Is it like this for most of them—is there a family problem or a personal crisis hovering over their lives as menacingly as this one hovers over mine? And is it drugs—alcohol, cocaine, marijuana? Or are there other American diseases?

Of course, there are problems, and many of them *drug* problems, and yet because these unseen strangers are American —or maybe simply because they *aren't me*—I imagine that somehow my life has become temporarily worse than any of theirs, because of my faraway family in Thailand, and the coming of the baby, and Richard's inability or unwillingness to arrest the downslide of his life.

As we wind our way out of the city and up the Northwest Expressway toward our cottage in the woods, though, I begin to realize that I am feeling very sorry for myself—for myself and the tiny life inside me. Looked at objectively, each aspect of a problem has a road around or through it: I hear from members of my family regularly, and, like Thailand itself, they are prospering under the functional "peace" in Southeast Asia.

The baby, furthermore, will be one hundred percent normal and healthy; that I can tell from many signs, including the absolute painlessness of the pregnancy and the constant reassurances of our obstetrician. I know, too, that the benevolent spirit of Sumwong is still with me; oddly enough Richard seems to think so too to judge by his steadfast claim that the infant will be a replacement for Sumwong in my heart.

From time to time I can feel little movements inside me, like the stirrings of some tiny furtive spirit as it awakens within its dark warm dream of life and makes ready to move toward the light. *All will be well*, is the message I receive daily from inside myself.

As for Richard, there is much working against him at this stage in his life: the growing drug dependency, yes, but also his precarious career and his apparent disregard of, or lack of respect for, the powers that shape individual destinies.

Yet all his troubles seem somehow superficial, skin deep, considering what he has going *for* him: physical strength, as evidenced by a handsome, healthy body; good genes, as evidenced by his intelligence and the success of his family members; and a wife who loves him from the roots of her soul.

Despite any petty arguments we might have now and in the future, Richard is my man, and as long as he stops short of either abusing me or falling into any real or metaphysical gutters, I will stand by him—no question. All women—Thai, American, or Ubangi—wish to live and love like that.

We have arrived on our winding exurban street. Everything looks the same, right down to the flowers I have painted on our mailbox to match the ones Richard tends in summer along the front of the house, a calculated and always flourishing mix—he has a green thumb—from early-blooming azaleas to late-blooming gardenias.

He stops and gets the mail.

I turn to him: "You drive long. I fix tea."

"I'd like that. Red Zinger, please."

"Yes, would be good. Much colder here."

He pulls up the driveway and cuts the engine. "Could you put a dab of honey in it—like usual."

"Okay. I make some cookie too, later."

He smiles, and looks in my eyes, and thanks me. No: despite his flaws, he is no senselessly cruel or cynical fool such as I might have married in Thailand—or in the States, for that matter.

And maybe I have been "haunting" him.

CONFESSIONS OF A MAIL ORDER BRIDE

If a marriage is not working out, over time, then one may contemplate divorce, even as one exerts more patience than seems humanly possible in order to make it work. But ours is way short of that point and, in fact, seems unlikely ever to reach it. It must be *kept* from reaching it.

We both sense something like that in the car, feel it as a sort of radiance outspreading from our hearts, warmth in the cool March air. We turn toward each other and kiss, very warmly. Love hasn't gone more than one iota off the mark—if that.

"Make me a cookie of yourself too," he whispers, "one I can nibble on for a long time."

"That exactly what I have in mind. Chocolate chip, follow by Wanwadee chip."

"Follow*ed*."

"Follow*ed*."

"They both sound awfully good."

We kiss again, and get out of the car. Twilight casts blue, peach and lilac shadows on the walkway as we carry in our few pieces of luggage. The house and all its furnishings are exactly as we have left them; not a knick-knack is out of place. It feels good to be home. Richard turns up the furnace, and we stand and hug for a while enjoying our renewed closeness.

There will be pot later, I know, but *ma pen rai*. It doesn't matter—for now.

13

A TRIP TO "PARADISE"

Atlanta 1977

It is a bright cool day in a month reputed to be the cruellest, April, but so far it has been exactly the opposite. There has been a week or more of perfectly cool, perfectly clear weather, of the sort rarely seen in Thailand except in mid-winter.

Actually in my native region *summer* and *winter* are misleading, for in lowland tropical areas there are only the two seasons of wet and dry. In my hometown, many of the houses are built on wooden stilts six to eight feet off the ground. They serve two purposes; they lift the house out of harm's way during the wet, flood-danger times, and elevate it sufficiently to catch breezes in the hottest weather. It never gets *cool* in the American sense of the word, and air conditioning exists only at luxury hotels.

On this particularly beautiful Atlanta afternoon, I return from an extended shopping trip—maternity clothing, things I cannot make for myself on the new sewing machine Richard's mother has sent, as well as food and drink—to find Richard and Robert under a small dogwood tree on the front lawn. My husband is lying on his back gazing up through the four-petaled white buds at the sky while his friend is propped on an elbow, intently studying one of these buds.

I watch them as I drive up and walk over with a bag under each arm. I see broad, peculiarly childish smiles on their faces, and hear their halting speech and giggles. They both have on sunglasses. Thus I am prepared for the worst.

When they finally notice that I am approaching, they stand up and, dusting themselves off, begin studying me curiously without so much as a nod to return my greeting.

Robert sniffs the air around me and says, his voice full of wonder, awe even, "A female. Oh, God, smell it—a *female.*"

Richard sniffs. "Umh. Beautiful. Like—like something from another world."

Robert laughs at that, and then they both begin laughing in short, almost out-of-control, bursts. When Richard mutters something haltingly and (to me) incoherent about yin-yang, the 180 degrees in a circle, and cosmic halving, Robert breaks up completely, and Richard joins him. Before long they are both on their knees under the dogwood tree, laughing like two maniacs, *howling* actually.

Thankful that we are fairly isolated on our three acres, I hoist my packages and head for the house. Over my shoulder I say, "Two more bag, Richard. Please bring in when—when you are able."

I don't think they hear me, but Robert stammers, "Wh-wh-when you are able, Ricky, when you are *able.*"

Seemingly that is the whipped cream on the cake, and they both fall over on their sides and roll around convulsing with laughter. Robert, on his back, kicks his legs wildly in the air like some monstrous dying insect; Richard, rolling up against the tree, slaps its trunk with his palm over and over again, emitting peals of glee.

I go back for the other packages and then flee into the kitchen. After depositing the perishable items in the refrigerator and shedding my sweater, I take a position behind the kitchen curtain and settle down to watch them, feeling disoriented, as if I have stumbled upon a secret American ritual to which I am not meant to be exposed.

As it turns out, that is not too far off the mark.

Their laughter trails off into giggles and guffaws, and they begin lolling and speaking again, most of which I cannot hear. What I can hear seems not to make sense, to be a sort of telepathic code, an unconnected word here, a cryptic phrase there, as if two aliens are communing—E.T. and Yoda. Yet they nod from time to time, enough to indicate that some kind of genuine, if uncanny, communication is actually taking place.

For a brief moment, I find the scene funny myself and laugh out loud. But my laughter echoes eerily through the empty house and comes back to settle on me, freezing the muscles of my face. Too, I feel a remote but palpable pain in my womb, perhaps from the strain of the long shopping expedition, more likely from the stressful contemplation of the activities I am witnessing. Husband and friend, on the ground on a quickly chilling spring afternoon, laughing at nothing, apparently, and conversing, if you can call it that, in a kind of oral Morse code.

This husband, *that* friend.

It adds up to dope. What else?

Catching sight of me at the window, Richard gets up and walks over very slowly, a smile on his face as ineradicable and unfathomable as the one on Easter Island icons.

When he gets to the window, he studies me through the glass and says, each phrase coming out very slowly, as if he is materializing them out of starstuff no one but he can see, with his eyes half-closed: "Beautiful Oriental lady. Far from home. Brave as any hero. Proud and singing. Good to the bone."

In spite of myself, I laugh again; the whole thing is ludicrous, impossible actually, as if we have stumbled into our very own Twilight Zone. Is there any way out?

I speak cautiously as he finishes and stands there in silence: "Sank you. Was like a poem."

I can think of nothing else to say. His smile broadens. After a long moment in which somehow I seem to have momentarily entered his frame of consciousness—perhaps by a form of osmosis—he opens his mouth to speak, and I know exactly what is going to come out.

And out it comes, through the beatific smile: "No, Wanwadee. *You* are like a poem."

That seems to satisfy him, and he starts back toward Robert under the tree. But then he stops and, wobbling just a tiny bit, returns to me. "Please call Anne," he says very simply, an attempt to be businesslike now—some semblance of his rational mode. "Robert needs to get home."

"How did he get here?"

Richard thinks for a moment, closing his eyes. It is a very long moment, more like a couple of minutes.

"Richard?"

"I—I can't remember."

He turns around and goes back to Robert, saying something, and they break up under the tree again, great howling hyena screams of laughter which I swear must be heard as far away as the nearest police station.

I hurry to the phone and call Robert's wife, describing the situation briefly as well as I can, and she promises to come right over. Fortunately (especially given the far flung reaches of the city), they live in the Buckhead area, only fifteen minutes away.

Between the phone call and Anne's arrival, Richard and

A TRIP TO "PARADISE"

Robert find something else uproariously funny, God only knows what, and laugh so hard they both start crying—tears streaming down their cheeks, making their whole faces blubberingly wet, contorted in the slanting light of the late afternoon, like the faces of two overgrown kids in pain.

Then Richard nestles up to the tree and, speaking with it as one would talk to a reasonable and sane human being, apologizes for hitting it each time he laughs. That's bad enough, but the crusher comes when he puts his ear to the trunk and listens, nodding, to the dogwood's reply.

It takes a while for Anne to get her husband into their station wagon. For one thing, she has made the mistake of bringing their kids (but what else could she have done with a six-year-old and a ten-year-old?), both of whom sense immediately that something is very different about Daddy. They study him intently through the open back window. For another, Robert doesn't want to leave his buddy Ricky just yet, they are having such a hell of a good time.

On their faces they still wear broad knowing smiles, as if together they have explored and communicated about life's greatest mysteries. While Anne and I speak distractedly about kids and school, they refuse to come out from their home at the center of the universe, under the sacred dogwood tree. It isn't until she has been there for some ten minutes or more that Robert gets up and comes unsteadily over to the edge of the lawn beside the car. As he approaches, the kids lean forward out the window, two puppy faces mooing curiously out a doghouse door, scrutinizing this unfamiliar aspect of a very familiar person.

"Can we go now, dear," Anne says, visibly struggling to sound eager and pleasant. "Pleeease."

"Yeah, I suppose so. I really didn't mean to keep you

and the kids waiting so long. What was it," he asks, turning to Richard behind him, his smile broadening, "a year or so?"

Hearing him, Richard cannot stifle a giggle—they are both at least tangentially aware of the queer dimensions of the warp they are in—but before they can stop themselves and focus on the reality of the situation, they are off on a flight of laughter once more.

Finally, very reluctantly, Robert gets into the car, in the front seat with the kids breathing down his neck. He smiles one final time at Richard, who winks and says, "Remember, guy: in every bud you see."

The smile drops from Robert's face and a look of awe takes its place. "Yeah. Yeah, man, yeah. But one thing, Ricky."

"What's that?"

"Does that include Bud*weiser?*"

They both start laughing again, and as Richard tells him to get the hell out of there, Anne takes off down the block at last.

Turning without a word, Richard walks slowly up the stoop and into the house. The door shuts with a neat little click behind him, and I am left alone in the front yard with the budding azaleas in front of me and the budding dogwood behind.

Buds. What is so special about buds?

I bend down over an azalea bush and inspect one very closely, from every angle, searching for what the two men found so interesting, if not profound. I whisper to myself, in response to my own baffled questions, "Not single damn thing."

Except for a handful of the tiniest white aphids crawling across its underside. These will need spraying.

Of course, there is spring, and the promise of floral beauty, and the implicit suggestion of rebirth and the cycles of life, but in my frame of mind—peeved and relieved at once—I cannot see a damned thing but the bugs.

So much for dogwood buds.

Inside, I refrain from disturbing Richard for an hour or so, until I have fixed supper and set it aside to be warmed when he is ready. Then I walk softly to the bedroom in which he has sequestered himself and tap on the door.

No answer. The room is on the northeast side of the house, and with the shades down and the curtains drawn, it is as dark as a tomb in the afternoon.

Figuring he is asleep, I start to tiptoe away. But then I hear his voice, low and slow, *different*, like a voice from beyond. "Yes. What is it?"

I go back. "It is Wanwadee. Would you like supper now?"

Another long silence. Then, "You must be kidding."

"No, I am not kidding. It ready when you want it." I start away again.

"Dee. Dee, come here. Come in, Doll." That voice from beyond.

I go to the door, push it open, and find him flat on his back on the bed with one arm over his eyes. Except for his shoes being off, he is fully clothed.

"Sit over there," he says, gesturing to the wingback chair in the corner.

I sit in the dark; a long moment passes. "Dee, this is incredible."

"What is?"

Another long moment.

"What I am seeing."

"Seeing? With light out?"

Yet another long moment in the cool dark of the high-walled room. "They call them eidetic images. Changing patterns of color and light. Shades, swirls, some things recognizable, most not. Like a kaleidoscope of all life, the entire universe, known and unknown."

"You have eye close whole time?"

"Eyes closed. If I open them, the images will go away. I don't want them to go away, they are so beautiful."

"Eyes closed. This very unusual. You sure you like—not scared?"

"How can you be scared of beauty. And truth."

"Truth in there too?" I don't know whether to take him seriously, humor him along, or call for Emergency Medical Service.

For the sake of harmony, and because he is taking it so calmly, so reflectively (at least he isn't howling like a hyena now), I decide to accept it all at face value for as long as I am able. But I have to know: "You all right, Richard? I am worry."

"Worried. Don't be silly, Dee. Of course I am all right. I am in paradise, in fact."

"Worried."

I sit and watch him for a while, lying so still and peacefully that someone just walking in could very well believe he is in paradise—has just died to get there, in fact. The only sound to be heard is the tick of the large clock in the hall and the bark of a dog so distant as to be more an afterthought than an annoyance.

Finally I ask him what he has taken.

"I don't want to talk about it," he says simply, without a stir, his voice still strange-sounding.

"But powerful."

"You bet."

"I thought all this stuff went out with hippie."

"Most of it did, along with most of the hippies." He

laughs, a brief semi-sarcastic snort that shakes the bed. "Tripped-out freaks."

"Robert be okay? I worry 'bout kids."

"Quit worrying. It's not going to turn either one of us into a fanged monster. Interesting stuff, actually. You wouldn't want to do it every day, though."

"What so interesting? What is 'bout bud anyway?"

"About what?"

So interesting, I think, that he can't recall the simplest thing. "The dogwood bud."

"Oh, that. Well, the main thing was that the meaning of the entire universe was wrapped up in that simple bud about to bloom."

"Oh. Simple like that."

"Simple, sure. But also profoundly complex."

"So I guess. What is meaning?"

"Of universe? I don't remember. It came and went like that. Robert and I had just enough time to work it out to our satisfaction, and then we lost it, most of it. It got away. You can't keep stuff like that, anyway. And you certainly can't transport it back over the line—like great wine, it doesn't travel well."

"Travel where?" What 'line'?"

"Between where I am now and where you are. Between my reality and yours. Between innately understanding and bio-logically surviving." I say nothing, not really grasping him yet, not sure if I can—or want to.

Reading my mind, he answers me.

"You can't get it, Wanwadee—not unless you were here with me. And knowing you, I wouldn't even ask. Even though you might be able to see and talk with your brother—"

"Please do not say. I would not have it that way."

"What way?"

"With drug."

"But . . . why not?"

"It cheap, for one thing. It dirty. It illegal. What why not."

He giggles, snorts. "Well, I asked for that. But you're wrong. I'm not scum, not a yahoo. Robert and I were on to something good, something deep."

"And funny, too."

"If only you would give it a try one of these—"

"*Please.*"

"Okay, Doll. I'm sorry. You can leave the room, if you want. I'll just spend some time in harmony with—with this."

"I will leave. But . . ."

"But what?"

"But I want to be in harmony with *you.*"

"Oh, you sweetheart. Thank you, my love. You are all the good things that I know of in the real world, Wanwadee—strength, patience, warmth, kindness, generosity."

I want to say *sweet talk,* but I hold my tongue; it is, can it be just sweet talk in his state of mind? It flatters me to think not, of course, but does one believe a drunk in a bar? It must be considered that he is off center just now; the tone of his voice is certainly other-worldly.

I keep the thought to myself.

Instead I say, "You say something like that outside, too. 'Bout me be like poem."

"I don't remember."

"No, I think not."

"Besides, I would not really say you are *like* a poem. The fact is, you *are* a poem. There's a difference."

"I'm sorry, dear. I'm begin to think is sweet talk after all."

"That's okay," he sighs. "Just as a noise is a noise whether someone hears it or not, truth is truth whether or not there is someone around to believe it."

"Well, that sound pretty good anyway. Maybe you are poet, after all."

He laughs. "Listen, Dee," he says, "in the bathroom medicine cabinet there is a bottle of niacin pills. In a half hour or so, bring me three or four and a glass of Coke. I need to come down . . . but not yet."

"Okay." I feel relieved.

"And, oh, one more thing. If anybody but Robert calls, I am not home. Say I had to go downtown for something. Consulting—say consulting. Yeah, that sounds good. And, who knows, I could very well be, if I hadn't gone to paradise today." He finished with a short rueful laugh.

"Food be ready when you want. It *tom-yum pla.*"

"*Tom-yum pla,*" he repeats. "That's lovely."

"It is sole fish in—"

"No, wait, don't tell me. Just leave it *tom-yum pla.*"

"Okay," I say, and leave the room, closing the door very quietly behind me.

As I start down the hall I hear him whisper over and over to himself, *"Tom-yum-pla. Tom-yum pla."*

Alone again, I feel suddenly frightened, for he hit that familiar nail squarely on the head when he said he could have been out consulting: like so many Americans caught up in a fancy for drugs, he could very well be more than he is now—a stoned, drug-prone, thirty-three-year-old man about to lose his job.

But it would be, literally, a hell of a time to bring that unpleasant subject up.

Instead I go to the front window and stand there for a long while, looking at the spot where he and Robert had set their little cocoon of paradise. What it is for him, obviously, is what it is for most people who indulge in drugs: an escape, albeit temporary if they don't kill themselves, from the strife and ugliness that comes creeping into life almost every day.

CONFESSIONS OF A MAIL ORDER BRIDE

Or so they see it.

It doesn't have to be this way, I want him to know—I want so badly for him to know and to feel and to believe. *It does not have to be this way.*

What it will have to come down to for the moment, though, is a little Thai phrase that I taught him long ago—the first ever I taught him, in fact. If nothing else, it will keep him from repeating *tom-yum pla* over and over in that voice, like some demonic mantra.

I walk to the second bedroom and whisper through the door: "*Shan ra-kun.* From both of us."

"Thank you, Dee," he says as he drifts in and out of his artificial paradise. "I love both of you."

But his voice still has that strange quality, as if emanating not from paradise but from its opposite.

14

OLD LIFE, NEW LIFE

Atlanta 1977

James misses being born on the Fourth of July by three days—he arrives on the first. He is a large baby, and is in the breech position complicating the delivery. Finally, the doctor tells us he will have to do a caesarian.

Hours later, tired and sore, I awake; it is a moment in my life that can never be equalled for magic or joy; in fact, it will *literally* never be equalled. A week later, after a post-op examination, my doctor says that as a result of a complex of symptoms known as "secondary infertility," I will probably never bear another child.

Still, the happiness James brings does not diminish. Not even in the light of serious financial trouble looming ahead.

From the first sight I catch of him after he is wiped down, I know he is my baby; *anyone* would know he is my baby: round face, tan skin, lots of black hair. I feel sorry for

CONFESSIONS OF A MAIL ORDER BRIDE

Richard, there is so little of him to see. (Actually as James grows he will stretch out like his father and always be above average in height. Too, his eyes will develop to be rounder than mine, more Western.)

Only a mother can know the pride felt at a new birth. Only an Oriental mail order bride could feel the sense of importance lent to a life led, so far, three steps behind almost everyone else's. I have brought into the world a new human being, and he is mine to raise—to feed, to nurture, to pray for —and to have.

Of course, I want the best of everything for him.

That much needs no voicing.

Richard understands when I tell him that I wish for James to be raised with American attitudes and values, but mixed with what is best from the Thai as well.

He understands me perfectly when I explain, for the first time, the basic concepts of Buddhism. He has some vague notion of patience and nirvana, et cetera, but he has no idea how it all might relate to a new life like James's.

Thai Buddhism teaches that everyone must experience unhappiness or dissatisfaction with life; that the human condition is one of flux, and nothing stays the same; and that individual behavior does not truly reflect enduring personality. Taken seriously and mixed in their proper proportion with a parent's worldview, each of these can enhance the way a child is raised.

Typical Westerner, Richard is surprised to hear all this said, but I tell him I wish to start with the right agenda. That makes sense to him. I go on to point out that any future unhappiness James might experience is basic to human life and is also certain to change to its opposite or to something in between. Furthermore, Thais believe that no single act a child performs, good or bad, intelligent or dumb, is a precursor of his or her enduring adult character. Tolerance must be tendered at all stages of growth.

Finally, what makes Thai Buddhism specifically Thai (as opposed to Indian or Japanese) is that it is profoundly, *uniquely* optimistic. My countrymen feel that each change undergone is for the betterment of the individual and of the entire race, as we move in ascending spirals through cataclysm, stasis, and ecstasy toward an ever higher state of being, an even higher level of consciousness.

This pleases Richard. It agrees with what he remembers of his reading in the Sixties, the lectures he attended, the music lyrics he heard, the things that were in the air back then. He is not so much convinced by my presentation as justified in his own convictions and habits of thought.

Thus James's life starts out on a very happy note, with a largely unspoken, yet profoundly understood, compromise between his parents. The meeting of two cultures; the meeting of two hearts. Coming to it from our separate angles, we manage to achieve accord.

15

THE OTHER SIDE OF
THE FENCE

Atlanta 1978

New Year's Day.

Unlike the previous year's New Year's Eve when we partied with friends (including Robert and Anne) until 2 a.m., we go to bed at ten the night of December 31, 1977. Richard, therefore, has no hangover to start the year.

Since being terminated by the university, he has not wanted to party or see his old friends. The past few months he has worked mainly at home as a "communications consultant," making enough for us to get by. He composes business people's resumes and writes and edits "farmed-out" technical and business reports. He waits for another major step in his life to begin: in just one week, he will start graduate school in spring term and be teaching again—both part-time.

CONFESSIONS OF A MAIL ORDER BRIDE

He would have begun graduate school in September, but he was either unable or unwilling to get his application done on time. In limbo, he has continued to have trouble deciding exactly what it is that he wishes to do. In the meantime, all our wheels spin, and life does not become any easier.

The only good thing to come from this current indecision and loss of direction is an accompanying loss of taste—momentary, as it turns out—for marijuana. He actually lets himself run out before he decides to go out and buy some more.

Through an unforeseeable turn of events, James and I happen to be with him when he makes his "buy."

It occurs on the day that he decides to take the Maverick into a garage for a tuneup. We all go together on a Sunday afternoon—nothing stops for any Sabbath in Atlanta—because I need to do some shopping as well.

Unfortunately, the automobile work takes longer than anticipated (and winds up costing more than expected), so Richard has to abandon his plan of dropping the baby and me off first if he is to get to his dealer's house before dark.

He has been told, sometime, somewhere, never to deal after night falls.

His dealer, Jeff, is recommended by one of Robert's friends as careful, circumspect, and a reliable supplier of top-quality pot. I have seen him once before in a supermarket when Richard pointed him out, a thin blond boy in his mid-twenties. He is married and the father of two kids.

Against my mild protests, we drive on this late Sunday afternoon to his house on a weedy road in Acworth, an exurb of Atlanta, so far out on the northwest fringes that urbanization has not really reached it yet. Surrounding the yard is a poorly erected chicken-wire fence with one thin strand of barbed wire along the top—as if *that* could keep out thieves or the police.

Richard pulls up to the fence in front of the house and

THE OTHER SIDE OF THE FENCE

honks two quick times, apparently a signal of some sort. It is then that I notice that there is no gate in the fence, that it goes seamlessly around the entire house.

I ask Richard about this and he shrugs. "It could be in the back where his truck is." I see a battered, peeling pick-up out back in some heavy weeds, near what appears to be a sort of pull-away section of the fence, more or less a flap.

It is a few minutes before Jeff appears, buttoning his shirt. He ambles slowly across the grassless, packed-clay front yard and shakes Richard's hand across the top of the fence, nodding to me. "Sorry, man," he says. "I was asleep. They got me working the damn swing shift. What can I do for you?"

He strikes me as a budding Southern "good ole boy," one of many in and around Atlanta, a friendly, lackadaisical young man with a drawl so slow you could lodge whole Thai phrases between each word.

"A couple of baggies is all," Richard responds.

"Sure thing," he says, and ambles back across the yard.

Through the open door we see him lift a loose floor-board in his interior hall and pull out two plastic sandwich bags full of a green-brown substance. Luckily there seems to be no one else living nearby. He brings the bags out and, in exchange, Richard hands him two, crisp, twenty-dollar bills over the fence. I wince to see the money passed: there goes a week's groceries at least.

"Thirty for anybody else," Jeff jokes.

"I'll bet."

"I'm serious, man," Jeff says. Through the open door I see a woman, his wife, pass noiselessly toward a room in which a baby bawls. "It's neat weed. Jamaican. Happy shit."

"Well, good," Richard says with just a touch of bitterness. "I could use a laugh." Jamaican, I learn later, is supposed to evoke humor in its indulgers.

CONFESSIONS OF A MAIL ORDER BRIDE

They reach over and shake hands again. "See you in a couple of months," Richard says.

"That long? You easin' off?"

Richard looks at me. "By popular request. Two, three joints a week." It was *one*, at least temporarily.

"Amazin' what a good woman can do." He nods at me again.

"You hit the nail on the head."

"But I tell you what. I can't make much at all off weed no more. People is starting to get into coke now, or crack."

"Is that right? I don't hear anything good about either one."

"Depends on your point of view, I s'pose."

"Like everything else."

"You said it. Come in for a beer?"

"No, thanks. We've got the baby in the car. Got to run. Take it easy, Jeff."

"*Adios*, man."

Richard will never know the hugeness of my relief when he refused that beer. I have been ready to leave since before we drove up.

As Richard eases the car back down the isolated dirt road, I catch a final good glimpse of the wife on the unpainted side porch. She has a flowered print dress on and a baby in her arms. Thin, haggard, she does not look young.

Jeff joins her, sticking our money into his back pocket.

When they see me looking, they wave. Jeff grabs the baby's hand and waves it, too.

I smile and wave back.

Reflecting on the totality of the situation—Richard's habits, this circle of people, the sort of thing one stoops to in order to make money—I cannot help but think to myself: *There but for the grace of God, of Buddha, go us.*

All three of us.

16

LOOKING FOR THE LIGHT

Atlanta 1981

In terms of perception and mathematics, time accelerates as one grows older.

The *math* of it is simple: when you are four or five, each year is one fourth or fifth of your lifetime—each day, not to mention a week or the epoch of a month, seems to last *so* long. Of course, in the growing self-awareness of the late teens and twenties, the years are now twentieths or so of a life, and they begin to slip away at a noticeable rate. And so time marches on at ever smaller fractions to an ever faster beat, and in the *terra incognita* of old age each year must seem a moment.

As a *perception,* if thought about too long it runs one up against death—one's own death. Think about *that* too long, and one had better have religion, or children, or both.

167

CONFESSIONS OF A MAIL ORDER BRIDE

I who have an ancient religion and Richard who as yet has none, though, are filled with equal joy at the birth of our first and last child: our one and only, a son. But one at least; and again in terms of mathematics and perception, the gap between none and one is everything.

Counterbalancing the addition of that life to ours is the subtraction of one *from* ours: Richard's mother dies suddenly, shortly before James's birth. She never gets to see her sixth grandchild.

The news is devasting to both of us. We have heard from her often, enjoying her many letters and phone calls, and were planning to fix our car after the baby's birth and drive to New Jersey for a visit. Now her death leaves a terrible hole in our lives that, for many weeks, nothing seems to fill. We think of her constantly and continue to speak of her with a great affection that makes it difficult to grasp that she is really gone.

Our one consolation in the face of such pain is the belief that, even though she lost her husband many years ago and lived a basically lonely life, she was blessed with three good children and half a dozen healthy grandchildren.

With not enough savings or time to have the car repaired, Richard is forced to borrow from a finance company for the air fare to go to her funeral. Sadly, I have to stay home with our son, miserable in the thought of losing that dear lady who, despite the miles between us, continued to mean so much. I am sorry also for missing another chance to meet Richard's family, most of whom will be in New Jersey for the funeral. Altogether, it is a low point in my American life, and I cry much of the time that Richard is absent.

The only good to come from this turn of affairs—and it is a minor thing indeed, viewed in perspective—is that our portion of her estate, when it is eventually settled, will be enough to help Richard complete his studies for the doctoral degree. It will not be enough to keep us from lingering near poverty, however.

We enjoy our tan-colored, dark-haired, Amerasian little boy from the day that we first bring him home. Knowing almost from the start that he will be an "only" naturally makes him all the more precious to us. For months after his birth, I walk from room to room with him in my arms, singing to him, hoping for the blessing of the very best spirits—including, of course, Sumwong's.

Richard sits and watches, wondering what the music is all about.

"That song sounds so plaintive, Dee. What does it mean?"

"Tell me what mean *plaintive* and I tell if you are right."

He explains the word. I like it and will add it to my vocabulary.

"You are right," I say, and continue singing, locked in a warm little one-on-one world that I did not imagine could mean so much. Is this Asian motherhood? I tend not to think so, if only because it feels so good to all three of us. James coos and gurgles constantly.

The birth has had its price, yet James, from his relatively peaceful infancy to his quietly curious but not rambunctious toddler stage, is an exceptionally easy child to rear. Most of the time, Richard and I hardly know that he is there except as another presence of love.

As so events pass and have passed under our cottage roof—"short and simple annals of the poor," Richard calls them, by turns moving and amusing. They get mentally logged and grow in emotional resonance to become our early family years.

New Year's 1981. *Tempis* does not so much *fugit* as simply disappear.

Publicly, the peanut farmer from south Georgia has been removed from office. The news is a disappointment to the thousands of people connected with the peanut trade in my native land, my letters tell me; to them he has been a shining example of what farmers can do if given a chance.

To most Thais, though, I suspect that he is just not tough enough on communism. A couple of years before I left Thailand there were university riots, and seared into my memory are the hanged and burning bodies of communist students who leaned just a fraction too left to suit their older countrymen's tastes. *De facto* death squads raided their campus havens to beat and kill them; one was literally flayed.

As anti-communist as I am, I wished then as I wish now that those 19- and 21-year-olds had merely been given a good talking-to. They were far too young to have paid that price, especially for what amounted to a peccadillo—political indiscretion in some cases, simple ignorance in others. It doesn't take much to teach a Thai what, in the real world, communism amounts to. All he has to do is look across his nearest boarders with youth's idealistic blinders off.

Water under the political bridge.

Now there is an *actor* in the White House. By nature of this trade, Ronald Reagan is suspect in Thailand, or so my letters say. His election has been seen by many Thais as bordering on the farcical but with the potential for tragedy if, for instance, in some move to cut defense spending he weakens any of the United States-Thai connections. He will have to be as strong on containment as he was, as governor, on Un-Americanism.

LOOKING FOR THE LIGHT

He proves to have no intention, of course, of cutting back defenses.

It is not until the autumn of Reagan's campaign that I am finally able to take more than one college course. I had made a B in my first college course (Math) and A's the next semester in my second and third courses (Philosophy and World Literature). Buoyed by those results, I enrolled in a second (required) math course and what, as expected, turns out to be my favorite so far, Introduction of Art.

Two more A's. I pinch myself when the grades arrive.

I take these classes at the state-supported, low-tuition urban Atlanta college where Richard once taught part-time.

Richard himself has become a student again, a doctoral student, at an expensive, prestigious suburban university to which he has been awarded a *partial* scholarship. I emphasize *partial* because the part of his tuition that the award does not cover is one of the things that reduces us, officially, to the poverty level.

The knowledge that we cannot go on to have a daughter hurts from time to time. But nothing really diminishes the joy of our main event of these years, which is, of course, the birth and growth of James. We remind ourselves that the Hope Diamond is an only; as are Mount Everest and the Eiffel Tower; and so, in fact, are the sun and the moon.

Compared to raising James, starting school again is very difficult, especially having to do it in a language not yet quite my own. Not fully understanding the teachers isn't troublesome— Richard is always there to help me piece my notes together from scraps. Nor is finding time to study, for I do that at home as I cook and clean and look after James.

No, the main problem for me (and, I suspect, for most foreign-born students) is reading the books—not just any books, but textbooks. And there the main problem is less the subject matter than the manner in which the books *as books* (as opposed to mere conveyors of information) are written.

But, then, I have been forewarned by Richard that the vast majority of them are put together by professors who know their stuff, sure, but who generally "can't write worth a plugged semi-colon." It is a bad situation made worse at each turn by my typical foreigner's trouble with a language as idiomatic and with so large a vocabulary, especially in its learned versions, as English.

Compounding that difficulty is the general run of classroom instructors in American colleges: mediocre. I speak only from my own experience and my limited exposure to campus scuttlebutt, of course. But in terms of taking the time and putting forth the effort to make a classroom the temple of learning that it should be, many American teachers seem to fall short of what I have been expecting.

My expectations have been honed by the disciplined atmosphere of Thai preparatory classrooms. There the students are as dead earnest about what they learn as a shipwrecked survivor is about knowing the ways of the sun and stars. Uniformed, alert, inquisitive, competitive, they are virtually ideal material with which to work. Most Thai instructors take advantage of the situation by utilizing skills acquired on *their* very competitive way to becoming upper-education level teachers, playing off the class's hunger for knowledge and the individual's desire to excel.

During my five-semester freshman "year," there are, nevertheless, teachers who whet my appetite to learn, to participate, to go on as an American college student. My determination to do so is always shaky, subject to cancellation, and I remain grateful to instructors like Ms. Hicks, who pours not only her knowledge but her soul into a course as potentially

LOOKING FOR THE LIGHT

tedious and intimidating as Astronomy, which I take in my third part-time semester.

A freshman option for the required natural science course, it roams the solar system and beyond in search of scientific truth. Ms. Hicks is more than a teacher, she is like the captain of a starship from whose helm we are alerted to the mysteries of the cosmos as we sweep outward from our moon and sun through the surprisingly (to me) populated void of space. Stars, dust clouds, supernovas, galaxies, *black holes*—things I might never have known about if I had remained in Thailand.

Especially if I had married Suwad—how mad a thought that seems now, how suffocatingly ludicrous.

Ms. Hicks advises us that no one really understands the black holes. They stand a better chance of understanding us.

Her tests are not easy, involving exotic names (none of them Thai) and a variety of calculations, but insofar as we have learned more from her than from the textbook, we are well prepared for them. When I make my A, I am prouder than if I actually were a Lewis or a Clark of space exploration.

It saddens me to learn later that, unmarried and forty-ish, Ms. Hicks, too, is about to lose her teaching position because she lacks a doctoral degree. The handwriting is clearly on the wall for such people—Richard among them—but what a nonsensical message it is: no matter how good a teacher you are, like Richard or Ms. Hicks, out you go if you do not acquire the union card of a Ph.D.

In terms of bureaucratic hierarchy it makes sense, I suppose. But I think of all the students who will not experience her and others like her *as teachers*. The difference between a Ms. Hicks and others seems totally inconsequential—a rose by any other name—from my perspective as one of her ardent students.

Just after finishing her course, though, I am given a

different foretaste of study and bureaucracy by my preparation for naturalization. From the Immigration and Naturalization Service building downtown one day, Richard brings home a hefty folder of materials and dumps them in my lap.

"Here you go, Doll."

James and I both look up at him in dismay.

He winks at James and says to me, "You want to be an American, no? This is the way it's done." Gesturing toward the material, he departs for his study. "I'll help you with it, of course. But you've got to break the ice yourself."

We have spoken of it before, but now that casual, abstract issue has become a pile of very concrete "material" that I am supposed to get through before the next testing and swearing-in dates a few months off. This in addition to studying for a big examination in Math 101. And there is James to care for. And meals to be cooked. And a house to clean.

Is this what being a wife, an American housewife, is all about? Doing most of the household chores, and working full-time or studying for a college degree? And what about raising children right? Having satisfying sexual intercourse? Engaging in spiritual or aesthetic pursuits, or just the plain old Constitutional pursuit of happiness?

The Labors of Hercules might seem an afternoon's diversion.

I suppose I would scream on the spot (the spot being the center of my tiny kitchen), if I were a real working-model American housewife. But I am not—I am ersatz, an Asian woman who by design and consequence of an "arranged" fate instead winds up on the floor of a kitchen in suburban Atlanta sobbing to herself.

Woman, I am; American Superwoman I am not.

By the time Richard hears me and realizes what is happening, though, I am back on my feet exercising what I am continually told is my race's most salient characteristic: patience. If that means stifling a scream and accepting the inevitable, then the characterization is accurate.

As he holds me in his arms, though, I wonder fleetingly what it would be like just to let it all out with a scream. Would I feel any better than I do now, sobbed out instead of screamed out, in my husband's arms? Being Thai to the bone, though, I remain in character. No screams for me.

Richard looks at me sympathetically. "I'm sorry, Dee. I thought citizenship is what you wanted."

"It is, but . . ."

"We can put it off."

Quieted down, I consider: perhaps it really is a matter of expectations, of doing what is anticipated of one under a certain set of givens. I do not want to disappoint Richard, and I do want to show him what I, his *American* wife, can do.

"No," I say. "I can do it. I have three month."

"Month*s.*"

"Month*s.*"

"It's not that long a time."

"Long enough. Thais have saying, translate as, 'If you do not use time, it use you.' "

"Yeah. We have something like that in English."

"It true, no? No one want to be use, by time or—or by anyone or any*thing.*"

Time to get in a dig; it helps drain off the pent-up emotions while reminding my husband of . . . certain things.

"That's right."

"*Anything.*"

"Can't argue there."

"Or won't?"

"Hmmm. Are we perchance talking about dope again? I've cut down to once a week, no?"

Actually I *have* made that much progress with him. But

it is like the tide: in and out. "Yes, and sank you." I kiss him. "Excuse me, I go now."

"Go? Out?"

"To the bedloom. To study."

He looks at me wanting to say something, hesitates, then tells me not to worry about "anything"—*that* anything.

"I am not," I lie.

"Good. And that's bed*room*."

"Bed*room*."

We kiss again, lightly. I take a deep breath—resignation perhaps—and go in, with James, to crack one or more of the dreaded textbooks and study materials lying around my room like dormant dragons.

Hats off to the American Superwoman, I think.

I would like to become one some day; but not, I admit to myself, at the cost of losing my essential Thai-ness.

At times, the two seem as far apart as antipodes; at other times, like this, with my book under my arm and my kid under my feet, they begin to take on an uncanny resemblance.

Three months later, through creeping morning traffic and a hell-for-leather rainstorm, Richard drives me to the I.N.S. building downtown. We get there at 8:28, dash to the door getting there under the wire. Richard waits for me, studying the books he seems to carry with him everywhere these days. By ten o'clock on that Tuesday morning, after a relatively simple test—doesn't everybody know that Jefferson authored the Declaration of Independence?—and an even simpler swearing-in, I am an American citizen with a social security number and a naturalization certificate to prove it.

We have parked in the parking tower of a large, expensive department store, and, before retrieving the car, Richard takes me to its fancy breakfast cafe to celebrate. Stopping at a newspaper stand we buy the morning paper. Sitting down in the cafe we order capuccino coffee and almond-filled croissants in the elegant room with damask draperies at each window—a rare and exquisite treat, given our financial status. I feel proud of my new identity, and, for a moment, completely content.

Trouble is never too far away, though.

We both keep glancing at our watches, for the sitter has agreed to watch James only until noon, at which time she has to be at her part-time job (there is no school this Spring Break week). So, although we could spend all morning nibbling and sipping and gloating over this immensely successful way to start a day, Richard calls for the check.

As we are waiting, Richard thumbs through the newspaper. Flipping a page, he does a little double-take and says, "Oh, no."

Trouble the width of newsprint away.

"What's wrong?"

"Drug-bust story. They got two dozen or so dealers in the northwest metro area. Jeff Beckwith is among them."

"Oh, I am so sorry."

The triumph of my day of naturalization has already lost some of its luster, placed up against the small daily disasters visited upon heads all around like the random and indifferent patter of rain. Then something else enters my mind: "You think he will give name to police?"

"What names?"

"Other seller. Other buyer. In Thailand, everybody connect go to jail. Rich one quickly bribe way out. Poor one rot in cell."

"That sucks. No, Jeff'll name sellers, maybe, but not buyers. That's not the way it works in the States. They're generally after the big boys, and the average dope-smoker is as small-fry as you can get."

"You are sure? I die without you."

"Thanks for the thought, but not to worry. What would the narcs want with a penniless graduate student, anyway?"

CONFESSIONS OF A MAIL ORDER BRIDE

He is right, of course. In that league, he is small-fry, especially since he wouldn't dream of selling it at any price or profit. He buys less now; in that tiny way—in his "voluntary" control of drug usage—my campaign of attrition seems to be very slowly paying off.

This is not to mention his renewed fitness—he is jogging again, and the paunch he has acquired lately has shrunk— and his reinvigorated ambition as a doctoral candidate has grown.

The tide is definitely turning.

Unhappily, our sex life is suffering, but I am ready to trade that, some of it anyway, for these signs of drive and determination.

I know for certain that he isn't fooling around on the side; Thai women pride themselves on being able to detect any infidelity in their husbands. It's a matter of careful observation of a hundred little things, tangible and intangible. Besides, I believe Richard when he asserts that infidelity killed off his first marriage, and promises continued fidelity to me. Other faults aside, he will prove to be a man of his word. That is the American Scout in him, and a good part of what I love.

The waitress is taking forever to bring the check. In the elegant cafe, people come and go, mostly business types garbed in suits and pant-suits, to confront the world over prices, deadlines, reports, mergers, stocks and bonds. Glasses tinkle, papers rattle, distractions in the distance, much like my concern over getting back to the sitter. I want to say something to Richard, but he has put the newspaper down and is glancing through one of his books, without which neither he nor I can be found much lately. It is as if we have become inextricably bound to paper and ideas, in an ongoing, uphill struggle to become masters of our bodies of knowledge.

In two years Richard has passed all of his post-Masters courses (with A's and B's) as well as his foreign language exam in German. He has also passed a preliminary oral examination, without which he could not have chosen his major areas.

One of these areas is the history of communication, and he has gone beyond the normal graduate-school requirements by presenting (at a convention) a paper on the ways in which scientists and technicians use language to manipulate readers as well as to convey information. The title of the study is "Emotive-Affective Aims: Morality in the Literature of Science and Technology," and it indicates his growing interest in technical communication.

I begin by being proud of myself for sitting down with the complex study one day and working my way through it; I end up being extremely proud of him. In his work I can see and appreciate the clarity of his undrugged mind—the bright interpretations of the ideas of others, the profound understanding of technology and science. The study does not deal with conventional notions of morality but makes significant points about adherence to data, and the manner in which fact and theory are differentiated.

I am not totally sure what Richard might, in fact, say on the idea of morality. He seems to believe more in *ethics:* that in our treatment of others we express our truest selves, our basic values, our sense of right and wrong. It would be hard for a Thai to disagree.

At last the waitress brings the check. It is after eleven o'clock.

We leave the cafe quickly and go right to the car. The rain has stopped, but scattered around the sky like a herd of dirty sheep are ragged, roundish, white-gray clouds.

On the way back out of town on the Northwest Freeway, I look back over my shoulder at the skyline of Atlanta. The city does seem a magical place, attractive, energetic, cultured—a sleek dynamo, defined by its ultra-modern skyline.

Maybe the "back-theners" are right after all.

CONFESSIONS OF A MAIL ORDER BRIDE

But surely other expanding Sunbelt cities are like this as well—Tucson and San Diego, names on a map—could be veritable paradises. There is no way, really, for me to know.

Besides, I may not want to know. I am happy enough in Atlanta, with my reinvigorated *can-do* husband, and our sturdy, growing son, and my fruit-bearing peach trees and scuppernong vines with their resident Mr. and Mrs. Red Cardinal (we have none in Thailand), and our student-level '70 Ford Maverick with its requisite dents and reliable engine.

Despite the major problem we have and the sometimes terrifying lack of money, I have little reason to suspect this morning that our generally pleasant Atlanta experience will end any time soon. But it will seem in just a moment that I have not been prescient enough.

Richard has several times mentioned how, outside the South, his degree from a prestigious *Southern* university will, paradoxically, mean more. Employers seek to cross-fertilize their institutions and workplaces with employees who represent a blend of regional backgrounds, he explains. He is prepared to accept a non-academic job virtually anywhere if it means he can work with computers and earn a decent salary.

Too, as an Easterner, there is the inevitable lure of the West for him. From time to time, he talks about it as though living out West is the Great American Experience. Having never been there, his enthusiasm is something I do not yet understand; I will not grasp it, in fact, until I take an Early American History course and read things by Bret Harte and Frederick Jackson Turner, and see such picture books as *Chromatic Utah* and *Beautiful California* in Richard's collection.

Suddenly Richard squeezes my hand. "You know, I would really miss this place."

"Freeway?" I kibitz.

He laughs. "No, Doll. Atlanta. This golden town."

Made uncomfortable by the voiced thought of moving,

of uprooting with the baby so young, I choose not to respond as we roll out of the congested areas of apartments and condos and into the greener suburbs.

But the handwriting on the wall is clearer than I have been willing to admit to myself. I dread the idea of *moving*, not just moving from Atlanta.

In Thailand, people rarely move, having roots sunk deep into their communities of birth; if and when they do relocate, their reasons are often unwise and the results often disastrous, as when they seek green pastures and find that, economically speaking, all Thai pastures are a uniform gray. Not-Americans in a third-world not-America, Thais are not really *meant* to move.

Now I feel sure that we, Richard and James and I, will. It is just a matter of time. Richard will be an A.B.D. (all but his dissertation done) at the end of the summer session. In any large city there are research libraries at which he can complete his dissertation. He is eager for work again, for income, for a change of lifestyle. To get from where he has been lately to where he—all of us, in fact—wants to be economically will definitely take a change of locale.

The handwriting is super-size, actually.

As we exit the freeway and pass into our neighborhood —a typical northside Atlanta neighborhood of well-cared-for houses on acreage filled with dozens of trees and bushes of many varieties—I feel a pang of wistfulness, as if we have already packed and moved. Like any back-then-er, I have started remembering what a fine time and place it was.

Richard has also been unusually quiet; we are often on the same wavelength, as happily married couples, even interracial ones, tend to be. He turns to me: "A penny—excuse me, a *baht*—for your thoughts."

"Oh, I just think 'bout Atlanta. We been happy here."

"And . . ."

"And now we will be leave, no?"

"Well, not *now*, not right away."

"But soon."

He reflects for a moment. "Wanwadee, I am not young anymore. I think you know where my best opportunity lies for a secure future for you and James, and I don't think it's here anymore."

I sigh. Memories of departing Nakhon Narai peck at me. I push them away. "I understand. It okay. We move when you ready."

He takes my hand and squeezes it. "We don't have to leave our happiness behind."

"Of course not. It just idea of moving. I'm scare."

"Scar*ed*. Not to worry. Everything will work out."

"Scar*ed*. I hope so."

"Remember, you've already made the major move of your life by leaving Thailand."

"That is true. But somehow different."

As our car crushes up the gravel of our drive, the sun peeks out from behind a massive cloud. Above us drab Mrs. Cardinal flutters on a nearby oak limb, emitting a burp-like chirp. On the screened front porch Susan, the sitter, already has her coat on. We are two minutes late.

"James is asleep," she says.

Hurriedly I get out and she gets in. When they drive off, I stand for a long time on the front porch contemplating the eventful morning. I am an American citizen now, free to drive, vote, work, live, love—and move. And move. And move.

The clock on our mantel strikes twelve noon, meaning 12:05; I heave a heavy breath and go in to check James.

As I walk between rooms, the sun retreats behind a cloud and the house goes suddenly, surprisingly dark. I nearly fall over an end table reaching for the lamp.

17

MANY WAYS WEST

Atlanta 1982

Once Richard definitely decides to leave Atlanta and head west, and I reluctantly but resignedly agree in the summer of 1982, we start to examine materials about states and cities before Richard sends out his first batch of application letters. He begins to bring home from the Atlanta public library oversize picture books on Colorado, or Arizona, or Washington, or California. After I get over the shock of having to depart Atlanta, this book-poring becomes an exciting diversion from our studies.

Although I have no reason to suspect otherwise, I wonder if most Americans appreciate the treasure they have in the West. I don't mean a specific treasure located out West, some old oaken chest in the desert or an abandoned silver mine near Carson City—no such romance nonsense. Rather, the West itself is a treasure incalculably more valuable than these.

CONFESSIONS OF A MAIL ORDER BRIDE

I may not be the first to have such a thought, but I may well be the first native-born *Thai* to do so; at the very least, the first Thai to do so on the basis of perusing picture books and studying *The Oregon Trail.*

But, then, I am surely the *only* Thai mail order bride from the city of Nakhon Narai ever to actually study and contemplate the West from a home base in Atlanta, Georgia.

Surely.

By *West* I mean the greater portions of such states as Colorado, Utah, Oregon, and California that man has not yet had the time, money, or inclination to befoul. They will, when I actually travel them, prove more attractive than any or all of the many photographs I have studied.

We eliminate several states because they are too remote or underpopulated; we cross off Utah because we are not Mormon. For hours we pore over pictures, wondering what the living places behind the colored photos are really like. Richard has some ideas of that reality since he took a vacation trip once to Denver and Colorado Springs. Because it was one of a series of failed attempts to save his first marriage, he prefers not to talk about it in detail. What I can gather is that he was impressed by the scenery: the clean smell of sage, juniper, and pine in the sunbaked high-altitude air—and buffalo burgers.

About this last, he is quite specific: not too different from a lean, good-quality hamburger, yet with a slightly gamey taste, they are always served, as far as he could tell, on a seeded bun or Vienna roll. Richard describes them as better than buffalo steak, which to Easterners is a bit *too* gamey and tough. He says they are the ultimate American burger. Beside them, a Whopper is paltry, the Big Mac an international disgrace.

"We serve buffalo meat in Thailand," I tell him. "Water buffalo. It rare, though."

"Cooked-rare or unusual-rare?"

"Cooked done. Thais do not like meat red. But they will

not kill valuable work animal like buffalo just to get steak and burger. These old buffalo."

"Meat aged on the hoof. Makes sense to me. I think the American Bison might be too dull to make into a work animal anyway. But, man, are they tasty."

First, because he has been there and, second, because he can read the intricacies of U.S. roadmaps, Richard maintains the role of trip-master. He buys a new road atlas, which he uses along with state maps from the packets of tourist information arriving on our living room floor with the same regularity as the oversize library books.

Practically oblivious to me and James and the television set, he calculates and examines the various routes west from Atlanta. Will it be through Birmingham, to begin, or through Nashville? Six of one, half dozen of the other. And from there, where? Kansas City? Or Oklahoma City? And then from there —Denver again? Or a southern route through the antique New Mexican highlands?

(I think for a moment of Marree, whom letters from home say divorced her American husband in 1980 and eventually returned to Thailand. I wonder if that could ever happen to me and conclude that it *could* but it won't.)

Decisions, decisions. "Many ways west," he mumbles over and over in a phony Amerindian accent. "Many, many."

James giggles himself pink.

More than a few times Richard looks up at me and says, "This trip won't get interesting until we get past the Mississippi River."

And each time he says it, I think, *He forgets that I am a foreigner and will find all of it interesting*—unless, of course, it degenerates into the roadside tedium of the rural South.

He pores and ponders, ponders and pores.

A mention of the Mississippi River evokes another train of thought for me. Closing my eyes, I am gazing out the plane

window once more, seeing far below me the broad brown water snaking its way through farms and fields under the July sun
of 1976. That was pre-Richard time, when more than half my
soul was still in Thailand, struggling with my decision to leave.

Now, six years later, most of my soul has made it here
to the United States—most, but not all. Richard still chides me
for singing only Thai songs when I sing aloud to myself. Most
of the time I am not even aware that I am singing; the remaining portion of my soul, the Thai part, has taken over.

"Let's see . . . let's see . . . ," Richard says, "St. Louis
or Memphis? What do you think, Doll?"

Shrugging, I say, "I think you should work on dissertation for while."

"Oh, that. It's in the bag. Not to worry."

And, luckily, this time he is right. No Tooth Fairy
needed—it *is* in the bag. He has been smart enough to use the
spring and summer days to just about finish this final obstacle.
Day after day, from mid-February through June, he headed for
the university library or holed up in his room to work on re-
searching, arranging, composing, revising. It was a Herculean
task, I knew, but he went to it each day with that blessed *can-do*
determination.

So totally into it was he during all of June that two
seemingly important things vacated his mind almost entirely:
drugs and sex. Of course, for him, if one goes, the other automatically follows; and when he does one, as he did only twice
that month (of course I was counting!), the other comes just as
automatically with it.

I was content to take it as offered. In fact, I would have
given up virtually any worldly pleasure to get the dissertation
out of the way, to help him complete this arduous phase of his
life and career.

Although in Thailand the Indian custom of *suttee* is not
practiced, women are used to giving up a good part of them-

selves to assist in their husbands' careers. We accept a secondary role for many reasons, not the least of which (in a fragile
economy) is our willingness to serve in any way possible as
support for the bread-winning power of our spouses.

One of the women in my native city did, in fact, surrender her life—indirectly. Due to her husband's incapacitating
illness she took his ten-wheeler (the Thai little-cousin of the
American eighteen-wheeler) out on a route and was promptly
run into a ravine. (There is little mercy on Thai roads.) Few of
us would go that far, but, with a workplace that does not
readily bend for women, much less merely *accept* them, we do
what we can, when we can, in our own way.

When, in July, Richard's dissertation is done—submit-
ted and accepted—acquisition of the degree involves completing just one perfunctory summer course (on "professional concerns") and passing a final oral-defense examination. This he
does by the late summer of 1982 as we plan our move west. He
sends out job applications to many Western colleges and firms
where he has heard or read that there are openings for technical communication specialists.

He is invited for a number of preliminary interviews,
and he goes to several at national-level communications con-
ventions and job-interview sessions in Atlanta. Unfortunately,
none of these academic jobs look all that attractive, financially;
furthermore, he seems eager to try something outside of
academia, not only because of the higher pay, but also because
of his interest in getting in on the ground floor of the burgeoning microcomputer industry. (IBM has just announced
that it is going to build microcomputers.)

Finally, after many turn-downs and turn-offs, he is invited to the interview of his dreams. A major computer-indus-
try firm with a branch office in Atlanta advertises an opening
for a technical editor at its West Coast branch; someone to direct the publication of all its manuals and reports from the

Coast as well as to train employees to create such documents. The man who supervises this position is in Atlanta temporarily and, through a contact at his university, Richard is able to lunch with him—he is a vice-president—toward the end of September.

They are mutually impressed: Richard with the man and his high-tech firm, and the man with Richard's background in both computers and teaching, plus the fact that Richard almost has a doctoral degree. Evidently, he really likes the idea of having material from his office imprinted with *Dr.*

One of the vice-president's major requirements is that Richard have the Ph.D. in hand by the job's starting date of October 30. We are on a roll—by choosing to skip the December commencement ceremony Richard can actually receive his degree by mail before then. That and a few other details dovetail together, including the firm's coast location in the hills above Los Angeles (in La Quiera) rather than in the clogged and smoggy streets down below, and, as Richard puts it, "It's a done deal."

By early October we are already, in our minds, denizens of the City of Angels. Orange groves! Hollywood! Hibiscus in the air! Creamy Pacific surf! Shopping malls on every corner! Our Los Angeles-of-the-mind blossoms forth in our dreams and conversations, like some flower improbably colorful and aromatic but somehow within grasp.

Letters from Thailand give me the names and addresses of Thai people to see, Thai places to go on the Coast.

Planning for our trip has reached a fever pitch. The Call of the West has become a deafening roar in our ears. We can smell the sagebrush, hear the curling crash of the Pacific, see the ridgeline of Coast Range hills. All I know, as a foreigner, is what I see in books, of course, but what I do see is so lusciously photographed and alluringly described that I cannot help but be excited by it all.

Beautiful California for real! More beautiful than Thailand. More beautiful than anything.

More beautiful, in our dreamy anticipation, than reality.

Almost to our departure date of October 20th (giving us over a week to get out there and get set up), Richard cannot be pried away from his maps and oversize books. Our living room floor looks like the war room of an army planning a long and arduous march. He continues to be oblivious to James and me, as if we are indistinguishable from the boxes and wrapped furniture scattered throughout the house.

Finally, the movers come. Can we believe the company will pay for this?

In a morning's time they have all our worldly possessions on board, and, with the signing of a slip, leave us with virtually nothing but the clothing on our backs. Actually, we do have a couple of suitcases packed with trip necessities already stowed in the trunk of our old drayhorse Maverick.

And so it is time to say goodbye to our cottage and our three wooded acres. Leaving James in the back seat of the car with one of his reading books, Richard and I stroll the grounds for a final time, noting this familiar nut tree here, that faithful gardenia bush there, the tall pines, the denuded oaks, the memorable sacred dogwood. It is a feeling of wistfulness and anticipation—the Great American Moving Experience.

You can't really be American without it, I have convinced myself. You have to try it *once*.

We walk through the house one more time, both to take a last look and to make sure nothing is left behind: empty, totally empty, as empty and dark as a tomb. Empty of things, empty of attachments, emptied now, as we leave, of life. We are ready to saddle up and head west.

CONFESSIONS OF A MAIL ORDER BRIDE

As we descend the front stoop, both cardinals land on a nearby branch, and, uncharacteristically, instead of fleeing they watch us. They perch and watch alertly, like two concerned spirits. Their heads tilt and bob. Eerily, they make not a sound.

They watch and watch until we get in the car and drive away down the block.

To Thais, a sign. Mixed, indefinite. Not really good.

18

BIG COUNTRY

Traveling West 1982

Judged from 35,000 feet of altitude, the United States did not seem so awfully large. Flying, one is able to traverse it, after all, in a matter of hours. And there are all those open spaces down there, the broad landscapes between relatively rare metropolitan areas which, surely (the foreigner supposes), one can motor across (at 55 mph) in a matter of hours. From up there, at that speed, everything seems convenient, tidy, *manageable*.

But from the road halfway across Kansas, Missouri or Oklahoma, smack dab in the rolling breadbasket of the country, perspectives change. Seen through panes of glass and the pains of cramped spaces, it becomes a very large country indeed. Mile after mile of concrete strip and green swatch, forest patch and townscape, grainfield and rangeland, bright, dark, bright, dark, bright. Mile after mile after mile. After mile.

James, too, notices that we are driving a lot, an awful

lot, and not seeming to get anywhere, as if on a treadmill. Every score or so of miles he will turn to one of us and ask plaintively where the West is. My thoughts exactly!

And I had thought the trip from Atlanta to Florida was long . . .

All I have between me and insanity is the ever-repeated refrain of Richard, "It'll get more interesting, by and by. Hang on." That, and the vision of us as Angelenos, surrounded by orange groves under a sparkling California sun.

The first portion of the trip has been rather interesting, if only because I had heard of, but never seen, Tennessee before. It is a state known in Thailand, since it is studied as a focal point of Southern U.S. culture—the home of the distinctive American music known as "country" (of which the GI radio station in Bangkok played a lot) and the equally distinctive American-type known as the "hillbilly." Thai kids are drawn to hillbillies because they see parallels between them and the hill people, the "tribes," of the northern provinces.

Unfortunately, across the entire length of Tennessee we neither listen to country music (Richard has little taste for it, even though he does appreciate its originality) nor see, as far as we can tell, a single hillbilly. At least we see no one who fits the L'il Abner stereotype of worn denim overalls, flannel shirt, shoeless feet, and corncob pipe. (Actually, we had the wrong state: hardly a year later we would see some stereotypical hillbillies indeed in Tennessee's neighbor, Arkansas.)

It is Interstate all the way. When we finally stop for gas and a late lunch at a mall just inside East Memphis, we are not at all surprised to see that the people eating, shopping, and strolling are hardly different from those we have left behind in Atlanta.

But it isn't for that reason that Richard and I like to stop at malls. It is rather that, in an intriguing sense, they are a uniquely American contribution to world culture—these giant, covered, shopping bazaars. Let a Thai or a Russian or a Bolivian loose in one for a day, and she'll never want to go home again. And to judge from news and magazine articles, they are catching on all over the world. In recent months I have read of American-style malls going up all over Europe and in many places in South America, as well as, of course, Japan and Korea.

In a letter from a cousin who had been to Bangkok recently, there was now a "Central Market" there, although as far as I could tell from her description it was—like many Thai adaptations of American ideas—a compromise. Covered yes, walls no; individual "stores" no, individual "stalls" yes; lots of merchandise yes, lots of credit, no. In other words, we (excuse, please—*they*) had not gotten it quite right yet.

Another thing about malls in America: despite the omnipresence of chain stores and franchises there are always surprises. In this mall in Memphis, Richard and I, pizza-lovers both, find one of the best pies we have ever come across. On a scale of one to ten, where the chain store pizza rates a 5 and a finely turned Chicago-style pie (outside of Chicago) anywhere from 8 to 9.5, this thin-crust, New York-style is clearly a 10.

In Memphis, Tennessee? The answer to this curiosity lay in the owner-operators. Born in Naples, transplanted from Brooklyn, these two brothers simply know how to knead a beautiful crust; mix a tangy, garlicky tomato sauce; and use a thick, first-quality mozzarella-provolone topping. This they bake to perfection in an imported pizza oven, letting the cheese reach to the edge and bubble up burnt while the rest of the pie stays a lovely streaked brown-gold color.

Thais appreciate the artistry.

I leave James a few feet away at a table with an ice cream cone and listen while Richard strikes up an after-dinner conversation, wanting to congratulate them on their cooking. They seem suspicious, reluctant, and we soon find out why.

"Boy," he says to one of the brothers as the other draws

Cokes for customers, "that'll take care of us for the rest of the day."

They both smile, weakly.

"What part of Italy you from?"

Hesitance. "Rio Nero."

"Oh, yeah, right outside of Napoli."

They look at each other. "You been there?" the younger of the two asks; his brother sullenly goes about his business.

"Heck, yeah. I studied in Italy. Was there for a year. Bologna."

"*La Grassa.*"

"Yep. *Si mangia bene a Bologna.*"

Both brothers smile more broadly. Later I will learn that they are complimenting the cooking of the Bologna region of Italy.

"I've been reading your reviews," Richard says. Plastic covered news clippings are taped to a wall on one side of their counter. "How in the world—I mean, why Memphis?"

The smiles disappear, and they look at each other. The younger says, "We do very well here. Mall location is very good."

"Well, I'm glad to hear that, but don't you guys miss New York—not to mention Italy."

"Business is okay here."

"I understand," Richard says, then goes silent for a long time contemplating his next conversational move while they both serve hot slices across their sparkling formica counter. When I ask him later in the car why he was so interested, he said he was always interested in the stories of transplanted New Yorkers who were usually no more able to shed their essential New Yorkerness than a leopard is able to discard its spots.

Finally, in a lull, the younger brother decides to fulfill

BIG COUNTRY

Richard's curiosity. "When you have to split your profit fifty-fifty with the mob," he says, "you know it's time to get out."

The older brother confirms this with a wink.

"Stupid me," Richard mutters. "I wouldn't have guessed . . ."

"It's all right. We are free now. And doing very well." He reaches his hand across the counter and Richard, shaken a bit, grasps it. "We appreciate your business."

"Unfortunately we are just . . . *passando, sai?*"

"*Eh, peccato.* We thought we had customers."

"The pizza was great. You have admirers instead."

"*Grazie,*" they both say. They are all like old friends now. "*Quest'e la sua moglie? Bellissima. Da quel paese?*"

"Thailand." I gather they are speaking of me, as I am standing there wondering about this flight to the midlands to escape metropolitan injustice and corruption; in a sense, it was like Thailand, for Bangkok, too, has "protection" gangs, modeled after the Japanese *yakuza* and capable of gangland-style warfare and killings.

". . . on our way to the West Coast," Richard says.

"*Ebbene.* Then," the younger says to both of us, in a sense dismissing us, as business has picked up, "have a nice trip."

"Sank you," I say.

"*Grazie a loro,*" Richard says, pleased with his Italian. If I had not tugged his sleeve and pointed to James half asleep, his face covered with ice cream, he would have been there the whole afternoon. "*Et buona fortuna nella sua . . . sua . . .* business."

"*Bottega,*" the brother supplies the missing word.

Aha, I think to myself; *how does it feel to be corrected?*

"*Si, bottega. Grazie. Et arriverdice.*"

"*Arriverdice, amico mio,*" they both say to him, handling calzone and Cokes for people in line.

Even before we leave the mall, Richard is congratulating himself on all the Italian he remembered. I take the opportunity to remind him, though, of the hazards of speaking a second language.

"You not know word for *business*?"

"It slipped my mind momentarily."

"Suuuure it has. Did."

He looks at me as we exit into the cool October air. "Okay, I get it. I know learning a language is tough, Dee. But you're doing fine. And look what it adds to your life."

"Then how come you never wish to learn Thai?" I needle some more. "You learn Italian well."

"It's not that I don't want to. It's just, I'd get it so screwed up with grad school German and street Italian. And I walk around with two *computer* languages in my head."

"Poooor baby." I love to use my new Americanisms at the right time—for effect.

"You've made your point. You don't like my encouragement?"

I put my arm around his waist. "Of course I do. You are very patient teacher. I just want be sure you understand."

"I do, Doll." He scoops James up in his arms. "Tell your mommy that I do."

Carried like an oversize football, James giggles and squeals all the way to the car. As Richard opens the door for both of us to get in, he leans over and whispers, "You *are* doing beautifully. One thousand percent better than when we met. So keep it up."

Seated, I smile up at him. "You also."

"Me, too," James says.

"Of course you too," we both assure him. And he *is*, sitting quietly, absorbing everything, as is his habit—more an Oriental child than an active American one.

"We be in Cal-fornia soon, Daddy?"

"We still have a long way to go."

I groan, as James curls up on the back seat with his nose to the glass. This is okay with him.

"Sorry, Doll," Richard says. "I'll continue to do most of the driving."

"It okay. We both drive. As long as we go there together."

He starts the old Maverick. It clanks twice, clinks, then, as if making up its mind to cooperate for a while longer, thumps into gear. "You mean, as long as we *get* there together."

From Memphis north toward St. Louis we roll, stopping overnight in a Motel Six—all we can afford—halfway between; then, in the late morning, we pass over the tawny Mississippi River (how broad it is up close; by comparison the Chao Phraya is a stream) and past the great gleaming Jefferson Arch. No time to stop except for gas, food, and sleep—just rolling, rolling, rolling over asphalt and concrete, past middle America, onward toward the West.

Across the center of Missouri, past Columbia (where a Thai prince went to journalism school), toward Kansas City. The trees are thinning out now, getting scrawnier, as if deprived of love. Rarely could so few trees be seen in florid, tropical Thailand.

I remark on it to James, who asks again about his mother's country, increasingly curious to know why he does not look quite like most of the kids he knows. I explain again where Thailand is, and who lives there, and what his many cousins are like.

Even if he has heard most of it before, he loves hearing it again. I know that when he gets a little older, and (God forbid) experiences the sting of name-calling a few times, the questions will get tougher and my answers not so comfortingly pat. That is still years away, though. Like me, he has not encountered overt racism—not yet, anyway.

For now, in the warm cocoon of our love, he spends most of his waking hours reading one of the many books or playing with toys. His favorites are decks of cards—anything from a plain poker deck to a stack of trivia items that he can hardly read by himself much less understand. But that is okay —as long as they are cards, able to be shuffled and peeled away one at a time with no way of telling what is coming up next. Though I hesitate to consider the idea at length, I suspect it all has something to do with the unpredictable ways of his parents.

On our Big Trip, he is content to stare out the window, asking occasional questions. The only things that seem to stir him are neon signs. When we pass an interchange with many of them, his head will bob back and forth like a spectator at a tennis match as he tries to take them all in. In a way, I suppose, they are like cards coming up randomly—no predictability whatsoever. A *McDonalds* here, a *Muffler King* there. *Red Carpet Inn. McDonald's* again (his "aces"?). Non-repeatables, like *St. Louie Rinks* and *West Mo. Truckstop*. A titanic *U.S. GAS* soaring alone above a small, flat town called Fulmore—equal to a royal flush, perhaps.

With that kind of game going on, I doubt that he notices the degenerating condition of the trees.

Richard has, though: "It's water. Lack of it. They get less and less of it from here clear across the Rocky Mountains."

"That why less farm then, too."

"Yep. And more rangeland."

"I'm sorry?"

"More land where livestock grazes."

"Yes, of course. We study rangeland in Geography course."

"Stud*ied*, past tense. You know, in Atlanta we were getting an average of 50 inches of precipitation a year. Denver gets twelve."

"Stud*ied*. Past tense."

We stop at a huge mall in Kansas City, so big in fact that billboards approaching it advertise it as the world's largest. Inside it indeed seems like the record holder, two stories high and perhaps a half mile from one end to the other. We don't have time to cover it entirely, but James and I have grilled hot dogs (we both love them with sauerkraut) while Richard strolls a bit further down in the food court and has a couple of slices of pizza.

"Mediocre," he says, recalling the recent pleasure of Memphis.

Before we leave the mall, I browse through a gourmet cookware shop and am delighted to find several cutlery and tableware sets from Thailand, the best we make: durable alloy nickel-brass with teakwood handles. In Thailand, c.$200 a mahogany-boxed fifty-piece set; over here, $595. Similarly, they offer copper skillets, which we learned to make from the French while they were in Indochina and which most Thais actually prefer to woks, for $95. Over there, about $30.

I ask the clerk if they sell well, and she says they do—remarkably well. And no one ever returns with a complaint. That information swells me with pride, proof again that (as Richard says many times) you can take the girl out of Thailand but . . .

We spend another Motel Six night somewhere in western Kansas, after driving for several hours through the dark. The October sun goes down early, cheating me out of the countryside but delighting James with nonstop neon. Richard says not to worry, that all I will be seeing is treeless, wheatless wheatfields, but I feel bad about missing part of America, nevertheless.

When we get out of the car at the motel, the aroma of the grasslands in fall is overwhelming—a sweet, fresh, heavy smell, like something good whiffed from a just-opened bottle. I

CONFESSIONS OF A MAIL ORDER BRIDE

drink it in as we climb the stairs, luggage in hand, sleepy James in Richard's arms.

The room is elemental but clean. We watch television for an hour or so, then fall into sleep as deep as James's—the pattern of each night of the trip. Fourteen hours on the road, ten in a bed dreaming of the road.

Thus, hour by hour, we work our way westward.

19

A SET OF CHAINS

Traveling West 1982

Even though I flew over the Rocky Mountains in 1976, it is especially exciting for me, from flat central Thailand, to *come across them* after all these endless, treeless rangeland and wheatfield miles of western Kansas and eastern Colorado.

After anticipating the mountains for days, I am beginning to doubt they exist; in fact, I think that my first glimpse of their snowcapped tops under the flawlessly blue-cold afternoon sky is a mirage. "Is it? Could it be?"

Richard laughs.

At five, James, inquisitive and curious, starts asking his *why's* and *how's*, sensing something big is up.

I look back at Richard. "So you tell me. Is it?"

"What, Mommy? What is it, Daddy?"

"Keep watching."

In a few minutes James and I can see an entire range of

mountains right down to their evergreen bases, and I let out a scream. So does James. Finally, Richard does too.

"Pike Peak or bust!" I shout.

"Pikes."

"Pikes. We make it without bust."

Just then the Maverick gives off a shudder—eager itself to get to Pikes Peak, we suppose—and we are chastened enough to slow down and contemplate rather than enthuse. "Beauties, aren't they?" Richard rhetorically asks.

"So clean-looking. Maj . . . Maj . . . majestic." New word.

"This *is* Pikes Peak, by the way. The big one in the middle. I recognize it from years ago. And you know," he winks, "it hasn't changed a bit."

"I wonder if it say the same thing 'bout you."

He laughs. "I doubt it. Less hair, for one thing. And what's left is getting gray. See what you've done to me, woman?"

My Thai tiger sniffs the air, but, realizing he is kidding as usual, I say, "That work two way."

Richard holds his peace.

It has rarely happened in our six-plus years together that my tiger has gotten out. Losing my temper is restricted to our arguments over—not money, not James, not even dope—but *politics*.

Both his social prejudices and his academic-liberal sympathies for communist governments and left-wing movements are virtually incomprehensible to me.

On the occasions that these subjects arise, Richard will be the first to back off; he has seen me once—only once—lose my temper completely in, ironically, a non-political situation with a Vietnamese-born plumber who overcharged us by about $50. Although I do not clearly remember, Richard claims that before he left I threatened bodily harm while shouting at the

A SET OF CHAINS

man. Since that incident, Richard has backed off from any serious engagement. Thus, it served its purpose.

Appearances aside, I repeat, Thai women do tend to sizzle in the face of incompetence, stupidity, infidelity, or dishonesty. And we fight not to fight, nor even to make a point. We fight to win, plain and simple.

Fighting is the furthest thing from my mind, though, as we speed over the last remaining miles of high plains toward the long range of mountains that looms before us. The snows of October have crowned them lightly with an icy white, below which shows their gray backbone of granite, itself girdled at the lowest level with bands of evergreens.

Afternoon clouds gradually wrap the tallest of the peaks. By the time we get to Colorado Springs, the mountains, as if aware that we have drunk in quite enough, hide themselves entirely in cloud, which they will not shed until the middle of the next day. But we have a whole afternoon of watching them through our windshield and are satisfied—surfeited, that is.

In Colorado Springs we forsake a chance to dine at a restaurant called Taste of Siam which we pass on the way to our Motel Six. Richard remembers a pizza place, one where he and his first wife Julie dined some years before, and he is determined to find it.

"Chicago-style. Nine-point-five, easy."

That is all the encouragement James and I need. We both love pizza and trust Daddy's judgment. Besides, to me eating it is an expression of my American essence.

As long as it is good and offered with anchovy, I am game. Anyway, Richard says, we can have the best Thai food in the world right at home, no?

"Sweet talk," I insist.

The pizza restaurant is practically around the corner from the motel. Break Number One: we check into the motel, get back in the car, and head for what we hope will be a nice meal to cap off the day.

Break Number Two: it is indeed a 9.5 pizza, possibly a 10, even though Richard insists (who am I to dispute, never having been there?) that no Chicago-style 10's exist outside Chicago.

It is a lovely sight, arriving at our table in a heavy black skillet, perfectly browned, bronzed almost, with the mozzarella bubbling away in the middle and burnt along the edges.

So American!

"Italian, *Italian,*" Richard always insists, but somehow I believe he is wrong on this one.

I feel sorry for my pizza-less Thai homeland, but the sorrow disappears as I take my first bite.

It is *my* addiction, pizza. I love it unflaggingly—but only (as Woody Allen answered when asked if sex is dirty) if it is *done right.*

Next day, just outside Grand Junction, on a major highway but not an Interstate, we pull the car over. Nothing is wrong with it; if anything, the old warhorse seems to be getting stronger the further along it goes. Maybe it reacts well to high altitudes.

We just want to rest and look around now that the sun has finally burned through all the low-lying clouds. We have just descended from a couple of mountain passes that were a disappointment because the peaks were cloud-covered, and all we could really see through our wet and filthy windshield were trucks, snow, and the center stripe.

Now it is gorgeous again.

For one thing, the landscape has changed from Evergreen West to Red Rock West. The air seems not only drier and cooler but virtually immaculate, the vistas more stunning because of their crystalline immensity. It is almost a desert land-scape, except for the flourishing sagebrush and the scattered leafless orchards of fruit farms. Off in the cool sunny distance lies Grand Junction, a good-sized town that is, nevertheless, almost swallowed up in the vastness.

For another thing, we are all feeling wonderful—reborn, in a sense. We have made it thus far without a hitch. Have slept well. Eaten another delicious pizza *and*, earlier this very day, a buffalo burger. Beaten the tricky late-fall weather. Car doing fine. Is this our paradisiacal entry into the promised land of the West? We are totally without foreboding or premonition (how could we be?), so we just stand beside the car, all three of us, basking in the replenished sunshine and in our continuing good fortune.

Unknowingly, though, Richard is about to make a decision that will begin to turn it all back around. Tide in, tide out.

"We are making fabulous time," he enthuses. "We're at least a half day ahead of schedule—no," he corrects, punching buttons on his chrono-watch, "make that almost a whole day out in front."

He stretches, poking his face up toward the sun. "Got an idea, Dee. Let's make a slight detour."

"I'm sorry?"

"Let's go out of our way to see something you'll never forget."

"Like what?"

"How about the Grand Canyon? You've heard of it?"

"Of course." I have heard of it as far back as grade school in Thailand. It is a world-famous wonder, of course. "But . . ."

"But what?"

"We not go too far out of our way? Everything holding up so well. Weather especially."

"Actually, it would take us down a more southerly

route. If anything, the weather might improve." Famous last words.

"Improve on this?" I gesture all around.

"We have the time. It's a suggestion."

I consider, honored to be consulted ever more frequently on matters of decision; it is a sign of the underlying health of our union. Actually, it does not seem like a *bad* idea, just a slightly disconnected or unnecessary one. "It okay with me."

"It's."

"It's."

We get back in the car and head, eventually, south.

One full day later, after a night in a Motel Six in Gallup, New Mexico, during which we hear a TV weather forecast calling for a winter-type pattern of high winds and heavy snow in some areas, we are on a two-lane blacktop following the signs to Grand Canyon National Park.

We have once more traveled through country so wondrously strange and beautiful that I could not have imagined it in my wildest dreams in Thailand. Twisted, tortured, soaring, enormous, multicolored, vast—just the fresh, high-altitude, sunbaked, sagebrush *smell* is sufficient to distinguish it from any other place in the world.

A chillier wind this day.

We can feel it leaking through the looseness of the old car's body as we creep over the immense red rock landscape toward Grand Canyon National Park. A sign we pass reads *Elevation 7200* feet. I translate that to meters and quote the figure to Richard. But he has already come to his own conclusion. "We're up there."

A SET OF CHAINS

"Yes," I agree. "And it get dark." Unnaturally dark for four in the afternoon, even in October.

James is napping, his small body spread across the back seat. We ride in silence, going constantly up, up, up, until we pass another sign: *South Rim Entrance 16 Miles.*

"That's good news," Richard says.

"We need some." Off to our left the wide open spaces are being eaten alive by a bank of clouds moving with the swift determination of a predator. Where half an hour ago we could see Mount San Francisco, highest point in the region, we now see omnipresent gloom. Visibility is at best a few miles in any direction.

We are climbing through stands of juniper, swinging wide of them now and then to run along the rim of a widening canyon which, it dawns on us, is the beginning of the Grand. Though we can see no river, we know it is down there, doing its ageless work of wearing down rock and sucking away the debris. We are excited by the prospect of seeing this wonder of the world, but we wish it could be under more pleasant circumstances.

At last the clouds roll over us, and I see it begin to snow for only the fifth or sixth time in my life, the other times being in February or March in Atlanta.

I am fascinated by the types of snow. This is a fine, icy kind that freezes to the windshield rather than being cleared away by the wipers. October snow? Western snow?

Suddenly the car slips and skids. *Dangerous snow.*

Richard turns the defrost fan on high. It helps a bit, but makes a demonic roar that awakens James. Disoriented, he looks out the window, senses our tight-lipped grimness, and starts to sob.

"It okay, baby," I comfort him. "Daddy get us to nice warm room soon."

"If they've got one in the Park," Richard says softly,

concentrating on keeping the car on the slowly icing pavement. "And if we make it that far."

A sign looms up, and I wipe the inside of the glass to read it. "Seven mile to Park Entrance."

"Not *too* bad."

Unfortunately, the last six of these seven miles are the worst of our entire trip; the road is ever slicker, ever more winding, and the car develops a case of giant hiccups, bucking and lurching as it strives not only to keep going (up!) but also to stay on the road.

"What is it?" I ask.

"Altitude—*too* high, I suppose. Playing havoc with the carburetor and my ears." James is still crying. "His ears too, I guess."

"You mean like swell and go pop."

"Yep. Swell and go pop."

"Good. I think it just me."

Richard laughs. I put James on my lap and we ride the last couple of miles—three Westward-Ho adventurers confronting a world gone treacherously ice-white.

We slip, skid, and fishtail the last half-mile on bad tires made worse by the conditions—double jeopardy—but arrive at the well-lit entrance gate just as full darkness descends. All three of us breathe a collective sigh of relief to be *somewhere* at last, and another sigh when Richard asks about accommodations and gets a laconic "Take your pick."

Meaning, of course, that few people are out vacationing on days like this.

But, since it is still only October, everything is open and available: hotels, restaurants, service stations, and stores. And there are, in fact, a fair number of guests. We check into the nearest accommodation, a rambling timber motel whose lit vacancy sign is the final confirmation of our relief.

Taking a double room, we are delighted to find that it is

A SET OF CHAINS

spacious, clean, and equipped with both a queen-sized bed and a rollaway for James. With the wind whipping after us like a scourge, we scramble inside, throw down our bags, and practically fall onto the beds.

"Turn on TV, Daddy," James says.

"Hmph, I wish I could."

There is no TV. James's face sinks.

But we don't really need one. The boy has his books, and I for one just want to relax. It seems that Richard should too, after the long day's drive made even longer by the last fifty or so miles. But now he seems restless, distracted.

Instead of remaining with James and me on the queen bed, he gets up and begins pacing the room as if it is a cage. He is also muttering something about forty-five dollars a night.

This behavior makes me, eventually, as uneasy as he.

"It hurt pocketbook, no?"

"It hurts pocketbook, yes. The bandits. They know we have no alternative. Charge what the traffic will bear, I guess," he says disgustedly.

Actually I have noticed the room price posted on the door, but I say nothing. Instead I ask if the trip is in trouble.

"If we have to stay here it is. Shit," he signs, "I wish we didn't have to scrimp every damn day of our lives."

"Don't worry. It get better soon."

"Sure," he says sarcastically.

"I can get job easy in L.A. Many Thai there."

"I told you, I prefer you don't work, not while the boy is growing up. So don't start that tune."

I shut up. He shuts up, too.

Finally, after ten minutes of walking and sitting and fidgeting, Richard makes another fateful decision. He glances at James drowsing over a Willie Widget book and says to me, softly, "Dee, I—I need a joint. My back hurts like hell."

I say nothing, glancing over at James, too, but it hits me

hard in the gut. He has been cutting down, holding off, and now this . . . *recidivism* is the word. My emotions teeter-totter between disappointment and fear. Things have been looking better for us. Why here, why now?

I know he has a sandwich bag full of marijuana stashed somewhere in one of the six suitcases, but up until this moment, I have preferred to forget about it and have actually been hoping that he would too. So much for hope.

I do not openly object. He *has* cut down, and at the present moment he *is* visibly on edge. And that wind! It's been an awful day.

I ask him to wait until the boy is asleep. And to smoke in the bathroom, please.

An hour later, it is a joint and a half. Six months after that, hundreds.

I simply have not been assessing correctly—or, rather, I have been unable to because he keeps virtually everything inside himself. I have seen his successes: a doctoral degree in hand, new parenthood, this move west to fulfill a dream.

But I have been overlooking the failures of a man nearly forty-years-old, not seeing things from his perspective. Now it is clear to me that he has been viewing himself as a loser in the rat-race of life. In early middle age, he is a relatively poor man, materially speaking: our savings amount to only a thousand dollars or so, currently in travelers checks. While he has an annuity left over from his years of academic employment, if he were to die suddenly it would pay James and me less than three hundred dollars a month.

There is no money, presently, for insurance.

This bleak picture will surely alter for the better when he begins work; there will be group benefits—health, life, dental—that we presently do not have. But beyond that to look

A SET OF CHAINS

forward to is Richard's continuing and obvious (then why could I not fully comprehend it until now?) assessment of himself as a failure.

The only part I have seen clearly is his persistent refusal to identify his "habits" as a reason for his lack of success. Drugs are only one piece, however, of the complex puzzle. The rest is locked deep inside him, and he will not let it out upon pain of losing his American manhood.

Comparing himself to many people his age, including his brother-the-doctor and his sister-married-to-one, he has no career to speak of, much less a respectable income. So far he has provided his family with, what he sees as, far less than many men his age: less housing, less automobile, less fringe benefits, less, in general, of all the material "goodies" that seem to abound everywhere. We have no slice of the pie. He has a wife and child, whom he dearly loves, but from his point of view he has not provided very well for them.

How that must be hurting him underneath the smiles, the sweet talk and the caring.

All he possesses, to deal with any of it, is a moment of forgetful pleasure, the all-important high. Now I can see what a part of him really is—a middle-aged man walking a thin line, one step short of going over the edge. And, all the while, keeping every bit of it inside. No wonder this seemingly easy reconquest by dope.

Locked in this tight cabin room hundreds of miles from anything we have ever known and loved except each other and James—without even a TV set to distract us—we have nothing really to do but quietly consider the truth. We are, in a sense, facing the music, and it does not sound good at all—a high-pitched whining wind at the door.

A few drags on a sinsemilla cigarette: one more escape from an ugly and unmanageable reality.

CONFESSIONS OF A MAIL ORDER BRIDE

So typical, my husband; so pathetic. And still so under-standable.

Perceived by Richard's eyes, our present situation is the very image of where we are in life. Surrounded by the immense and famous beauty of the Grand Canyon, we have neither the means nor the opportunity to enjoy it. Instead, we are cooped in a tiny, costly room by circumstances that seem as far beyond our control as the changes of climate. Trapped—that's what we are—trapped in this room not by a blizzard but by time and fate and mistakes.

Ice crystals sweep against the windows like breakers over a bow, and they and the larger snowflakes pile up against and on top of everything that isn't locked and huddling in-doors. Already our car right outside the door is blanketed in white, formless, like a body in a shroud.

Small mistakes. Recent ones.

If we did not detour southward, we might be on the San Bernardino Freeway now, in the sunshine of Los Angeles. So it isn't just the fault of the stars; it is, in fact, mostly in ourselves. Our mistakes. Our ways of doing things. What a realization to come to at nearly forty years of age, and what a time and place for it.

I am fearful that he might see me and James in that light, as part of a massive and essentially insoluble problem, and in the gloom I turn to face him, to talk, to try to get it out and soothe it over before it gets any worse for all of us. My thoughts reach toward him. Ricky, Ricky, Ricky. We will find a way out together. Trust me. Trust Buddha. Trust your own God. And trust yourself. But I say nothing.

But, shoes laced up again, he is putting on his jacket.

Despite the joint-and-a-half, he seems reasonably steady

in his movements, adjusting the knit sleeve-ends, zipping up the front in one controlled movement.

Made immobile by fear, I cannot get a single word out, not even to ask where he might be going in the dark and driving snow. He smiles, a red-eyed, masking kind of smile, behind which he has been concealing a substantial part of himself from the first day I met him.

It is pure bravado, of course, but I find myself admiring it—the stubborn silent *maleness* of it reminds me of what is best about American men, their strength, their solidity; as a result, paradoxically, I find my fear melting away.

There is that in Richard, counterbalancing the escapes into drugs: the quiet inner strength, the *can-do* backbone. There has always been that ineradicable American part of him—thanks be to Buddha and his God.

"Be back in a while, Doll," he says.

He will walk out the door saying just that much if I do not rediscover my voice: "Where, Richard? Please."

Pulling out his wallet, he checks to see if he has the travelers checks in it. As he replaces it, he takes the time to wink at James's sleepy and confused face before he answers me.

"I'm going to fix things so we can drive the hell out of here in the morning."

With that, he opens the door and almost gets blown back inside the room. But he fights through the wind and gets out quickly, before he lets in too much snow and before I can think of a reason to stop him.

And before I can scream *come back*.

But, actually, there is no reason to stop him. Quite the opposite: I know he *can do* it, whatever it is.

And besides, it is a Friday; the movers are scheduled to arrive and unload on Sunday at the rental house the company has selected for us. We *have* to drive the hell out.

I return to the bed and sit down.

CONFESSIONS OF A MAIL ORDER BRIDE

The next hour and twelve minutes I spend looking at my watch and wondering how much time I should allow before racing outdoors myself and screaming for help. Finally, the snowfall begins to slow and I am at the point of putting on a pair of high-heeled boots to go out through the drifts and seek help—when in he walks.

"Whew!" he says, shedding his jacket. That is it—all he has to say for himself for the first couple of minutes. Here comes that scream for help again.

It just about gets out when he asks me how long he has been gone. I take a breath to restabilize myself. "One hour and twelve minute and forty-six second."

"Minutes. Seconds."

I don't feel like correcting myself.

"I would swear it was half the night," he says. "Anyway, they got the chains on. Thirty bucks, the pair. I tipped the guy a five. His fingers were absolutely blue by the time he finished."

"So we have tire chain now."

"Yep."

"And . . . you were okay?"

"It's raw out there, but I've seen worse. Hardest part was shoveling the snow off the car with my arms."

"I mean, you were able to function well?"

"Hell, yeah, it was a blast. I had almost forgotten how grass kind of heightens everything, you know. This past hour and forty-six minutes has been a genuine adventure. An odyssey, in fact."

"Hour and *twelve* minute. Minutes."

"Whatever. It was fun. And I'm not really high now. Just relaxed, more so than at any time since we left. And for a long time before that."

"I am glad for you." I smile. I mean it, poor man. At the moment it is difficult to deny him his escape.

A SET OF CHAINS

He glances over at James, asleep where I put him on the rollaway—the one thing I accomplished in Richard's absence. "Hey," he winked, "you wouldn't want to, you know . . . ?"

I know what he means, of course; and shake my head *no* —not here, not now. He shrugs, and smiles, and tries to make me promise *yes* for Sunday night.

"Maybe," I say, and add, "You be high like this?"

"I told you, I'm not high. Cold air cleaned me out."

"Well, then, like this anyway."

He studies the rug in the middle of the floor for a long while, lost, it seems, in the intricate Navajo designs that embellish it, on one of those interior odysseys that people in his condition seem prone to.

Finally he says, "Probably."

I choose not to say anything else.

After an interminable moment of silence, with the only sounds being James's breathing and the eerie rustle of drifts shifting against the car, he speaks the words that reawaken the pain inside me, making everything seem as fathomless and icy as the night outside.

"I can't help it. I like the stuff."

I think of all the excuses I have made for his smoking tonight and shake my head resignedly. One joint? I am kidding myself.

I say nothing. Long moments of silence, that scream stuck in my throat, ready to erupt again. But what would *that* solve, now?

Instead, I say, "You *like* stuff. You *love* Wanwadee?"

"You know I do, Doll."

"Then make promise, please. Just try to stop. You come so close already."

He looks into my eyes and says, "Okay, I promise to try. But it will take time."

I relax a little.

"I can beat it, I know I can," he says, studying the rug. "But not right now. Just give me time. Please."

"As long as you try, it okay."

Sitting at his feet on the Indian rug, I lay my head upon his knee. The fear inside me has begun to melt again—that is all it takes. When I look up into his eyes, I think I see tears but, whatever it is, he quickly blinks it back. "Still some smoke in here," he says, and gently strokes my hair.

There isn't any smoke. I have let it out a cracked window long ago, for James's sake.

But there is still time, I think, lost for a moment in my thoughts. As long as there is still commitment and love, there is still time.

We both listen to the sound of tires crunching through snow as another guest pulls into the motel lot. The place is filling up and we find comfort in the thought of not being so alone.

"I'm glad you get chain, though," I say at length. "We got to be in La Quiera by Sunday."

"Yeah, the movers."

"And . . ."

"And . . . ?"

"How quickly he forget!"

"Oh, yeah–that! Do you remember how it's done? It's been so long, you know?"

"If not, you can teach me over again. Best teacher in world."

"Sweet talk," he says.

"Of course. I learn that from best teacher," I say, and we both giggle loudly enough to stir James.

"Go on back to sleep, son," he says. "Everything's okay. Except Mommy's learning some bad habits."

He winks at both of us. James grunts, turns, and, like a

stricken little ship rolling over before it finally sinks, slowly settles back into a sound sleep.

Silent and full of passion, we cannot wait until Sunday night.

20

ALIEN PRESENCE

Los Angeles 1982–83

To late-twentieth century Thais, who continue to trickle into it, Los Angeles is attractive for its climate and the chance that it presents for a better life, the same reasons that caused earlier immigrant floods. There is no doubt about it's being a magical place.

It now has the largest Thai population of any city other than Bangkok. Thais love magic in whatever form, and they are always proud to say the magic words that they have been to Southern California, they have relatives living there, or, best of all, they live there themselves.

But Richard and I have been here less than a month when we begin to suspect that it has some *black* magic about it, too, a dark side that manifests itself with the most bizarre happenings under the sun.

Every day in the newspaper, and every night on the

219

local television news, there is one more story of teenager Satanist suicide pacts, rock musicians electrocuted by their sound equipment, rashes of bag and box people found with their throats slit and various appendages cut off; plus headlines like "Irate Father Slays Sons in Bad Drug Deal" (East Los Angeles), "Dead Shut-In Eaten by Own Dog" (Manhattan Beach), "23 Actors Busted in Gigolo Ring" (Beverly Hills); and the topper, from Los Angeles proper: a nurse confesses to poisoning over a dozen ill, elderly male patients in eight hospitals, then asks the court to consider them all anti-sexist revenge-euthanasias rather than murders.

It is an even bet that, eventually, a jury may.

It gets to be too much. Richard and I begin to ask one another: *what next?* We have the feeling that we are living either a sunlit public nightmare or the pages-come-to-life of the *National Enquirer.*

"Do things like this happen in Thailand?" he asks one night in front of the TV.

"Sometime. Not quite so crazy, though."

"I didn't think so. It's all blacks and Mexicans anyway."

"Oh, come on."

"No, seriously. I'm not talking opinion or even prejudice. I'm talking statistics."

"What statistic?"

"State of California."

"My old teacher say there are three lie—big lie, little lie, and statistic."

"What does he know about it?"

"She. This was course in sociology. Much statistic."

"These particular stats said that blacks commit more than half of all urban crime. And by the way, that's statistic*s*. It's one of those words that is almost always plural."

"Statistic*s*. Thank you."

"You know, you're not saying 'sank you' anymore?"

ALIEN PRESENCE

"Really? That good new."

"Still leaving your *s*'s off, though."

"It tough habit to break. Anyway, black—blacks—probably have much less than half the opportun*iteez*."

It is another political argument that we often have, and our lines are well drawn, but now another news item has popped up.

Motorists are shooting one another on the freeways.

Let's see him blame that on blacks.

On the floor between us, James fiddles with his toys, puzzled by it all. It worries me that one day he will understand.

Still, it does not take me long to realize that the media is in part responsible for the outlandish nature of the broadcasts, pandering to a need in its movieland audience for this sort of sensationalism. Then I feel stupid, suckered into craving more, more, *more* of the depravity of mankind. Smug in the safety of our dens, Richard and I cluck over this gang rape, that Satanic murder, and lead our lives of lewd anticipation.

I recall Thai television's strict, government-enforced code of censorship. The only dead bodies shown, for instance, are those of Communists slain on one or another border. These have socially redeeming value; i.e., one can see, even call the family over to see, the wages of that particular political sin.

But, then, that may be changing—may even have already changed in the nearly seven years I have been in the States. Much has probably changed.

A commercial is on. My mind wanders.

Has it been *seven* years? I pinch myself and realize that the three thousand miles closer to Thailand I have come by moving mean absolutely nothing.

Yet the seven years and the three thousand miles are more than just numbers; they are like blocks of stone in my mind, gravestones, markers over feelings I have almost laid to rest, almost for good.

Almost. There are always memories of my brother, Sumwong, close at hand.

Commercial ends. Sports. At Santa Anita, a horse drops dead in mid-stride. Doping suspected. Arrests to follow.

At the end of our second month in Los Angeles, disgusted with ourselves for being duped, we find other things to do with our early evening hours—anything, in fact, to avoid the temptation of watching the local newscast and seeing another on-camera police shootout. Living less than a mile from a huge, tri-level, temple-like shopping mall, we spend some evenings there, shopping, or having dessert at a little *gelati* store, or just watching people.

We also enjoy puttering in the garden of our small rented house, particularly on the weekend evenings, when the mall is too crowded. We have yet to make any real friends in these early days. In fact, we make hardly any friends at all in the ten months we are in Los Angeles. Perhaps we sense, with the passing of time, that Los Angeles is not the way we would like it to be for ourselves and James; perhaps it is Richard's growing need to return to a life in academics; perhaps, ultimately, it is just the slow dissolution of his dream of the West.

Things out here are, after all, not that much different from what they are back East; prettier country, maybe, but basically, as Richard phrases it, "the same old shit." I don't know *exactly* what the phrase means, but it has the ring of authenticity.

Foreign-born, I still have a comparatively dim sense of what the West is supposed to represent to Americans—escape, release, the archetypal Frontier, what? I can appreciate its beauty, of course, but one has to grow up with the myth to catch all its nuances. In any case, I am able to share the feelings of many Easterners like Richard who heed the old advice to

ALIEN PRESENCE

head West but wind up disillusioned, discontent, and even, in a sense, disenfranchised. Dislocated, too. That's why so many move back.

We are, nonetheless, thankful that the company asked someone with decent taste to rent us our home—an efficient house with a yard full of exotic flowers and fruit trees. I can even grow extensive vines of yard-long drooping *buab*—Thai "zucchini." Sometimes we have the feeling that the only thing unique about our Los Angeles experience is those trees and bushes. The city itself is too much like any other, only magnified: the traffic, the crime, the bad air, the ever-expanding exurbs.

It is easy to pick on Los Angeles—that's why everybody does it. It is urban America writ large, a naughty star always looking much less than "mahvelous" under klieg lights; but not worse, really, than other cities its size. Somehow, though, it seems that it ought to be better—given its jewel-like setting. But, then, to someone like me, all American cities ought to be better, given their relatively jewel-like settings *in America*.

Sadly, though, I have seen and read of too many to know that the opposite has become true. *America Brucia* is the title of a Sixties book in Richard's bookcase. In Italian, by an American, it was a worldwide best seller back then. *America Burns*.

At least its cities do. Civilizations cycle, and big cities are the first to be crushed by the wheel.

I begin to wonder what small-town American life is like —how it is different, if not better, and whether people find a bigger slice of the American dream pie there.

Because of a combination of traffic and the exurbs, getting in and out of the city either east to the beach or west to the mountains is something of a day-long proposition. Of course, the

CONFESSIONS OF A MAIL ORDER BRIDE

Pacific Ocean and the San Gabriels are outstanding attractions —Venice is a "trip" in all senses of the word—but to have to *drive* to either one can ruin the trip.

And yet one cannot make such a trip *without* driving, a paradox explained by the total lack of public transportation. In Thailand, virtually all holiday trips are taken by bus or train.

Besides the transportation problem, Richard comes home each day fed up not so much with his job as with getting to and from it through freeway traffic. He is happy to be able to return to the garden, sometimes for an entire weekend. Things get so cabin-feverish for us in Los Angeles, in fact, that we feel a kinship with those pre-Cambrian creatures trapped in the tar of La Brea.

For Richard it is, in a word, hectic. In another word, competitive; in yet another, tedious. In a fourth and summarizing word, stressful. Or, in other words, he does not like it.

To be more precise, he grows to hate it. At first, he gives Los Angeles his very best shot, heading off each day in one or another piece of the "Coast Look" wardrobe it has taken much of our remaining money to buy for him. He believes that, in the business world at least, clothes maketh the man. And it is a high-fashion denim, brightly colored and patterned, leather booted, tieless-casual and sunny urban-cowboy Richard taking off down our suburban street at eight each morning.

And driving back up at six, seven, sometimes eight or later, looking frazzled and much the worse for wear, bright shirttails hanging out like a panting tongue.

At such times, he manages just a couple of words before sitting down to dinner: "This sucks."

Or: "Traffic bad."

Or, after dinner, heading for the garden: "Where's the trowel?"

And James and I will lose him for the rest of the day,

usually to the garden, but too often to marijuana and the head-
phones.

Among the redeeming features of Los Angeles is its selection of FM radio stations, which, like New York's, offer every possible shade of musical distinction. He often fiddles with
the dial for twenty minutes before settling down to progressive
jazz or the latest evolutionary stage of his "sophisticated funk."
Once or twice a week I awake at two o'clock in the morning to
find his side of the bed empty; he is in the den, half-asleep,
headphones still on, a look of intensely studied *escape* upon his
face.

And always it ends the same way. Awakened, he asks
what time it is, expresses surprise, brushes his teeth, kisses
James and me, then totters off to sleep until the alarm goes off
at seven sharp. In a quick hour after that, he is gone to work.

We are definitely seeing less of one another. Strangely,
though, our sex life has ironically improved. He claims it is the
often cool West Coast winter nights, but we both know it is
because he is smoking more. Thais have a saying: collect with
one hand, pay with the other.

And so it goes, day after day, week after week, in the
buzzsaw of Los Angeles. Lonely nights for me, frantic days for
him. From time to time I have contact with someone from the
city's huge Thai population, but with so many miles to travel,
friends meet but do not stick. As far as I can tell, there are few
if any Thais in our immediate neck of the suburban Orange
County woods.

The marriage, however, remains secure. Our real problems are only two: infrequently flaring political disagreements
and, of course, more importantly, his use of drugs; the former
is a hot spot, the latter cool. I am sure, however, it is only a
matter of time before I win him over on both.

Americans tend to act on hunches in short-term matters; Thais use them to make long-term commitments. My

CONFESSIONS OF A MAIL ORDER BRIDE

hunch is that Richard can be made to see the light. He is a good man, as solid as a rock and as sweet-natured, beneath the prickly skin, as Durian.

(Durian is a tree-fruit cultivated in central Thailand for its creamy texture and delicious figlike taste; unfortunately, it has a rough horny exterior and somewhat unpleasant aroma—a paradoxical fruit, in other words, which is surely why it is so highly prized. It is also, of course, that paradox of strong-weak, sweet-flawed Richard that appeals to me—the idea that I can love everything he is and yet want desperately to change some things that are so essentially him.)

Los Angeles is a time for contemplation, for retrenchment and adjustment, a sort of early mid-life crisis for our marriage which will alter at least the material circumstances of our lives; each month Richard brings home a paycheck that is nearly twice what he made when he was teaching. We are finally able to save and even invest in a mutual fund. He signs up for life and medical insurance. That feels good, too.

But Los Angeles is also an opportunity for us to consider what we really want out of life instead of what we thought we wanted or what our societies—American and Thai —have taught us to want.

There are also James's needs to consider. Becoming more Oriental in looks as he grows older, he will have less trouble fitting in with the tides of multi-racial people in the Los Angeles area than in other places in the United States. Counterbalancing that consideration is the nature of American city life itself—this particular city, for instance, where, under endless sunshine, people perform some of the most outrageous atrocities upon one another since Attila the Hun blinded and castrated an entire army of Bulgars. We have not sent James to public school so far, keeping him instead in a private kindergarten.

Apart a lot, being to ourselves, depending on ourselves,

we manage to grow. Richard and I grow as individuals, a growth that has to precede any we can possibly have as partners.

For several reasons, I become more Americanized, although I manage to take only one college course, a six-month community college reading-writing course for foreign-born adults. The teacher has us read American literature, including some essential works that I have heard of *(Huckleberry Finn, Leaves of Grass)* and some by non-native English speakers that I have not heard of but wind up enjoying immensely *(Democracy in America, Lolita)*.

She also leans over our shoulders as we write our impressions of these works and teaches me more about expressing myself in writing than anyone before or since, in either Thai or English.

Driving around on my own in our new Ford Escort station wagon (how tearfully we bade the old Maverick goodbye!) helps in my Americanization. Out there, coping with traffic, with people, with only my six-year-old for company, I have to speak and *think* American. It is a daily challenge to function, almost as if I am an alien "presence" adapting to the ways of indifferent mankind (Los Angeles is nothing if not indifferent) while trying, basically, to blend in, to go unnoticed.

It is confirmed what I have suspected that, as an American, you go less with the flow than Orientals do. You establish yourself as an individual, shopping for bananas or even sauntering down the street; you operate behind a self, an ego, rather than as a blended member of a large organic body called, fondly in your heart, Siam, ancient Siam. It is far less an issue of patriotism—Americans are, in the usual sense of the word, more patriotic than Thais—than it is a concept of *self* and *society*.

In America, generally, the emphasis is on the former; in Thailand, and in most Far East countries, it is on the latter.

CONFESSIONS OF A MAIL ORDER BRIDE

I have to adjust to being *Wanwadee* first and foremost, as distinct and separate an "other" as all the June's and Jane's and Juan's and Yvonne's out there walking the streets of Los Angeles. Make that *driving* the streets of Los Angeles; outside of ambling through malls, no one actually walks in Southern California.

It is best for me to do so, and educational, and wholly necessary, since we are so very alone in Los Angeles. Our neighbors on all sides are hardly ever home, and among their kids James makes only two or three friends.

Despite my growing independence, I don't think such a place will ever be safe for any of us, even this far up into the hills. There is always some dreadful mayhem going on, somewhere, anywhere, in the sprawling city. *Parolee Goes On Crossbow Shooting Spree, Kills Six.* That sort of thing.

Daily.

Ultimately, the *why's* and the *what-for's* of such events make one search inwardly for answers, if there are any to be found. Too often, there are not.

As titillating and diverting as these times become for us in the mishmash of Los Angeles, Richard still clings to his old buddies in Atlanta more than to any one else—especially Robert, with whom he exchanges letters and occasional long-distance calls.

For one thing, he has known them for a longer time, during his period of adult maturation when the bonds of friendship form deeper. For another, he has shared with them his most engrossing avocation, experimenting with drugs.

Richard and Robert let their friendship drag somewhat while we were still in Atlanta and did not see each other in the six months before we left. A few days before that departure they had a long phone conversation, during which they laughed and reminisced a lot, but that was all.

That's why it is with great excitement that he greets the news of an impending visit by Robert and Anne. They are flying out to San Francisco in March to attend a lawyers' convention where Robert will be presenting a paper on—what else?—"Legalizing Recreational Drugs." He urges Richard to attend because he will be "giving out free samples." Richard gets a kick out of it, but that sort of joking becomes a reason why I myself am more or less dreading a visit from them.

He might indeed show up with acid or cocaine or something else worse than the grass to which Richard has been limiting himself, fulfilling his promise of *trying at least.* Unlike Richard, Robert has always seemed to me to be more apt to experiment and to take a variety of stuff with him wherever he goes. It might be a rationalization, but I also tend to see him as an instigator, one who has already led my husband down the wrong path in their early days together.

Of course, I do not have a shred of evidence; for all I know, it could have been the other way around.

I hate to be thinking these dire things, especially when this friendship means so much to Richard, but I continue to live in dread of his getting arrested for possession—an unlikely event, given his caution, but a source of fear with careless people like Robert around. Nevertheless, I try to look forward to seeing Robert and Anne.

If nothing else, Anne and I can sit around and trade our usual small talk about kids and prices and our husbands' bad habits, as we used to do in Atlanta. She does not particularly like Thai food, but she has taught me a few things about American desserts, the end results of which—cookies, cakes, pies— have been pleasing to Richard and James if not necessarily to me.

(Thai people have a difficult time developing a sweet

tooth because sugary sweets like cake, cookies, and candy are virtually unheard of except in Bangkok, where they have been introduced by Westerners. When we crave something sweet, it is almost always some sort of fruit or preparation with fruit.)

Over the phone, as we plan the visit, she intrigues me with talk of a country applecake that just might make a convert of me. Unwilling to divulge the recipe until she sees me, she makes it a "hook" for our getting together in San Francisco.

A few more negotiations, and Richard and I agree to meet them at the Hyatt on San Francisco's Market Street on a Saturday at the end of March.

Something to look forward to—and to fear.

Meanwhile our education on the streets of Los Angeles goes on.

Ironically, self-search and discovery are exactly what Richard and I have determined for ourselves, whether we know it or not, by departing Atlanta; what I long ago laid out for myself, in fact, by departing the Far East. As a Buddhist, I believe that it isn't really by accident that Richard and I have met. We have been heading more or less toward each other, and toward this place, all along. We just happened to intersect, finally, along a patterned course.

Maybe we all harry ourselves onto a certain path in life; and to alleviate a sense of personal responsibility for what we can find there, we blame "Fate." The cards. In Thailand, we call this *chokchatha*. Nice to have this character Fate in the wings, like a seasoned performer, a rough-and-ready buffoon with all the straight lines, whenever we make fools of ourselves on the stage of life.

Fate delivers; his timing is superb.

I am out there in the suburbs, hanging on at the edge of the San Andreas fault, being pulled, *pulling myself* in several new directions at once—being on my own, being American, being, or at least becoming, Wanwadee. In more than name. On more than paper. Wanwadee: someone I have lived with all my life but hardly known. A pretty little Oriental girl, so they once said; married now; a mother; an American housewife, amazingly; and growing up at last.

I have never told Richard of the fence my father had built around our family house in Thailand, how he and my mother had clung so hard to us two girls, how our lives were thus encircled, circumscribed by love, hemmed in by devotion and protection. At the time, I did not realize it for what it was; but on my own now in a foreign land I could put it in perspective, appreciate what it offered and despise what it denied.

It was a transcendent and all-inclusive love known as the Oriental family.

The social "glue" provided by the family is essential; without it, Thailand itself would be unthinkable. In a land of few government hand-outs or self-proclaimed "support groups," there is really *only* the family. Why search outside, around, or underneath it?

Or, to phrase it as my Mom would—a Delphic proverb —if the *masman gai* (chicken stew) is simmering well, don't meddle with the heat.

By coming on my own to the United States and gradually establishing myself *on my own* as an American, I have ensured myself a somewhat different set of codes in the conduct of my thought and life. One of these is in fact the inward-turning search for self. I feel blessed, in this respect, just to have the Western-style self-awareness that my cross-cultural experience has brought.

At no time has achieving it been as easy for me as it seems to be for the millions of American-born women who speak, boast, complain, and write of it as if it were as much an inherent part of being woman as menstruation or childbirth is.

All of this I say without rancor, as I look with anguish and fondness upon the City of Angels that has proven to be so full of the sternest challenges. It all started with a dose of lone-liness, in this great and busy place that spreads out and down from our haven in La Quiera like a smorgasbord of the grandest aspirations *(I'm gonna be a star!)* and the dumbest fol-lies *(I'm gonna be a star!)* of the American people.

In desperation, I sought to alleviate the gnawing condi-tion of my life at that time, being foreign, being alone. My child was there for company of a sort, but the only adult close to me, my husband, was either off at work or under his head-phones. Two female friends, Maxine, an American, and Sheila (nee Shera) a Thai-speaking Laotian with whom I enjoyed rem-iniscing in Thai about Southeast Asia, lived so far away in L.A. that they might as well have been in Mexico or Nevada.

Seeking someone for company, then, I eventually found a twenty-nine-year-old woman, Thai-born, named Wanwadee.

I am glad to have met her at last.

I am even gladder that, by becoming American, I did not miss the opportunity to do so.

21

ENCOUNTER ON THE STREETS

Los Angeles 1983

Although Richard first claims that he merely made a wrong turn, later he will admit that he entered the area because he wanted to check out *the* place in Los Angeles for an easy buy of marijuana—you don't even have to get out of your car.

No more than two minutes after making that turn, he is out of the car and looking into the faces of two uniformed members of the L.A.P.D., as stern and spitpolished as stormtroopers.

We happen to be within a little City of Sin in Los Angeles—one of several, we later learn.

Richard has made a wrong turn—a very wrong turn.

It is 12:30 a.m., and we are returning home from a Los Angeles Lakers basketball game. One of Richard's friends at work offered him a pair of $25 tickets to a playoff battle for $5 each, and Richard couldn't resist even though it is a weekday night. We ask Maxine to sit James late—no objections from either one.

It turns out to be an overtime game and so exciting that neither of us cares much about the time. Although I don't grasp all the nuances of the first complete basketball game I have ever watched—I never played the sport (popular in Thailand) while I was a girl—I try to remember to cheer every time someone in a purple and gold uniform throws the ball through the hoop, and to groan with every L.A. foul.

"Just watch Jack Nicholson and do what he does," Richard advises.

I do know who Jack Nicholson is, six rows in front of us. And I do, in fact, exactly as he does. That makes it easier.

The Lakers get it in more times than Houston, and everybody leaves the game in one happy throng, us included, exiting the Coliseum lot toward the Boulevard.

If we were just a bit more careful we would not have missed our Freeway entrance; but since we do miss it, Richard (as he explains it later) knows another way home through the dope-buying hotspot—just to "have a look."

Because his supply is low, I suspect that he wants to do more than look, but with me in the car he says he will not stop if the place looks too grungy.

And grungy indeed it looks: lurid neon signs blinking *NUDE* and *SEX SHOW,* and packs of hookers, gaudy birds of prey, on every street corner. There is an equally gaudy pimp recessed into one of the darkened doorways like a city rat.

As we swing a U-turn to get out, the cops, on foot with their cruiser visible down a side street, whistle us over right behind another car. It is a large Buick or Cadillac, and a third officer is writing a document—ticket, summons, fine, whatever —to the well-dressed white man standing uneasily beside it.

ENCOUNTER ON THE STREETS

As Richard gets out of our car, I have a sinking feeling all the way down to my feet. It dawns on me that most of the women on the street are Oriental, and here I am seated beside a white male in a car on this street in this part of the city.

An open and shut case of whatever they want.

The longer Richard stays outside speaking with the police officers, the more I feel like crying. In my imagination I can see us being fingerprinted, mugshot, spending the night in jail, and then having to pay a huge sum for one violation or another.

For what? A wrong turn? Or because I am Thai?

The more I think about it, the less I feel like crying and the angrier I grow. At the thought of being blackmarked as the end result of an evening of professional basketball, the tiger stirs. I am about to get out of the car and swipe at somebody, but as I slide to the door Richard comes over and gets back in, tucking his driver's license into his wallet along with the Laker ticket-stubs, which, miraculously, he has saved.

"Jeez," he says, "it's a good thing I never had my driver's license and plates changed to California."

"There is no trouble then?" By now the police have moved off down the block, and my question is rhetorical.

"Not now. The one thing I thought might some day get me in trouble turns out to save us."

"Buying drugs?"

"No, I'm referring to my license. We are both still driving with Georgia licenses. He saw that and took me for a tourist, and before he could ask for anything else I showed him the Laker ticket stubs. He handed them back, apologized, and told me to stay out of this neighborhood."

"Good advice."

"I'll take it. I'd rather go without smoke than have to hit a place like this. Whoo-ee!" he concludes as he turns onto a wide main street and speeds away.

CONFESSIONS OF A MAIL ORDER BRIDE

But for me it isn't *quite* finished: "Did they say anything about me?"

He glances over. "They wanted to know who you were. Why?"

"You did not notice that some of the girl out there is Oriental—Vietnamese mostly, I think."

"Girls are."

"Girls are."

"You think that's why they stopped us?"

"What you think?"

"I thought it was because we had slowed at the exact wrong time and place. They were just waiting to nab someone. Anyone."

"Anyone who looks suspicious, no? Like Oriental woman. They always expect worst, the police—they encourage it, in fact."

Richard glances over again. "You really think so, Dee?" he asks in a serious voice.

I consider the question.

I do not answer.

We have come to a Freeway entrance. Down the far reaches of the eight-lane street, looking toward one or another of the city "downtowns," Los Angeles looks empty, brazenly yellow under the mercury street lamps, hollow and hellish. How different from the Los Angeles of sunshine and golden beaches and hills in the distance.

We accelerate onto the Freeway and head for home in silence.

Just a few miles from La Quiera, Richard exits and goes to a late-night pizza drivethru (everything in Los Angeles is drivethru) and gets three slices, one with black olives for himself, one with anchovies for me, and one with pepperoni for the babysitter. We have stopped here before; the pizza is very good.

ENCOUNTER ON THE STREETS

I sit in the car and chew. Still good. Crust cheesy and bubbled along the edges. Eight, eight point five.

And luckily so, or Los Angeles would have lost *all* of its blue sea-brown mountain charm by now.

I am still sore, but I'm finally ready to reconsider the question: "I take back what I say about police."

"What'd you say?"

"Encourage crime."

"Oh, that. I knew you, of all *conservatives*, didn't mean it. Anyway, some Americans don't need any encouragement. Did you see that pimp?"

Here's that Voice of America again. But, after being exposed to one form of racism, a person does not wish to hear of another. "It big hang-up you have about black. *Mister* Conservative."

"Tit for tat."

"It true. You are paranoiac."

"Maybe I am, but—"

"No *maybe* about it."

"—but score a few for Wanwadee."

"For what? Truth?"

"I'm talking about language—vocabulary, idiom, inflection, the whole schmear. You handle it all a lot better now."

"I try. Teacher help."

"Except for those *s*'s."

"Don't change subject. It still hang-up."

Munching, he chooses not to respond. If he cannot change the subject when he knows I'm right, he shuts his mouth.

My Ricky.

22

ON A HILLTOP

Northern California 1983

Winter fades; by March spring is in the air! A California spring, to be sure, but spring nonetheless. We have been told that the only way you can tell the change of seasons is by the increase in talk of Angels and Dodgers (Angels? Dodgers? the *baseball teams,* it is explained to me) and a corresponding decrease in talk about skiing in the Sierras.

But it actually does feel briskly spring-like, as I have at last come to understand that term (along with the nature of deciduous trees), and the smog seems to vanish for days at a time—gone with the wind, the Pacific onshore wind.

Having just about decided to leave the company and Los Angeles, Richard asks for the last Friday in March off in order to have a three-day weekend so we can go to San Francisco. He is good at his non-academic role as technical editor and is greatly appreciated by his immediate supervisor, Ian,

239

who knows that Richard deserves an unscheduled day off. He has been putting in long hours on various company documents without complaint.

Also, we know we have to get out of Los Angeles, as the prisoner of Chillon has to get out of Chillon and the prisoner of Zenda, Zenda. Prisoners around the world will understand.

To be fair, it is not really that we feel like inmates, in a prison of our own making. It is more a result of a form of cabin fever. Little have Richard and I—urban American, Thai gal— suspected that we love the great outdoors so much until we moved to smog-saturated, eight-laned, many-downtowned Los Angeles.

Also, we are too locked into routine, and we are simply not routine-loving people. If we were, Richard would be in New York City somewhere selling stocks and bonds, and I would have settled into a role in my hometown (had I never married) halfway between a *femme fatale* and an object of pity. I can see myself—and it is no joke—walking to and from market with whispers about bad luck trailing me down the narrow streets like a cloud of bothersome flies.

We leave James in the care of Maxine, whose maturity, childless condition, and basic good-hearted nature make her a near-perfect long-term babysitter. When he understands that it is Maxine with whom he will be spending a couple of days, he almost pushes us out the door.

"Mommy, when are you and Daddy leaving?"

That done, we manage to wipe all other obligations out of mind early on Friday and hit the Great American Road.

Coastal Highway One is aptly named, for it may be Number One in beauty in the world, unwinding like a ribbon of wonder between wrinkled brown hills on the inland side and the sun-struck blue Pacific seaward. This Friday, huge late-winter waves cream themselves against coastal crags hundreds of feet below as the road dips and rises like music.

At seven, as darkness descends, we take an inland turn to a bed-and-breakfast room (what a wonderful idea, these rooms—someone in Thailand could make a fortune introducing them for tourists; someone probably *is*, by now) some forty or fifty miles south of San Francisco, and spend a restful night in the quiet of the Coast Range foothills.

A joint seems the furthest thing from Richard's mind as we take an evening walk in an open meadow.

Tentatively, I mention this impression to him.

"You're right," he says. "I'm almost there. It's almost history."

"I am so grad."

"Me, too. And look, for you, no more grad's. You're almost there, too."

"What you think it is has change you?"

"You know the answer to that."

He is going to say *Wanwadee*. "Please, tell truth, not sweet talk."

"If you won't let me tell the real truth, I'll just say that I heard an old Sixties song on the radio a while ago. The title explains it all—'I Got Stoned and I Missed It.' I used to think it was hilarious; now I think it's pathetic."

"You know, you are right."

"What?"

"It pathetic."

"Ooops, there goes that missing verb again."

"It *is* pathetic."

We have come to a little, quick-running stream, gurgling along beneath the purple twilight sky. A small beaver sees us just as we see him and waddles into the water, slapping its surface with a warning flap of its thick, dark tail.

"I'll tell you what else is pathetic," he says. "That you won't believe you are the best thing ever to happen to me."

"Oh, no, I believe. You won't believe opposite is true."

"I believe it, too, Doll—if you say so. But listen to us, we sound like a Mutual Admiration Society."

"It okay. It *is* okay. Way it should be."

"My mail order bride," he smiles. "That's *first-class* mail."

I smile back. "I be pleased to come to you parcel post."

He lifts my chin and kisses me lightly, and we hug, holding on to each other as tightly as we did on an evening in New York years ago, only now for reasons almost infinitely deeper.

By eight the next morning we are back on the road and by nine inside the upward-sweeping lobby of the Hyatt, where epic poetry and far-out architecture meet, and our reunion day begins with the shock of seeing two old friends looking slightly older. Both of them, as if driven by identical clocks, have flecks and streaks of gray in the same areas of their hair.

Curious what time can do to a couple: brand them.

Wrinkles I did not notice before now hold Anne's eyes hostage, looping the green-gray pupils in a tell tale net of age. Robert is, if anything, more visibly aging, with a stoop to his back that seems positively judicial. Is this new, or was I not paying attention back in Atlanta—so self-conscious was I? He reminds me of my father in this respect, and, in fact, of many older men in Thailand; they seem to develop a male version of dowager's hump.

And it has been only a year or so! Do people age faster in America? Am I blind to my own signs of aging, or just newly alert to them, now, in others? Or—and this seems the oddest but likeliest explanation—have we, Richard and I, living on the frantic, often chaotic and superficial Western edge of civilization where everyone is addicted to the value of appearances, simply become more aware of the various forms of corruption to which flesh is prone, including aging?

Whatever the reason, the visual shock is erased by the happy aura of seeing old friends and anticipating an outing with them. We hug, joke, have a noisy breakfast in a snack bar open to the towering lobby above, and, because it is getting well into the morning—Robert has an evening conference—head for the car.

Sunny, happy California day. There have been too few of them for us, less a gripe against the Golden State than against ourselves for not taking advantage of them.

It takes a couple of hours to get to the Napa Valley, more than we have anticipated. The Saturday traffic is heavy with tourists heading for one or another of the things that Americans do to legitimize their getting "out of town." On the way we notice two or three billboards advertising a spring wine festival that same day, which explains a portion of the heavy traffic. There is also something called the Highland Games going on somewhere nearby, as well as a NASCAR road race in Fresno. We are on the main road to Fresno.

There are more "outings" on this one weekend, it seems, than during an entire year in central Thailand. But, then, most Thais do not have the access to automobiles that Americans do. They have not cultivated the habit of getting out of town.

During the drive Richard and Robert joke and banter—that conversational trait in American males that I observed long ago. To avoid talk of any substance or seriousness, they turn to joshing and quippery. Some get so good at it that they turn it into a sort of folk art, skimming everything lightly, making everyone laugh.

Richard once explained this tendency as one more manifestation of a long history of anti-intellectualism in this country ("whole *books* have been written about it"), but that explanation does little to relieve me of the feeling that these men are missing something in life, something that Thai men, as well as I can recall, usually choose not to miss. That is simply a *lively exchange of views*—on politics mostly, but also on history and culture, less often on sports and business—that is often the content of conversation among educated Thais, as well as among other Orientals and Europeans.

There seems to be no other explanation for this tendency to cover everything with a laugh than the American national manias for surface humor and inner privacy. Can these both be by-products of the lack of community in the States and the resultant thinness of trust among people who remain essentially strangers to one another?

Whatever the cause, Richard and Robert talk lightly about old times in pre-Beltway Atlanta, but not, thankfully, about drugs. Richard has not brought any.

"You get too old for that shit," I hear Robert say.

I breathe a huge sigh of relief in the back seat.

Richard listens, says nothing.

Anne and I speak of kids and food and prices and schools. She asks me how I like living among so many of my fellow compatriots, and I have to tell her that I actually see no more Thais here than I did in Atlanta.

"Isn't that strange!"

"Not," I say, "if you know Los Angeles."

Before long, we arrive at a castle-like fieldstone structure that, on a huge sign out front, hails itself as the oldest winery in the Valley. It really doesn't need to boast for it certainly isn't short of visitors. People, hundreds of people, swarm all over the parking lot and grounds; they line up dozens deep at the entrances marked "Shop" and "Cellars" and even deeper at the one marked "Tasting Room."

California weekend. Thais queue up like this only for fresh fish on seafood market day.

ON A HILLTOP

Richard is tempted to by-pass this winery and head down the road, but Robert's guidebook calls it the most beautiful establishment in the area. So, dutifully, we stand in line a half-hour for our half-hour tour of the cellars—cavernous and dank, overwhelmingly aromatic—and exit through a tunnel anticipating an hour's wait for fifteen minutes in the tasting room.

But surprise: the line has dwindled to about ten people. Anne remembers that the wine festival entertainment at a larger winery many miles up the road is to start at noon, with the Beach Boys, Natalie Cole, and Jefferson Starship. It is already well after noon and the crowd of people has fled to get there—before the crowds get there, of course.

The end result is a mixed blessing. We stay much too long. Richard and Robert drink too much and have no desire to fight any more traffic. Besides, the place is much too beautiful to leave.

Neither Anne (semi-sober) nor I (sober as a clam) can dispute that point, situated, as the place is, three-fourths the way up a hill that looks out over vineyards and rolling evergreen forests. So we stay put to give the men a chance to shake it off.

And stay put.
And stay put.

At three o'clock, with Robert asleep on a bench in the almost deserted Renaissance Italian garden that is the vineyard's backyard ("jet lag," Anne explains, winking), and Richard and Anne chatting desultorily about computers (she works at home on one), I decide to take a stroll.

I make my way over the acres of vineyards that spread upward beyond the garden, enter the forest, and climb still further upward over boulders and around trees. The ground is covered with evergreen needles which, heated by the sun on an otherwise cool day, emit a clean-smelling but heavy aroma almost as intoxicating as the wine itself. Over my head, in the topmost branches of a fir, a large blue bird—Steller's Jay—chirps away endlessly. The bark of the trees that I touch as I climb is pleasantly rough against the palms of my hands.

When at last I reach the top, I find a clearing. Some rusty junk, and scattered paper and plastic remnants (rubber, too—a condom), tell me that I am far from the first person to stand (or lie) in this spot. But I may be the first Thai—a still-awestruck newcomer to the United States; I am willing to overlook the marks of man and concentrate instead on the scene.

As in most of the Western United States, it is arrestingly beautiful. Grandeur of landscape seems always here, around the next bend, directly in one's path, routinely accessible wherever man has not destroyed or otherwise interfered with it.

If there is one clear debt that I owe California and the West it is the arousal of my sense of aesthetics, dormant in my Thai youth, awakened by the fresh New York and Atlanta experiences, and now in full bloom. I will be impelled to take many art courses in college, which in turn will direct me to art as a pursuit and, eventually, to portrait sculpture as a career.

Suddenly I am aware that I am not alone up here.

A twig snaps, some leaves rustle, and I turn to face a tall, emaciated, middle-aged man with a scruffy beard and two bleary but piercing blue eyes. He watches me warily, ferally actually, like some wild beast disturbed in its habitat. Dressed in torn overalls and a rag top of indeterminate origin, with shoeless and filthy feet, he seems like a character out of some horror movie.

He takes a few steps toward me, and I look around to

calculate my next move. I see a canvas lean-to in a small clearing to my right. Some clothing, more rags actually, are hung on a line; wisps of smoke emanate from the remnants of a campfire.

This guy lives up here!

He is no more than twenty feet away, still eyeing me wordlessly, when I try a scared little smile. "Hello," I say. "It pretty up here, no?"

He studies me some more, spittle forming at the corners of his stubbly mouth, then says, "Suzie Wong?"

"I beg your pardon."

"Suzie Wong?"

When he decides to take one step closer, *I* decide that discretion is by far the better part of valor, and I edge back as slowly and carefully as I can. He appears not to like this, but I don't care since the situation does not look healthy at all.

"Suzie Wong?" he says again, a little louder, a little more insistent. He stumbles another step closer. The situation begins to look extremely unhealthy. A thought crosses my mind—but no, this is definitely not the time and place to test the value of my karate training in Thailand.

One more step, and I panic: I turn and run.

Down through the pines and boulders I retreat as quickly and nimbly as I can, over fallen branches, across a dry gully.

Although I do not turn to look back, I sense, with relief, that he is not following me. This feeling is confirmed when I hear a cry like that of a sick or wounded animal from back up at the top of the hill: "Suzie Wong! Suzie Wong!" it says. Then a veritable howl: "Suzie Wong! Suzie Wonnnnggg!"

For one brief moment it seems the sky will split if it gets one decibel louder.

But it stops, and I slow down, breathing heavily, perspiring in the bright California sun but still not looking back. I am in the vineyard now, among the tiny grapes, well out of harm's range.

I continue downward very slowly toward the winery, thankful to be far from danger and musing to myself: *Is there something like this on every hilltop in California?*

By the time I get all the way back down, Robert is up on his feet, and the three of them are engaged in lively conversation; I decide to keep the incident to myself, lest it disturb the remainder of the afternoon. Later, perhaps, I will disclose it to Richard.

It was unpleasant, but an unsteady emaciated drunk—poor man!—is nothing that the new Wanwadee cannot handle.

So I think.

"Did you hear someone shouting, Dee?" Richard asks.

"No." I think of my encounter with that poor beaten homeless hopeless man in the wooded hilltop wilds of America. "Not a thing."

"Hey, it's after four o'clock."

"Okay, Dee, where have you been?" Robert asks. "And do you have Ricky's permission to wander off like that?"

I smile to answer both queries and to cover up any lingering sign of disarray.

"Ah, the mysterious East."

"No," I say at length, "I have answer. I do not need Ricky permission. He does not want me to ask for it."

"Enlightened guy! And, hey, I thought it was *Reeky*."

"Oh, no—it *Ricky* now."

"Yeah," Richard says. "She's been taking this reading-writing course. She's getting to be whiz-bang at everything."

"Heck," Anne says, "it was just a matter of time. And opportunity. That's all a woman needs nowadays."

"Even a *Thai* woman," Robert says, being smart.

"Thank you," I say mock-sarcastically.

"That used to be *sank you*."

ON A HILLTOP

"You used to be nice."

"Hey, I'm gonna keep my mouth shut."

"You'd better," Richard steps in. "She's done a lot of growing up out West."

"You know," Robert says to him, changing the subject, "speaking of East and West, I recall your saying in your last letter that you two—three—are planning to return East. True?"

Richard shrugs.

"That says it all," Robert shrugs back, and they stand there smiling at each other and the world for a moment or two. "Look, I've got that eight p.m. meeting at the hotel. Let's start back toward the city and you can tell Anne and me all about it."

Slightly groggy from the afternoon wine but functional, Richard agrees, and we hit the road again just in time to catch the first wave of people heading back from the festival. A long line of cars winds down the dusky road below us toward the Bay Area like a glittering, endless serpent.

Eventually we slow to one of those famous urban first-gear crawls.

Infamous California traffic: now there's a reason to consider moving, we all agree.

We are going to miss some aspects of California, leaving as we are for yet another unopened door back East. Looking out to the blue heights of the most distant mountains, I find myself wondering—as I never really did at home—exactly why we are moving again. The issue is like a jewel of indeterminate worth held up to the light: from one angle it appears to be a certain way, rare, valuable; from another angle, entirely worthless.

I suppose it is the residual Thai in me that is ready to do whatever is necessary to support my husband in his search for the right job, for a satisfying career. But I am not at all sure that a move East is what is required. Relocating, furthermore, is always a risk. It is gratifying, on the other hand, for the *American* me to be able to have these questioning thoughts, and to voice them freely, whenever I wish, to my husband.

As for James, his suburban kindergarten is excellent, the best equipped and staffed school he will ever attend. But the city itself lies all around him like a huge La Brea pit. Just the other day a couple staying at a Brentwood motel lost sight of their six-year-old girl for a moment and didn't see her again until the next day when a maid found her—stabbed to death in the vacated room directly below the parents' room.

Terrible stuff.

Late getting back, we have only a minute to hug and say good-bye.

By the time we have rolled into San Francisco proper and up to Robert's hotel, Richard has been convinced, more or less, to move back East. Robert has done some arm-twisting, so that Richard's projected cut in salary, as he once again changes fields and jobs, is balanced nicely by the emotional peace of a return to academics and to the settled East.

"Eastward-ho!" Robert shouts in farewell.

Richard laughs and says *we'll see*, and Anne and I exchange waves as the car eases out of the Hyatt drop-off and onto busy Saturday-night Market Street.

We stay again in the Coast Range, and, after another scenic and enjoyable drive down Highway One the next day, arrive home very late Sunday afternoon after picking up James from Maxine.

It is nearly dark, but not dark enough for us to miss the damage done by neighborhood vandals in our absence: chalked graffiti on the front door—nothing racial, just nasty—and toilet paper unraveled all through the branches of our two quince trees. One of the panes of glass in the garage in broken out.

April Fool! is scrawled in chalk on the driveway concrete. And I thought that sort of thing was reserved for Halloween.

It does, however, fit a general pattern we are familiar with: random, violent, senseless.

Silently calculating as I stand there with a sleepy but curious James, Richard (always quick with the math of anything) comes out finally with "Forty bucks, maybe fifty."

"Could be worser."

"Worse. It would be if I had my hands on the little bastards—worse for them. Did this stuff happen when I was a kid?"

"Worse." I decline to answer the question because I wasn't around when he was a kid. In Thailand, at water festivals, people sop and spray water on each other with sodden towels, garden hoses, and all sorts of waterguns. Some clothing inevitably gets ruined, but it's all done with the utmost good humor. There is some religious significance as well.

Richard wouldn't want to hear about this now.

Going against his own advice to stop blaming all the world's ills on cities in general and Los Angeles in particular, he mutters conclusively, "Eastward-ho, Dee, Eastward-ho."

I could, maybe even *should,* argue the point, but I resist the inclination. My thoughts will remain my own. For all practical purposes, the matter seems to have been already decided. By both of us. Eastward-ho indeed.

But even after Richard has resigned—with surprisingly substantial severance pay that will keep us going for some time financially—and it does come time to choose a job and relocate, we find ourselves still drawn several ways, and we make and unmake several "final" decisions. We cannot tear ourselves away immediately or completely from our vision of life in the West. Like a bittersweet dream, it just keeps hanging around.

The eventual compromise outcome is that we will try to move only *halfway* east, to the *middle* of America—an odd but somehow satisfying solution for me. After all, I have never really seen the middle of America—don't even know exactly where or what it is, as a matter of fact.

So: solution to dilemma. Or so it seems.

Blessed with a number of options in academia because of his "real-world" experience, Richard finally decides on an attractive job in the state of Arkansas, exactly midway between where we are and where we started out from over a year ago. From there, he says, we can "visit" both East and West—the best of both worlds.

It makes sense to me. As does his claim that it is a Sunbelt state with a good future in education thanks to an enlightened governor. And his assertion that he could be getting in on a ground-floor academic computing position in this self-proclaimed Land of Opportunity.

Brilliant! I think, and my fear of the unknown is allayed. Temporarily.

Arkansas, Ricky? Robert writes a week later. *Are you kidding? They don't even wear shoes over there.*

Now I am worried again, picturing a compulsorily barefoot James, with a corncob pipe in his mouth.

Other people, trusted Maxine included, seem surprised at our choice.

Are you sure about this? they ask him.

Do you know what a billbilly is? they ask me.

Because of Richard's ideal job offer and because it is sort of "halfway," we turn deaf ears. We are convinced that, if we must make a move, this move is the one to make.

So, curious about small town middle-American life, and

hoping that we can make this East-West idea work, we decide on Rousersville, Arkansas, population 20,000, wherever in America that happens to be.

Richard accepts a job at a four-year technical college where he feels he can be both inwardly satisfied and outwardly successful—teaching technical communication courses at undergraduate and graduate levels. The people he interviews with are impressed by that non-academic experience, while he is equally impressed with their intention of placing him in an advanced, quasi-administrative position.

Of the jobs available to him, this is exactly what he wants at this point in his life.

"And, of course," he says, "we don't have to stay there forever."

"Of course," I agree.

We are ready, by summer's end, for another turn of the road. Goodbye, Los Angeles. So long to the beaches, the barrios, the brown hills, the bizarre news. Farewell to all you American Thais at the exact opposite end of the county.

Goodbye to my best American teacher and my closest American friend.

Beyond the unknowns in the curve, to me as a foreigner trying to get to know America ever better, ever more intimately, the road we have chosen looks interesting—adventuresome and challenging.

23

AMERICAN LANDOWNERS

Rousersville 1983

It is *hot.*

If someone told me, when I was growing up, that there is a place where the August weather is as hot as in the central valley of Thailand, the steamy Rice Belt, I would have thought that they are either crazy or speaking of a literal Hell—that is, if I had a Western notion of Hell.

But, to me at least, the center of Arkansas qualifies.

I realize that there are places on earth hotter than both Thailand and Arkansas, but they must be sparsely inhabited, like the equatorial Amazon; or reserved as places of punishment, like Devil's Island; or populated by people who believe that dry heat will cure everything from sinusitis to gout to old age, like Tucson or Phoenix, Arizona.

255

CONFESSIONS OF A MAIL ORDER BRIDE

But few places on this globe are as relentlessly hot as the two in which, by accidents of birth and marriage, I have spent and will spend considerable portions of my life: Nakhon Narai, Thailand, and Rousersville, Arkansas. Just the names bring perspiration to my brow.

Richard and I spend a three-day weekend searching for a house to buy. We decide that we have had enough of rental living and wish to become people of property, a notion which I in particular find appealing: me, Wanwadee, mail-order bride become *American landholder.* A person of property in the New World. Like George Washington. Like Thomas Jefferson. Like Donald Trump.

Besides, it will do James good to set down roots for the first time in his young life. Here he is about to begin public school, and his family will buy their first home—three bedrooms, two baths, a double garage, and a backyard (not to mention a place to leave his bicycle without fear of it vanishing overnight).

As exciting a prospect as home ownership is, it does not take the searing edge off this early-August weekend during which we scurry over a small Ozark Valley city looking for a dream. The heat is not moist heat, as I'd known in my native land, nor is it truly dry, as it can be in Southern California when the Santa Ana blows. It is somewhere in between, and, in that sense, it is quirky, unpredictable. You do not perspire as much as in Thailand, yet neither do you run short of breath as in a dry-hot climate.

Actually, we do a little of both, so that by the time we finish mopping our brows, for instance, we are thoroughly winded. But I exaggerate again.

Just say that it is very hot and that the heat is very uncomfortable. (Later on, I will learn that the entire central plains of the United States is suffering a severe drought this summer, temperatures being well above average for a 45-day period through the beginning of September.)

The house we finally choose at the end of the harrowing weekend, reduced in my memory to a blur of heat and kitchens and house-for-sale signs, is, in fact, being constructed on a tiny lot no more than a mile from the campus where Richard will be teaching.

We choose it for several rather specious reasons, among them the privacy of a backyard that backs up to a seven-foot cedar fence and Interstate 40; the fact that we can make minor alterations in the cookie-cutter plans as the house goes up; and the 7.25% mortgage, which is low.

The paper-logged maneuvers involved in our deal remind me of Richard and Lee-Lee in the New York airport. As well as I can remember my father negotiating with his clients, I recall many conversations, a few swift handshakes, and the signing of a single document—that was that. In an American real estate office, there is enough paper at a typical transaction to start a large bonfire: deeds, insurance, tax documents, inspection papers, financial instruments, et cetera, et cetera.

I understand that in America the rule of law is paramount, but in such a situation it is more like the rule of forms. The *spirit* of the law, if by that phrase justice and trust is implied, does not prevail, much less even exist.

Worse than the mere paperwork, however, is the premise upon which it is based: simple mistrust at least, complex fear of litigation at best. Or should that be reversed—is the fear of ensuing lawsuits, with another paper avalanche, worse than mistrust of the strangers with whom one is often forced to risk business? A lack of faith in strangers, after all, is as universal as its opposite, the trust and love experienced among family.

Whatever the case, the typical American seems to relish these signing rituals, and in fact shows the high regard in which they are held by climaxing a deal with them. In America

such deal-making approximates orgasm, with negotiation act-
ing as foreplay and the pen-wielding affixation of signatures
coitus itself. The participants sigh, sit back, and often even light
up a cigarette afterwards.

For Richard and me, signing all the papers is more
trauma than pleasure, however.

The move from Los Angeles is more expensive and
emotionally exhausting than we have anticipated. Not only is it
hard to give up eight thousand dollars a year in annual income,
it is at least as difficult to surrender a metropolitan lifestyle—
even though we have unquestionably chosen to do so.

Arkansas, in our minds, is not exactly the Middle Ages,
but we knew we were giving up the bright lights and big city—
forsaking, literally, life in the fast lane. For another thing, we
were, in a sense, buying a pig in a poke. True, Richard had
traveled to Rousersville for an interview. At that time he said
little to me other than a mumbled comment that he liked the
people he met. But he did not really have a chance to scrutinize
the place, to check out the entire scene, from the housing potential to the cultural amenities to the very air we would be
breathing.

For all the *planning* (as opposed to *worrying)* we had
given it, the move itself is like stepping into a dark and unfamiliar room.

Yet we still see it as something we want very much to
do—I do anyway. Perhaps to Richard, deep down, it is just
another move to be made. He is nothing if not a movin' man.

On the other hand, knowing that we can actually *afford*
a place helps to salve the wounds. What we are paying fifty-
eight thousand dollars for, a new three-bedroom house on a
quarter-acre lot in a middle-class "suburb" with trees and
shrubs, would have set us back *three times* that much in any
decent area of Los Angeles.

Correction: it would not have set us back at all; we simply could not have afforded it. Ever.

By the middle of August we have a brand-new house to live in with virtually nothing to do but unpack and get to know a west-central corner of the state of Arkansas. The apparent benefits of our reasons for buying the house go up in smoke as we realize that an Interstate highway, even in Arkansas, generates nearly as much noise as any runway at Don Meung, especially when it's part of your backyard; learn that cookie-cutter designs have a *raison d'etre*, and if you really don't know what you are doing you can wind up, as we do, with a dining room that looks directly through an open archway at the cook in her kitchen, and a master bedroom without direct access to a bath (no *wonder* the builder kept scratching his head). Worst of all, we have paid a grand total of $2,500 in "points" to acquire rights to a 25-year low-interest loan that would require ten years of payments of recoup the $2,500.

But, when it has risen above 105 degrees for three days running (and above 100 for weeks before that), one is not thinking especially clearly, not even in an air-conditioned motel room or real-estate office. Knowing the heat is out there waiting for you twenty-four hours a day (it dipped only to 86–88 overnight) is like being one of the three little pigs. Sooner or later the Big Bad Wolf called HEAT will get you.

Richard introduces me to his associates, one of whom, Burt Greider, the college dean who hired him, causes me a slight shock remembering Richard's words in passing about having liked all the people he met. Also, he will cause Richard to reassess some of his past viewpoints.

In his mid-thirties, Burt is young for a Dean; furthermore, he doesn't actually look like one. His standard mode of dress is flannel shirt and fancy jeans, with a belt buckle that looks as if it could brand a steer. That doesn't play badly in Arkansas, and, in fact, helps him establish solid rapport with faculty and students on campus, and businessmen and legislators off. Besides, he is a good-looking man, as tall and straight as Abraham Lincoln, with a firm, warm handshake and a piercing gaze. To me, when I meet him, he looks like the Archetypal American.

Except that he is black.

And, as such, he will be a revelation to Richard.

Like: *So, give any of them a chance, and . . .*

Like: *Well, Burt may be a forerunner of a new type . . .*

Like: *Okay, so they can do more than play basketball and make the best music . . .*

Richard has no work obligations until the very end of August, and James no school, so it amounts to two weeks of relatively (relative to the stress and press of Southern California) blissful freedom.

Nor do we know a soul in the area yet. We are on our own and loving the "breather."

The first thing we have to do is get used to living with the heat. Inside the house our air conditioner runs virtually twenty-four hours a day. Moreover, we do not dare venture outside into the blast furnace at all between the hours of 10 a.m. and 6 p.m.

Almost every night on the local news we are reminded that the great heat wave is expected to last through the summer. We take some perverse consolation in the discomfort of others, for there is always a picture in the paper or a segment on the news showing people doing what they can to stave off this unexpected monster called Summer. We take less comfort in the disasters that hit, including numerous forest fires in the Ozark National Forest and the failure of whole crops of soybeans, rice, corn, and cotton.

One crop that does not fail because of the drought is the

fruit. The smaller size of the fields on which grapes, peaches, and nectarines are grown allows them to be irrigated by the Ozark Valley watering services that are raking in a windfall. The grapes go to make wines in several little wineries west of Rousersville—all of them, paradoxically, in dry counties (half of the counties in the state are dry).

The peaches and nectarines go to make our introduction to our new home state.

Specifically, an orchard: set across the tops of several hills a few miles north of Rousersville (the hills grow progressively larger north of town, eventually becoming the Ozark mountains of "Scenic Route Ten, One of the Most Beautiful Roads in America"), eighty acres of fruit flourish under the sun, with the help of weekly irrigation by trucked-in water. Row after row of peach and nectarine trees bring forth fruit as large as baseballs, softballs even, and as succulent as one who has been raised on Thai fruit can wish for.

Each morning for a week during the peak of the season the three of us head up winding two-lane roads toward the orchard. The heat is already up percolating by eight o'clock, opening time for the "pick-yore-own" acres of Moorhead Farms. But it is still bearable, especially when you know that by 8:10 you can be sinking your teeth into a nectarine that makes the ordinary supermarket variety seem like something concocted in a food-chemistry lab.

By nine, usually, we have consumed a half-dozen each and filled two bushel baskets, and there is hardly a soul around —just the chirp of birds and the green hills of Arkansas rolling pleasantly off into an invisible blue distance, like dreams that never quite get completed.

"This is what we missed in Los Angeles," Richard says toward the end of that August week.

James is over in the next row, munching and sucking on a peach that looks bigger and moonier than his face.

"You mean, the nature? Being out in the nature?"

"Yeah, sure. That, Dee—and something else."

"I think I know what you mean. Listen: no airplane."

"Airplane*s*. And no police sirens. And trees and hills all around instead of eight-laner strips."

"Airplane*s*. Also air is so clean—smell fresh and new. Somehow is more like Thai imagine New World to be."

Richard pulls down a medium-sized nectarine, as perfect in color and shape as if it were painted by one of the Old Masters. He scrutinizes it for a moment, inhales its fragrance, then takes a sinfully juicy, sloppily audible bit. Juice runs out of the sides of his mouth.

"New world," he says. "That's right."

By the time we have paid for our bushels and the dozen or so pieces of fruit consumed on the spot, the heat has risen. Richard turns on the Escort's air conditioner, as we ease down the dry, rutted dirt road and head for home.

Our rural American routine. It seems so natural, like something I would do in Thailand.

A couple of times that week we have to go for groceries, and we shop quickly and late, like hungry midnight rodents, afraid that we'll be spotted by someone Richard met on his interview trip—so deeply do we treasure this brief interstice of leisure and privacy.

But no one sees and few speak to us—only strangers.

What does happen, happens to me: for the first time since arriving in the U.S.A., I am made acutely aware of my differentness.

People stare.

Richard explains to me that in a deep-country, middle-American town, people are awed by the strange, piqued, if only because they are so unused to it. Most of them live and die in these small towns and cities without ever seeing Paree, and anything different is as much a source of wonder to them as snake-oil salesmen and bellydancers were a century ago.

That is explanation but not consolation. By the time that month ends, I have the feeling that I have been studied by every citizen in the Valley. Not that there is any maliciousness in their stares; the people are not like that at all.

But, not all of them confine their curiosity to stares.

On more than one occasion, I am approached by a total stranger whose interest overpowers his or her natural small-town reticence. They smile and clear their throats, preparing to see whether they can communicate with the odd little creature of dark skin and semi-slanted eyes.

The brief conversations that ensue usually go something like this: "Where you from, miss?"

"I am from Thailand."

"Thailand, huh? Seems I've heard of it."

Or: "Thailand, eh? I've got a brother-in-law served over there."

Or: "Taiwan, you say? Well, you're a long way from home."

"It is Southeast Asia country," I say.

"Yes, I know. I heard of it on TV."

Not that I censure them in any way. Any American in Nakhon Narai has found himself subjected to the same sort of interest, the intrusion of simple curiosity.

It, the reverse, would go (in either Thai or English) like this: "San Francisco, yes? I have six cousin live in Bay Area."

Or: "San Francisco, no? That is in North America, yes?"

Or: Fran San Cisco? You be long way from home."

Although I understand the origin and operation of xenophobia, why it exists should be incomprehensible to anyone who takes the time to think about it. People are so much alike under their differing clothing and skin shades as to be *all* cousins living in the Bay Area.

One of the lasting lessons I have learned as a stranger in America is that, if natural curiosity can be channeled into open exchange before it degenerates into sullen hostility, the human race might eventually achieve peace—even by so simple a path. It takes less a new millennium than a few simple and contagious acts of communication.

And yet people keep waiting for the thunder and the lightning of a New Dawn.

Done shopping, we cruise the town for an hour—an hour being quite enough to cover it—from the Blatkin Kosher Pickle Company at the east end (founded by Saul Blatkin, a New Yorker) to Nuclear Unit (a power plant) in the west, from Skyline Drive in the south to the Interstate along the north.

Rousersville is, in fact, the very definition of Small Town, Small City America. From coast to coast such towns are all pretty much the same, with their Sears outlets and well-stocked hardware stores and dull-food supermarkets and franchised fast-food joints and country music and petty-crime problems and friendly folks and town drunks and endless gossip and suspicion of strangers, et cetera.

Nothing has changed but the surfaces—smoothed over by technology, broadened somewhat by cable television, diversified by the appearance of the likes of me and the two East Indian doctors in town and a seasonal influx of migrant workers from Mexico and Jamaica.

In the case of Rousersville, the advent of nuclear power has had a different sort of impact, bringing with it good news, bad news. The bad news is a mild sort of us-against-them community mentality ("They'd better keep a tight lid on the damned thing in *our* town.") while the good news is an excellent school system—the best in the state. According to native Rousersvillites, the latter is largely the result of an expanded tax-base that allows the county to pay top salaries for good teachers from all over the state and even neighboring states.

"Tax-base, humbug," Richard says. "It's because they have no blacks here."

He is almost right—about there being no blacks. The entire county, I will discover from one or another source, has a 3% minority population. This is quintessential White America.

Whatever the reason, we have no quarrel with a good school system, for James will be a prime beneficiary.

We have, in fact, little quarrel with anything in Rousersville. The three of us throw off the yoke of general discontent we have acquired lately (in Los Angeles if not necessarily from Los Angeles) and become, as well as we are able, Arkansans ourselves, eventually smiling in public (an old Thai habit!), speaking to strangers on the street (not usual in Thailand, even in the small towns), buying a few things over Radio Swap, and cussing the heat of summer and the ice of winter.

We know we have begun to acclimate in earnest when Richard buys a pair of overalls in which to work around the house. It is a purchase he would not even have considered in Atlanta or Los Angeles, but, smack in the center of the continent, it seems not only appropriate, but absolutely requisite. Besides, as an active homeowner, he has to have sturdy apparel in which to mow the lawn and clean out the gutters, as well as a variety of pockets for nails, steel-wool pads, and pliers.

Once Richard has overalls, James has to have them, too. At first we think there will be difficulty locating a pair for kids, but we soon find that Boward's, a general store cum clothing outlet, has sizes from toddlers to big man's, with every possible stop in between. It merely becomes a problem of deciding what brand, what color trim, how many pockets, et cetera. When we finally get him home and decked out in new flannel shirt, new overalls, and new brown work-quality shoes, he looks something like a newly-minted hillbilly, junior variety.

Richard and I laugh ourselves silly—until we look in the mirror. He has a burgeoning beard to go along with his flannel shirt and overalls, and I, although I certainly cannot pass for Daisy Mae, have at this time of leisure let my hair grow down straight and long, so that it covers the shoulders of *my* flannel shirt. Too, *my* overalls have paint-and-grass stains all over them, as if I have just quit a twelve-hour day of chores (which, of course, I just have—we are still "moving in").

So we become, in six or eight short weeks, a family of embryonic hillbillies.

Richard has a theory about hillbillies, and their camouflage-garbed high-riding counterparts in similarly isolated pockets all over the country. Under the right circumstances, they exhibit some of the patterns of behavior most lauded by society. He refers in particular to wartime heroism; like locusts, they seem to come out of nowhere and perform some of the most incredibly altruistic feats imaginable under the worst battlefield conditions.

It doesn't really matter much that they tend to take a bunch of lives—enemy lives—in the process; that, after all, is a "given" of war. What matters, fundamentally, is that they are there when they are needed, ready to don, Achilles-like, the armor of warfare. Hillbilly Sergeant York, poverty plainsman Audie Murphy, reservation Sioux Isaac Hayes—in any list of heroes, such men will invariably appear. It must be war making itself that channels their otherwise destructive energies in directions useful to society, however temporary the conditions are.

So Richard believes. And that is one of at least two reasons he, too, finds hillbillies as interesting as I do.

The other is the fact that they have turned the Ozark mountains into the world's largest outdoor pot garden. For each year we are in Rousersville, marijuana is known as the state's leading illegal cash crop, bringing millions into the economy.

Most of it is grown just to the north of our county, in the remote reaches of National Forest land. Aerial surveillance is virtually useless, given the vast areas to be covered and the fact that forest growth and coloration is such that a plane must be directly over the pot for it to be spotted. Surveillance by any other means is, for one reason or another, totally out of the question. Uninterested in the corn and rye liquor stills that have given their fathers and grandfathers an alternative life-style, the hillbillies have made the mountains their own preserve for the cultivation of ever-more-potent strains of marijuana.

One of Richard's students loves to brag about and bring to campus sinsemilla-grade cigarettes that wipe out whole dormitory rooms full of upper-classmen. No one is ever arrested, no one openly complains. The local attitude is lax at best. One reason is surely the newfound prosperity of a lot of Ozark communities—like Jasmine, the largest town between Rousersville and the Missouri border. Like those northern California towns and counties transformed by the drug trade, it is a completely renovated, upscale, indeed "gentrified" little town.

On the other hand, there are solid citizens all over the state eager to shut the Ozarks down. Some are afraid for their children, naturally; others don't like to see the law broken so flagrantly; and still others are just plain jealous of the profits being made in one part of the state.

Storm clouds thus gather on the horizon, and every night on one or another of the Little Rock TV stations there is a story of a huge bust here or a sting operation there. It begins to take on aspects of both a range war and a soap opera, and, like the rest of the citizens, Richard and I sit back and watch with interest.

CONFESSIONS OF A MAIL ORDER BRIDE

For me, it is almost like being back in Thailand, for acts of violence and vengeance over the drug trade are daily occurrences in both places.

Given the volatile atmosphere—which he laments as "so different from the laid-back Sixties"—Richard decides not to seek out a dealer in Arkansas. I breathe a sigh of relief. My long term strategy has worked. I congratulate myself and him —prematurely, for he continues: he is not going to buy pot; he is going to grow his own, "just a little bit."

I vow not to be discouraged. I try to see this decision to break free from that sordid, awful world of drug dealers as a move in the right direction. I have chosen to fight a long war of attrition where one step forward often is followed by two steps back.

Even the smallest light is welcome in the dark.

24

YANKEE DOODLE DANDY

Rousersville 1983

It is a cloudy morning, with a threat of rain after a sunny Labor Day weekend. James is six years, two months, and one day old.

It is time for school.

After a year in the paradise of his Los Angeles kindergarten, at which he spent an average of three or four hours a day coloring, playing games, and watching "Sesame Street," he is ready for public school. *Ready* may not be the right word. He is *prepared* for public school. No, not that either.

He is *going* to school, whether he likes it or not. We are both dressed and almost headed out the door for the six-block walk. "Finish oatmeal, please. Do you have jacket?"

He goes back and slurps it up, neglecting to answer, lost in apprehension.

He doesn't like this one bit, and I think I understand why. Compared to what he knows of schooling from the aptly-named "Velvet Mittens" preschool, the idea of Valley Elementary threatens, like the rain. Books, teachers, hordes of strange and possibly hostile kids. Who needs it? Kindergarten is fine, a comfortable, known quantity; home, with Mom and friends Waynie and Robin and all, is even finer.

The limited horizons of youth.

From what I remember of schooling at that level in the Old World, though, I find it hard to understand or sympathize with his fears. I see it as I still tend to see most things—from my Siamese angle, which I refuse to give up.

School is to be treasured, not abhorred. It is one of the most precious jewels that society offers to youths.

"Don't worry," I tell him. "This will be piece of pie."

"Cake," Richard says from the other room. "Piece of *cake.*"

"Piece of *cake.*"

And it will be, son, I promise, it will be—chocolate cake with a cherry on top.

And yet . . .

American schools seem too chaotic for me relative to the school in Thailand I knew.

Like the small city one I attended in Nakhon Narai. It was and surely still is (things change slowly in Thailand—a strength and a weakness both) fairly typical of the whole country. For one thing, we all wore uniforms, gender-determined outfits that parents bought or made for their little ones. The girls wore navy blue skirts and white blouses; the boys, khaki trousers and white shirts. Both sexes wore black leather shoes and white sox.

Given the fact that Thais tend more than Americans to be all basically of the same size and coloring, the school scene is one of uniformity and order beyond what mere identical clothing can render. The children sit at their seats quietly, black haired head after black haired head, with hands folded before them. Before they speak a word—and they do not speak to anyone but teacher during class—they raise their hands.

Teachers, too, have a comparatively uniform dress code and mode of behavior. The males wear conservative slacks and white shirts while the females wear dark skirts with white or lightly patterned blouses. They remain calm at all times, and their most common expression is a smile, although they can be awfully stern with sluggards. They are used to being obeyed.

When one day I tell James's first-grade teacher about this Asian pattern of behavior, she practically drools at the thought of a classroom full of alert, polite, cooperative children. It is no surprise to hear her, hardened front-line soldier, asserting that the greatest problem with American education is the lack of discipline. American kids are among the most unruly in the world, and the likeliest explanation has to be this reign of the ego. It is an idea, a cultural lifestyle, that bears good fruit in some areas of life; but in the schoolroom it has proven a disaster.

In Thailand, on the first day, the most common sight to be seen is one or two older children calmly leading their beginning brother or sister through the streets (school buses do not exist) and right up to the schoolhouse door. They leave him or her there with pride and confidence, for he or she already has a homemade name tag which tells teachers and monitors who he or she is and where he or she belongs.

Everything is done in an atmosphere of caring and concern, so it is extremely rare to encounter one of those awful images of a first-day child bawling his lungs out the whole morning long (as Richard told me he did long ago, insecure, war-orphaned middle-child that he was).

When a Thai child is directed to his room and seat, he is ready from Minute One for the long haul of books, games, uniforms, tests, and, above all, *learning*. The odds-on chances are that, for years, his parents have drummed into him the importance of an education.

Of course, the same thing happens in the United States, but I think I will be excused by even the most patriotic of Americans when I say that it does not produce quite the same result. The majority of kids here seem totally disaffected by education and would far rather be out in the streets or fields, playing ball full-time.

While Thai children love to play ball, too, they seem to love to learn equally well. I remember that I did, as did my older sibling and most of the children whom I knew. School was, if not an outright pleasure, then at the very least a pleasant place to be doing things as pleasing (and necessary, and practical) as learning about words and numbers and maps and, later on, ideas.

The only real exceptions to this rule are the kids who, because of family situation or trade, have to be out working as early in life as eight or ten years old. Education in Thailand is every bit as compulsory as it is in the United States (our laws are, in fact, based on the American), but it is, alas, far easier for Thai parents to plead hardship. Thus it is that fully 20% of Thai children drop out before the legal age of fourteen—but not to play pool.

Most of them go directly to work in fields and factories, or on fishing vessels, or at market stalls. I still have images of boys and girls like this from my home town. Their faces have the harried, world-weary look of overworked adults; their eyes are sunken, most of them, defeated-looking, like the eyes of caged beasts who once knew, or should have known, the freedom of the rain forest.

Or, on the streets, they are sharp and aggressive, like predators.

There are kids in such situations in the United States, of course, and we all know them personally or at least know of them. They are to be pitied as much as the Thai kids—maybe more, for a striking contrast exists.

Here in sunny, prosperous America where a properly extended education for a child can open so many doors to adult opportunity, school is taken for granted, abused, even scorned. In Thailand, even the hardest-working child has no guarantees whatsoever of opportunity, much less of eventual success. It is awfully tight at the top, with nothing but the barest cracks in doors that are figuratively flung wide open in the United States.

So the chance to become educated (at state expense!) is universally regarded as one of the greatest gifts of progress, as Thai children seem to know by instinct, or by some kind of societal osmosis. As a rule, they give their studies everything they have, and let the chips fall—or the cracks open—as they may.

School is the first step of the thousand-mile journey toward enlightenment and fortune. Thus it is that I am somewhat dismayed, in Rousersville, Arkansas, U.S.A., to see the sloppy dress, the unhealthy attitudes, and the fights. It is like seeing someone casually toss their own most prized possession in the trash—a jewel, a family album, a treasured book.

And perhaps, later on, want it back.

With no job to hurry off to, I hang around on the first day, sitting outside the Principal's office, speaking desultorily with a few other non-working mothers. James has been properly herded to his "home room," where he has stayed behind locked doors for half an hour or so. Intermittently I hear several young souls wailing in despair at having to leave the comfort of home—boys crying their eyes out in the halls outside their rooms. I feel terribly sorry for them—to be so unprepared for, so uninstructed about one of life's incredible opportunities.

Strangely but explicably, I suppose, given the greater emotional strength and social adaptability of females, there is not a single girl among the half dozen bawlers. I am glad that my son, despite his earlier whines of protest, is not among them either.

Gradually, satisfied that all will be well for their little Johnnie's and Sue's, the mothers depart one by one, leaving only Mrs. Wharton, whom I know from my neighborhood, and myself. Then she too smiles, and bids me good day, and I figure that, at nearly nine o'clock it, is time for me to leave as well.

I walk down the hall and am almost out the front door when over the loudspeaker, unannounced, blares some loud martial music. It has a fast, bouncy rhythm to it—I have heard it before—just the kind of music to get you up and moving. And that is exactly what it is intended to do at Valley Elementary, move the kids quickly and in step from one room to another and drown out their noise as it does so. A cute idea.

But what *is* the name of the song?

I linger at the door for a moment hoping to catch a glimpse of James, and sure enough I do, as he emerges in the group from his room. His seems to be the only first-grade class that is moving, but then I recall that nine o'clock is his gym time—a good time, too, to wear off some of that early morning physical energy.

The music continues blaring out of the strategically placed speakers as the kids line up outside their homerooms and start marching in place, with teacher sweeping up and down the row to make sure no one is kicking from behind or pulling hair.

Doodle, doodle, doodle, DAH! Doodle, doodle, doodle, DAH! Where have I heard it before?

Silent, shrunken back a bit from the light, I watch my son begin to march away down the hall toward the gym. Even from the back, he looks slightly different, of course—thick, straight, black hair (like mine, not Richard's), perpetually tan skin (again like mine), but taller than almost anyone else too (like Richard).

There are few "ethnic" people in this part of the state: in the entire school, only a handful of blacks and the children of three Chinese families. With the exception of one bully-type boy who cultivates the habit of calling James "the Jap," no racial hostility will come his way; for that I am grateful. Even this first morning I can see that he is in step with the catchy tune, marching right along with the others, who do not seem to pay him any special attention. He will become one of them, just as surely as his young, long legs can step along to the rhythm.

And then come the words of the song, sung in a whisper by three or four of a group of older kids passing right by me as James disappears around a corner: "Yankee Doodle went to town a-riding on a pony" . . . and something incongruous about "macaroni."

I smile to myself as I leave, and button my jacket against the mist that swirls through the air, cooling it, promising the end of summer and the beginning of another of the academic years to which all three of our lives now seem attuned: Richard teaching; I, a twenty-nine-year-old junior art major; and James, finally away from the starting block.

All of us going in the right direction.

As I near home, someone driving by honks—Rose Anna, Waynie's mother. She stops and asks if I want a ride, but

CONFESSIONS OF A MAIL ORDER BRIDE

it is only a few blocks. I thank her, saying that I would rather walk in this weather so refreshingly cool.

Good neighbor. Hardly a bad one around. Hardly a bad anything around. This is fine now; this is super. We like it here, I think as I approach our tight little sub-development house—James off and winging; Richard the new Golden Boy on the faculty with journal articles and two successful grant applications for computer equipment; and I, adjusting and adapting more completely than ever before.

Yes, we like Rousersville a lot. There is no reason to move again. Not from here—no reason under the sun.

Or so I think, as I turn a corner and get a face full of mist in the whimsical breeze.

25

GREENHOUSE BLUES

Rousersville 1984

Richard has been keeping the promise he made in Los Angeles of gradually cutting down, not so much on his habit, as on the *idea* of habits. He has stopped using other drugs and any form of alcohol except an occasional bottle of beer—two or three a week. For that, I breathe a daily prayer of thanks.

It is the notion of other drugs, cocaine in particular, that is strangely enough encouraging him to toe the line: he doesn't understand coke, much less have a desire to try it.

"That stuff wasn't around when it counted," he says. "Who knows what it does to your brain."

"Marijuana bad enough for brain," I chirp in.

"I'm serious. Anyone from the Sixties would know better than to stick powder up his nose or inhale a bowl of hot gas —for what? A thirty-second thrill? Give me a break."

"It make no sense to me."

CONFESSIONS OF A MAIL ORDER BRIDE

"And acid nowadays? It's not the same stuff it was back then. You're better off playing Russian Roulette."

"I think you are right."

"Pot is the only safe stuff left. And even that is losing its kick or appeal or something."

"Something."

Nevertheless, before the beginning of another hot summer, our doorbell rings—the UPS man with three very large boxes containing the 1,001 parts of a California greenhouse kit. Richard has ordered it from an advertisement in *High Times* magazine.

It takes me all of three *seconds* to figure out what is up— Richard has said he wants to grow his own pot to get away from buying. The stuff he brought from Los Angeles, although he is using much less of it, is almost gone. "Down to stems and seeds at last," he says.

Once the greenhouse is erected, he begins to grow specimen after specimen of some of the healthiest plants I have ever seen in my life. Thais are universally plant-loving people, and his plants *as plants* grow admirably, thick-stalked and arrow-straight. They bush out uniformly full and green, and blossom forth elegant purple-white *fleurs de mal*, and yield ounces and ounces of high-grade pot.

I have to hand that much to him—when he sets his mind to something, he is able to do it as well as any so-called "expert." That old American *can-do.*

Regardless of my admiration for his skill, though, I never stop emitting subtle groans of dismay and not-so-subtle howls of protest over the entire idea.

Pot again. This time in our backyard. In a close community like this? Are you insane? No way! No way at all!

Unfortunately, what I actually say never gets phrased with quite that type of vigor and determination.

Again, I choose disapproving silence and long-term

cunning. I may have lost more battles than I have won, but I still firmly believe that the war can be mine. I have to believe that or give up on a marriage that is otherwise loving and satisfactory. If he were meaner or rougher or less faithful to me or not devoted to James, my campaign might be different. But I am not about to, as Thais say, discard a good vegetable because of sand on its skin.

And so to work . . . on the small things.

The first concession I wring from him is to lay a patio on which to place the greenhouse close to our sliding back door, and then seal the area off with a cedar fence from all angles but overhead—from which come the sun but, in a subdevelopment, hardly any surveillance aircraft.

By the middle of August, he has bought huge (21-inch) clay pots (plastic will not do), Pro-Mix growing medium (the most expensive—plain dirt is not even a consideration), two kinds of fertilizer which he mixes in precise proportions, and various additives which he has read in *Head* magazine are as absolutely essential to successful cultivation as the six to eight hours of direct sunlight per day.

By the end of October (it is a good warm autumn) he has grown his first two plants (both five feet tall, three or four feet in diameter), plucked them up carefully from the medium, hung them upside-down in the hot greenhouse for a few days to "cure them," and gotten a yield of two pint-size Mason jars of high-quality, *leaves only* marijuana.

This is more than he can use in a year, even if he smokes every night.

He seems as upset at the success as I am. It is the sheer quantity that is disturbing; it is too much marijuana to have around.

In his discomfort, I take some qualified joy; light is again appearing in the tunnel, and, if it isn't the end, it isn't another oncoming train either.

CONFESSIONS OF A MAIL ORDER BRIDE

The rest of the plant goes into the garbage and down to the county dump, in plastic bags that also contain envelopes and other documents with our names on them. He does this with two crops until I realize what he is doing and convince him to let me grind and flush the "waste" (three-fourths of the plant) in the kitchen disposal. This is the second concession to my concerns—a small matter, but I know he isn't ready yet to yield on any of the major ones.

The third concession has to do with his health. I have read somewhere that, compared to cigarettes, marijuana *just as smoke* is actually worse for one's respiratory and general health. The tar content is substantial, and THC, ingested through the lungs, is thoroughly toxic in its effects. The same source claims that many old potheads and several knowledgeable physicians are recommending eating marijuana instead of inhaling its smoke.

When one doctor and this same concept appear on "Donahue," I and the rest of the country know, of course, that it's for real.

To the fuel of that argument, I add the easily substantiated claim that the smoke is dangerous in other ways. With neighbors thirty or so feet away on each side, any escaping fumes can clearly be smelled and traced; the end result might be what I have been dreading from the moment I first smelled the stuff as it drifted downstairs into Richard's Mom's New Jersey living room: simply put, loss of job. Worse, loss of career. Worse yet, loss of personal freedom—*jail.*

That gets his attention.

And there is James to consider. Even if Richard smokes a room or two away (you can't get much farther than that in our small house), the fumes will find their way to and *into* James, and who knows where that might lead. Besides—and this is taking a longer, larger view indeed—what will the boy eventually make of a pothead father? Will he want to copy him or be ashamed of him? Think about it, husband and father.

That also gets his attention.

So, he takes to baking his dried marijuana leaves into cake recipes, primarily bran-honey muffins and chocolate-nut brownies—the one for its health benefits, the other because it masks the green-veggie taste of the pot. He claims that the results are "yummy." I am content to take his word for it.

He lodges a familiar complaint that I have never shared in this significant side of his life—not even once. Pot cigarettes I have been able to decline because I cannot smoke, but with muffins and brownies can I claim that I don't eat? No, I am forced to be more direct, as on the following occasion: Richard, slicing up a newly-baked, cooling pan of pot-laced brownies: "Care to try one? For once?"

"No, dear. I'm sorry."

"You might be sorrier if you don't. I got the album by the Reddings—the one with 'Hand Dance' on it. Dynamite."

"I would like to hear song again." W have heard it on a high-watt FM station out of Little Rock that plays "sophisticated funk" which has become, over the years, my favorite American music, too. "It really nice. Original."

"Yeah, Otis's kids are doing him proud." He looks at me: "How about it, Doll." The implication is there will be sex afterward.

I shake my head sadly. "I will listen with you and . . . and other things. But I do not wish to smoke."

I slip and he catches it. "Smoke, hell. You can eat this stuff. It doesn't taste bad, and it gives a body-stone—a really deep, relaxed feeling."

"I might fall asleep."

"The music will keep you awake."

"I can enjoy without dope."

"I don't see how."

I almost tell him that he has just pinpointed the root of the entire problem—that he *can't see how*—but I hold my tongue.

"I'm keeping my promise," he says. "I've stopped all other stuff and cut back slowly on pot. It's just that—well, I've got so much of the stuff now."

"That is not reason of any kind."

"Okay, then—it's good weed."

"The answer," I say, mildly but firmly, "is *no.*"

It is as assertive as most Asian women are likely to get over anything—from money to kids to drugs—in a good marriage.

He shrugs, and smiles, and finishes slicing, thoughtfully. I do listen to the music with him an hour later, after the drug has taken full effect in him—the entire album. And we do make love after that—very sweetly, in fact.

And I make another tiny but significant advance along one of the many fronts in this ongoing war. I have shown him that regardless of how accessible the drug is, I will not fall into its trap—ever. Even though he never regards marijuana as any sort of trap, and always insists *(ha!)* that he is never in thrall, my attitude does make another nick in his armor. I plan that the nick will become, over the months, a chink; and that chink, in the long run, a substantial, and then ultimate, crack.

In the long run—literally.

One of three keys to the gradual decline in Richard's use of this last drug is, in fact, the easy "score." It is right in our backyard, after all, and in our refrigerator, grown, dried, baked, and ready to consume. No longer must he go out on a hunt for it, into the seamier side of society, bickering over type and price even as he keeps an eye over his shoulder and wonders whether he is face to face with a narc and ruination. Now all he need do is open the fridge.

The second favorable factor is his age. Closing hard on forty-one, he occasionally tells me (an indication of how much it concerns him) his fear that he will become, in the words of poet Gregory Corso, "an old man with pee stains on his underwear"—victim of irredeemable habits. That possibility strikes him as particularly worrisome since, without any other bad habits, he will have this consuming one to dwell on endlessly over the years.

The last key is truly "in the long run."

Ever so gradually, Richard is becoming positively addicted—actually, re-addicted—to running—he has been fretting over slackening muscles, an expanded paunch, and his bad back.

Quitting *any* smoking habit gives such movements impetus.

He starts to try to get back in shape by running several times around our block in the early morning, and, within a couple of months, has lost fifteen pounds, is running five or six miles three times a week, and has subscribed to *Runner's World* magazine.

At just about this time, as if the gods are truly on our side, the Army Corps of Engineers completes a 120-acre nature preserve adjacent to huge Lake Dordone as part of an ongoing project to develop a dam site. As part of that preserve, they are nice enough to include an eight- to ten-foot wide jogging and bicycle trail that winds through trees and over creeks for a 3.8 mile circuit.

It isn't long before we have a thrice-weekly twilight routine worked out whereby James and I complete a circuit of the trail going one way while he does two or three going the other way. So, while he runs much faster than James and I, we at least get to pass him and say, "Hi, Daddy!"

CONFESSIONS OF A MAIL ORDER BRIDE

When we finish before him, we take a few minutes to cool down in the near-dark by walking around a smaller (.4 mile) strolling trail. At that hour there is no one on it, and I use the time to be with my son outdoors and to reflect on whatever happens to be important in our three lives at the moment.

As time goes on, I find these moments devoted to considering how the more Richard heads toward the light, *mens sana, corpore sano*, the more he heads away from the dark.

By the start of our second and final academic year in Arkansas, he is using marijuana once or twice a *month*, and it isn't unusual for me to end one of those exercise cool-down periods with tears of thankfulness in my eyes.

"Mommy?" James will say curiously.

I take him in my arms. "It is okay, son. Everything okay."

Something has worked—a combination of things, actually—and I am a step away from winning this protracted Thai-American war. It may turn out to be a longer step from 1 to 0 than from 3 to 2 or from 2 to 1. But it is a single step, one more battle to go in the campaign. In real life, as opposed to soap operas and romances, major defeats and victories are won such as Iwo Jima was won, inch by inch of territory, grain by grain of sand.

In the meantime, Richard is looking better and better—more like a young man. He is feeling better, too, and in fact *doing* better. His weekly running mileage is up over 25. Each morning he springs out of bed like a jackrabbit to tackle his professional world. The people with whom he works comment to me that he seems like a living dynamo, and his classes are in high demand even among students whose curricula do not require technical communication courses.

I know for certain now that it is only a matter of time

before he quits eating the stuff and quits growing it, too. So confident am I that I find myself looking forward as much to the latter event as to the former. After all, I need the greenhouse for chilis, lemon grass, and bantam bananas.

One more push is all that is needed.

On some cool fall nights after the heat of another Arkansas summer has lifted, we pass a large milestone on the road to where I want us both to be. For the first time virtually since I met him, he is able to make love to me consistently—once, twice, four times—without being high. And to enjoy it. And, most importantly, to *prefer* it.

Lying back afterward on the fifth or sixth of those nights, with the incessant hum of I-40 traffic in the background and a lively dance of headlights on the ceiling, he asks, "Where have I been all these years?"

His voice is husky with emotion, and I know exactly what he means, but I take time to ask back, as I reach up to his face, "You mean at time like this?"

He can't answer; I feel some moisture on his cheeks. "Away," I say, "away . . . from me. As away from me as if you not here."

"*That* far?"

"That far."

He takes a sharp breath and shakes away the emotion, the part that shows at least. "Why didn't you tell me?" His voice is firmer but still distressed, faltering as if caught, momentarily, in a high tight spot.

"I try to."

"Did you really?"

"I did—really."

"Thank you for trying."

"I still try."

"You may not have to much longer."

"I hope not."

He removes my hand from his face and holds it tightly, tightly in his hand. "I'm so sorry, sweet doll."

"It is okay. All time, I knew you be back."

"You'*d* be back."

"You'*d* be back."

26

LEARNING TO MOVE

Rousersville 1985

Now it is *cold*.

I have heard—it must have been in Thailand when we studied climate in a geography class—that so-called "continental" regions are supposed to be unpredictable and subject to extremes. But this weather is ridiculous. Worse than ridiculous: painful. Especially for a displaced denizen of the Asian Rice Belt.

Whereas truly hot weather (such as we knew during our first Arkansas summer) creates discomfort, cold weather such as we begin to experience in mid-December 1984 is "downright hurtful," to put it as an Arkansan would. People who come from tropical climates never quite realize that fact until they are subjected to it; then they realize what *cold* means. And *pain*.

The weather has changed abruptly for the worse midway through exam period. On Tuesday Richard went to his

287

Technical Communication examinations in shirtsleeves. On Wednesday he left for a mid-morning committee meeting wearing jacket and gloves. By Thursday morning a light snow has fallen, and to get to his Applications Software exam he has to don a coat and a scarf to go along with the gloves.

I myself go to my Modern Art exam on Friday afternoon in an Arctic windstorm.

After that it gets worse.

People have been telling us that the summer of 1983 was atypical; summers are not normally so Ethiopian. Now they are telling us that this winter is a record-breaker.

And the ugly part may be yet to come: big snow, bad ice. I shiver at the thought, while James looks forward to missing some schooldays and Richard goes out to buy a kerosene heater. Given the underground utility lines of our newly-built sub-development, the purchase seems unnecessary, but he is bound in the memory of the ice-storm that hit Atlanta, when our neighborhood was without power for nearly forty-eight hours.

Americans say: once bitten, twice shy.

Although we will never use the kerosene heater, it gives us a sense of security that is probably worth the $89.95. Spending so little in low-cost-of-living Arkansas, we feel entitled. It is nice to have money and to spend it.

A day later, Richard buys James and me high-quality coats, mine a rich camel's-hair and James's a lined nylon with hood and pro-football logo on the back. It helps the boy blend in better—how many Amerasian kids are Patriots, after all—Boston Patriots?

Given the weather, the three of us spend a lot of time watching the NFL Playoffs on television that winter. Even though James nor I can never make much sense of it (and even less of baseball), it gives us a warm, secure feeling to be sealed up against the howl of Central Plains winds and the drift of

LEARNING TO MOVE

Ozark Mountain snow, doing nothing better than watching grown men grunt and perspire over an inflated pigskin.

No matter how gloomy the skies become, we have the colorful spectacle of an athletic contest in front of us, the very image of limberness and warmth. Let it snow.

And snow it does.

The deepest snow accumulates over a forty-eight hour period about a week before Christmas. We are well supplied and do not need to go out in it until we find the cupboard bare of everything but leftovers. Finally, we have to brave the bitter storm for food.

We prepare for our sojourn through deep snow. Richard is cursing his decision to throw away those precious Grand Canyon chains shortly after our arrival in Los Angeles. We will have to rough it now.

Actually, there is no snow falling when we go out at nine o'clock on Monday morning. It has all fallen the previous weekend. It had come down as if someone upstairs left the drains unplugged. News media speak of inches, but in the real world, blown around like New Year's confetti, it has accumulated into drifts measurable by *feet*. Unlike some cars we can see from our front window, shrouded over with white, as still and hopeless as death, ours is luckily in the garage.

James is sledding, so we leave him in the care of his playmates' mother. We will be gone no more than an hour, just long enough to swoop down on the Safeway and make a getaway. Before we can get started, though, there is a minor problem that Richard takes care of with twenty minutes worth of hard labor: the driveway. I help as much as I can, but we have only one shovel, and no one in Thailand ever told me exactly how heavy snow can be. It looks so airy, so light and feathery . . .

I mention this paradox to Richard.

"Shit," he grunts.

He has broken into a sweat, anyway—a good way to start the day! I mention this to him as well.

Same response.

But a well-shoveled driveway is easier to back down than one under a foot or so of ice-encrusted snow. I am about to mention this also to Richard but change my mind since I can guess how he will respond. Instead, as we get in the car, I inquire whether it is the ice in the snow that makes it so heavy.

He looks at me as we crunch backward through the little barrier of snow that a plow has left. "Do you really want an answer or are you tormenting me?"

The tone is friendly; we love to "rag" each other now and then, as Thai couples do. Americans tend to react more often and with more venom.

"I take any answer except 'shit'."

"How about . . . never mind. Yes, the ice makes it heavier. Powdery snow almost blows out of your way."

"Just how many types of snow there are?"

"Eskimos have sixteen different words for the white stuff."

"Because they see so mush of it, I guess. That make sense. Thais have ten kind of banana."

With a slight spin of the front wheels, we take off down the street, waving to James and his friends Robin and Waynie who do not see us. But Waynie's mother Rose Anna gives us an "OK" sign through her front window to let us know that all is well.

At the end of our sub-development street the road rises sharply to a stop sign, after which it empties onto a highway that leads into the town center a couple of miles away. Here we encounter another problem—and not a small one.

Under the snow is a sheet of ice that has lain in the shade most of the day—certainly overnight—and has not melted. I have no idea the stuff can be so devious! And slippery!

LEARNING TO MOVE

As we ascend the slope, the front wheels slip and the car turns sideways, ceasing all forward motion as it obeys the Law of Inertia, then begins to slide of its own weight back down the hill, obeying the Law of Gravity.

These are forces normally beyond human control. Luckily there are no other cars at that moment, so we come to rest plop in the middle of our sub-development street. At about this time, the sun peeks out from behind a bank of clouds and, although it has no strength to warm, it offers an overabundance of brightness. That's another bit of street lore one is unlikely to pick up in Nakhon Narai or Bangkok: sun on snow is bright, a blindingly bright *problem*, to be precise.

That we don't *really* want to go to town happens just after we find ourselves wishing for sunglasses. We can return home for them, of course, but Richard is determined to get out and back as fast as possible. He insists that we can go an all-flat route through residential streets to the Safeway—no problem, right?

Wrong.

A combination of three amazing (to any Thai) factors yields one result: factor one, the streets were plowed early the day before but not since; factor two, a number of cars have gone over these streets since—but, significantly, not a great number of cars; and factor three, the present temperature, after a high of about 35 degrees Fahrenheit the day before, is presently in the low twenties.

Result (surprisingly evident to a tropical person): the residential streets are so deeply rutted with ice that it seems our compact Escort can easily get lost in one of the grooves. The sound of our tires crunching the re-frozen crusts must be similar to what passengers on the Titanic heard at their fateful moment. And Richard has as little control over the direction of the car as a drunk playing Pole Position.

Secondary result: within another three or four minutes

we are harbored in our garage once again, feeling lucky to be there, safe but breathless—and grocery-less. Of such crises, it dawns on me rather pleasantly, is small-town American life made. No assassinations, no revolutions, no massive demonstrations with brutal government crackdowns—just a failed grocery trip.

I like it.

"Shit," Richard says at length as we sit there, and I haven't even asked him a question.

We sit some more, both of us pondering in our individual U.S.-male and Asian-female ways—he, mad that we could go only so far out; me, glad that we have made it this far back—as the engine steams off chunks of ice and the sounds of children at play drift to our ears like the cries of creatures so remote from this frozen reality as to be from another world.

I do like it.

"Shitaroonie," he repeats for good measure, on a different, darker wavelength from me, and we both get out of the car. The morning's domestic drama is done. Back to the television set. Leftovers it will be.

At least until it gets above freezing out there in the continental U.S.A.

Regardless of the weather, it is nice to get to know the citizens of the Heartland. Far too often foreigners remain in large coastal cities and imagine that the United States is made up on endlessly interlocked ethnic "neighborhoods," alternately feuding and learning to live together, surrounded, as they are, by the asphalt of superhighways and the concrete of office buildings and condominiums. We are hardly aware of the denizens of deeper America, as remote from us as the great interior basins and the snowcapped mountains.

When we do get to meet and know them, however, it is like a whiff of fresh air blown right through the stale attics of our Old World attitudes and biases.

LEARNING TO MOVE

In my sculpture classes at the college, I also learn new ways of thinking. Maury, my instructor, is a devotee of Oriental art. His *sensei* at the Pennsylvania institute he attended was a Japanese-American, and his usual method of decorating his work is Korean *hakeme*. I tell him on one occasion that I cannot see any qualitative difference between his work and the work of Masters that I have seen in photos and museums. He smiles and tells me that the secret lies in focal-point concentration, an old Oriental technique which he implements with a chant. With his help, I consciously adopt the technique for my own work. But whereas I chant to myself, Maury does it out loud. I do two busts of Burt, Richard's Dean, who is nice enough to have patience with me through the first effort. I ask him to pose several times because I feel that the work is not coming around.

Richard is there one of those times, and they kibitz.

"Time is money, Ricky," Burt complains. "Tell Dee to hurry up, or there goes your Christmas bonus."

"What Christmas bonus? Or is this something new this year?"

"You mean you didn't get yours last year?"

"Heck, no," Richard says.

"Oh, that's right. It was your rookie year here—no bonuses for rookies."

"If I don't get one this year, it'll be sophomore jinx?"

"And after that you'll be a grizzled vet, and they never get *anything*."

"I didn't think so."

I break in: "Go now, Ricky. You two guy keep me from concentrate."

"Really?" Burt says. "I swear I feel your eyes burning a hole in the side of my head."

"No, not today."

"You should see her when she's cooking *panag mou*," Richard says as he leaves the studio. "Total concentration."

"Is ancient Oriental custom," I kibitz back.

"That's the stuff we had at your house a few weeks ago?" Burt asks Richard.

"You got it."

"Did I ever. It was *hot*—and *good.*"

I smile. Stir-fried pork served in spicy-curry sauce; everyone loved it. Nice to recall, but they really are keeping me slightly off-target.

For the second bust, using Maury's concentration chant *(focus, focus, focus)*, an intense half-hour is all I need to get the features—flaring nostrils, stubbly hair, big Nubian eyes—exactly right.

People will tell me later that I have made him a perfect African prince—everyone except Richard, who insists my sculptures all come out looking slightly Thai.

Being a city boy himself, and a coastal citizen for most of his life, Richard is also enjoying small town life in the middle of the country. Or at least he seems to be.

Thus it is a distinct shock when he comes home one afternoon and announces that we might be moving.

Again.

"But, honey . . ." I begin, and do not know exactly how to finish the sentence.

"It's just an idea so far," he says. "But a serious one."

He waits a few minutes, studying me to see whether I have any question or comment. I do not. So he leaves for the backyard to play with James and friends before settling down to work on a grant proposal.

Later, he explains to me that it has to do with opportunity, but I doubt that. By now I have come to the conclusion that Richard is addicted to moving, as addicted to it as to— other things. That is a gloomy prospect. On the verge of achieving success with one bad habit, now I have to begin work on another?

That's how it seems to me as I watch the news distractedly (oil tanker breaking up at sea, blizzard in the Rockies) and look forward with dread to packing the dozens and dozens of boxes.

Perhaps I should be satisfied that moving isn't anything like being hooked on dope, from which nothing good can come. At least with moving, there is a 50-50 chance it will work out for the better—this Arkansas move has done so, after all.

But then there was Los Angeles.

Is it by moving from time-to-time that Americans express a basic attitude about the transient nature of their history, their great moves westward, first, then from the farms into the cities? Or is moving a small scale personal reenactment of that history—unconscious homage to transience? In any case, it is anathema to Thais, who rarely have a need or desire to relocate.

There is nothing that I can say to Richard. From experience I know that once he makes up his mind, rightly or wrongly, that opportunity is knocking, he finds it hard to resist answering. As a no-income housewife, I cannot lock on to the larger concept of "career."

All I know is that we like it in Arkansas, and we are about to move away. As an only child, James has enough trouble making new friends without being plopped down like an alien among a different set of kids every few years. He especially likes Waynie, and a few other boys and girls down the street, and I know that he will find it very difficult to leave the endless games they play right under my window.

I will find it equally difficult to see them end.

Suddenly a sense of loss overcomes me, and I begin to feel suffocated, leaden, as if I am about to drown. It is all to be lost again, left behind, as I left behind Thailand years ago. My family, my youth, part of myself—left behind, lost in Thailand.

The trees outside the window blur in my vision as I grip the rim of the sink and hold on as if to the end of a life raft.

But I bite back the tears, finally, and resolve to see and do it this impermanent American way (or is it just restless Richard's way?) one more time at least.

Later that day, Richard promises me that this will almost certainly be the last of our moves.

Good thing.

I feel better. He is very faithful with his promises, never breaking even one of them. That is one reason I have been disappointed; he has not actually *promised* to give up pot. He has been so good the last year or two about cutting back on it, almost *(but not quite)* to the point of quitting altogether.

This move just has to be made, he insists. There is one more bend in the road ahead, after which it will straighten out beautifully and lead on to success. He makes it sound convincing, as anyone can about his way of life.

An ingrained, culture-conditioned, *inflexible* way of life.

But, no, no, no, I am not bitter. I will accept it, as well as any housewife in the "corporate sector" whose husband simply must be transferred from time to time. What does IBM stand for, after all, but *I've Been Moved?* So: adios Arkansas. Goodbye, Middle America.

Once we have indeed made up our mutual mind to leave —or at least once I have been reasonably well sold on the idea —Richard and I both try to justify the decision to ourselves: by economics, necessity, that old standby opportunity, whatever. That's awfully hard when you like a place as much as we both like Arkansas. But Richard has convinced *himself* that the time has come for a final move. Just as, I believe, the time will come for him to quit marijuana after trailing off for months. I think a lot of the key decisions in life are made this way: the *time has*

come for this-and-that; it is *time* for such-and-such. All it takes is
the slightest little push, like the puff of wind that finally knocks
over a huge, dead oak tree.

As for moving, the puff of wind here seems to be that
Richard has gotten a job offer which he feels he must consider
seriously because it pays five thousand dollars more per year,
and it will bring us all the way back East.

Robert, old friend Robert from Atlanta, has made his
way up the ladder to a judicial position of some influence. (In
an aside in a letter, he claims that his rise is a consequence of
his abandonment of dope and some of the attitudes that go
along with it; I read the letter first and underscore that passage
for Richard.) He has mentioned Richard in apparently glowing
terms to the chairperson of an academic department at a me-
dium-size college in the Carolinas.

Robert called Richard in February, Richard responded
to the chairperson's ad in *The Chronicle* in March, and since then
things have taken off.

Richard loves the area because of the beaches where he
used to vacation before he met me. He also loves the idea of
being back East not too far from his old flame Atlanta.

Money and love. Deciding factors in so many things.

After a flight east to interview and check it all out, Richard is offered a spot on the faculty as developer and instructor
in a business and technical communication program. While he
is not being "promoted" to administration—which he does not
want anyway—he can pretty much do as he sees best. In addition, he will be the prime introducer of computer equipment
into the various humanities departments on a basically liberal
arts campus. Big fish in a—not *little* but—rather—*different*
pond.

It looks ideal for him, but the clincher is that, while we
no longer crave life in a large city, we are beginning to long for
a somewhat bigger place than Rousersville. There are so few

cultural opportunities—or outlets. I have begun my art career as a sculptor, but, so far, I have had commissions to do only two portrait busts, both of local church leaders. There doesn't seem to be any secular market at all.

So *mea culpa*. Eventually, it begins to seem, we have *both* decided to move.

Curiously enough, a glance in a recent atlas shows that the population of the small Carolina city where we will be going is almost precisely that of Nakhon Narai: about 40,000 in the city proper, with another sixty or seventy thousand in surrounding towns and villages. A sign.

The omens are right. *The time has come.*

With misgivings still malingering in our minds like gnats in late summer, we reluctantly begin planning our move. As in Los Angeles, my body moves very slowly into the "packing mode" that is familiar and depressing. James goes into an uncharacteristic whining phase. Even Richard walks about with his face as overcast as a cloudy afternoon.

I finally voice my feeling that perhaps we are forcing ourselves into a get-up-and-go pattern from which there might be no escape.

I remind Richard that, in the 20-plus years I spent in Thailand, my family moved only once—and that was the only time they had moved since years before I came along.

Richard's response: a curt *This ain't Thailand.* He is edgy.

"*Isn't,*" I say. "And do not bark, please."

"Okay, sorry. *Isn't.*"

End of conversation. No hard feelings, just deeper thoughts.

Like a runaway freight train, the three of us hurtle through our days toward the move with a blind and restless resolve. Grimly determined, we start the heavy-duty packing of

LEARNING TO MOVE

cartons and suitcases, making all the proper phone calls, arranging things with a mover, and cleaning, cleaning, cleaning.

We list the house with a realtor, and the first person who looks at it buys it—at a very good price. Another sign I think.

When Richard's job-offer letter arrives, it verifies what is taking place, a written confirmation of our waffled-over decision.

We are going to move. The Thai in me resists the idea to the bone while, for the American, it bubbles right along in the blood.

27

FOOTSTEPS IN THE SNOW

Rousersville 1985

In February, Richard writes an official letter of resignation to his closest associate, Burt Greider, the College Dean.

Thereafter, news of our move is generally known, and all our Arkansas friends express regret at our decision but wish us well. We have no answer for their questions about our leaving except to say, in effect, that *the time has come.* To us there seems little reason of substance.

The *why* will remain answerless.

Everyone we have interacted with these two years, both personally and professionally, comes over or at least telephones. I am moved by this more than Richard. Of course, the idea of acceptance has to mean more to me than to him.

CONFESSIONS OF A MAIL ORDER BRIDE

Everyone comes over or telephones, that is, except Burt. We are faced with a *why* of a different sort—why not Burt?

The answer comes in the form of a phone call late on a Friday afternoon in March. He asks us both to come in the following afternoon for a chat. We go to bed that night—after another evening of packing and cleaning—with yet another *why* whirling in our heads.

Richard, who rarely dreams now that he has almost given up pot, and even more rarely speaks of his dreams, says the next morning that he dreamt of serpents washing in from the sea. He interprets it as guilt over deserting his newfound, but nonetheless dear, friends just to be near a beach. I agree with the reading, but I remind him of the lure of the salary increase as well.

Then he tells me that the serpents had dollar-sign markings on their skin.

As for me, I dream every night, and, like most Thais, I love to interpret my dreams. But my dream Friday night is of ice, walls of solid blue ice. Impossible for a Thai to interpret since ice is not in our lexicon of dreams!

Richard sees my dream as any senior psychology major would: a closing of the heart to something or someone held dear. Under such circumstances, who can dispute that?

We arrive at Burt's office early and sit in the waiting room, both lost in our own thoughts. The bust portrait of Burt I did several months before has just been awarded First Prize in category at a show in Little Rock. A color photograph of it has appeared in one Sunday newspaper. I could hardly believe I had done it with my own hands. The writer said that he looked like African (not Thai, Ricky) royalty. *Not bad for a mail order bride,* I told myself. From that work I get two more commissions from a church—the largest Baptist congregation in the state—to do church fathers.

The first thing Burt says to us when we walk into his

office is a forthright declaration: "You two are precious to me. Both of you."

"Why, thank you, Dean," Richard smiles. We feel the same way about you and Vera—right, Dee?"

"Of course."

Burt lowers his thick-lashed, brown eyes and frowns, seeming to push aside this kind greeting as superfluous.

When he looks up, he is ready to return our smiles. "You know, we really hate to lose competent faculty. It diminishes the college."

"I can understand that," Richard says. "And if you are referring to me, I'm quite flattered, Dean."

"*Burt*—please. Of course I'm referring to you. You turned our communications program around, not to mention your help in getting the big federal grants."

"It's part of what I was hired for."

"What *I* hired you for."

"You don't think I've forgotten that, do you?"

Burt frowns again. Something is definitely on his mind. "Not until recently."

Richard returns his frown, and they eye each other cautiously. They seem to be playing one of those games American males play when, in business dealings, they are trying to conceal the way they really feel. It involves gestures, shrugs, smiles —and a few, very few, telling words.

It pleases me to see Richard playing it, man-to-man, *mano a mano*, with a black man; I have a feeling that it pleases him as well.

"Recently . . . as in *since I quit.*"

"I didn't say that."

"But."

"Okay. But."

"Hey," Richard says, "have I lost your love?"

"Almost."

"That's okay—as long as it's *almost.*"

Burt pushes his seat back and puts his leather-booted feet up on his big Dean's desk. Time to get down to business.

"Ricky," he begins, "you might be interested to know that although we haven't filled your position, we have found someone in foreign languages. Trilingual, can you believe it?"

"Incredible. I know what you were looking for. English, French—and what?"

Burt gazes out the window. When he decides to answer he looks directly at me. "Thai."

We are both speechless. "Thai," Richard finally says, "as in Thailand?"

Burt the Dean, the negotiator *cum* manipulator is at work. "You bet," is all he needs for the moment.

Silence.

I speak: "He is from Thailand, then?"

"She. Yes."

"I—I mean, what part? She is real Thai?"

"If someone comes from Nakhon Narai, they are authentic Thai?"

"Is she really from there?"

"Close enough. *U-ta-ta-ni,* I believe is how you pronounce it."

"*Uthathani,* yes. It very close to Nakhon Narai."

Richard looks at me. Both our brains are working. We both know what it may be but are afraid to confront it.

Burt, dear Burt, you shouldn't have done what we think you have done. Burt, Prince Burt—say it isn't so.

To forestall the inevitable, I ask the next question on this strange agenda. "What is her name?"

"Aree. Pretty name. Aree Panrun."

I breathe a sigh of temporary relief; I know no one of such name.

"You may not know her," Burt goes on, divining my

thoughts, "and she may not know you, but she has heard of your family." That is possible; the Chancharons have some small influence, mainly in building and commerce. "She is eager to meet you."

"Where is she now?" Richard asks

"Well, still in Seattle."

"Ohhh," I say. "Oregon so very far away."

"Washington," Richard says.

Burt perks up: "Then you would like to meet her, Wanwadee?"

"Of course. Very mush. She will come soon?"

"Actually, she has to finish up her degree there before she can join us."

"But you've got her in the bag?" Richard asks.

"She signed last week. You know, we had a bunch of strong candidates. She looked the best for a variety of reasons." He pauses, and smiles, obviously relishing this sort of power game. "Frankly, Dee, one of them was that you must be lonely —I mean, in a sense, with no other Thais around."

I feel suddenly uncomfortable. Yes, I am lonely for Thai company from time-to-time, but I thought I had kept that part of me to myself; I never said a word of it to anyone, not even Richard. But now I realize I have been wearing my thoughts on my sleeve all along.

Or perhaps as the only Southeast Asian for miles around I am assumed automatically to be in need of the company of someone of my own race and sex. I feel *quite* uncomfortable.

Underneath it all, though, I feel sorry most of all for Burt, hating to lose a valued employee in his little academic Ozark kingdom, and hating to lose friends as well.

For the second time, Richard and I are caught without words. Burt, our Prince Burt—we think of him more than ever as a black prince since I completed the sculpture.

But Richard has found the words. "Burt, you know we think as highly of you as you do of us. That was so very thoughtful of you—incredibly so. But it looks now as if I'll be signing a contract. It's—it's in the bag as well."

Burt swings back around and looks directly into Richard's face: "Is it, though? If the contract hasn't been signed?"

"An oral agreement has been made."

"Oh, hell, Ricky, you know what weight *they* carry. Remember last year we lost that engineering candidate in *June* to O.S.U.? This is only March—they can find any number of people, still."

"Burt," Richard says in his most carefully measured manner, "I'm afraid we really have committed. I don't know what else to say except *that*—and to thank you for being such a prince of a guy."

Deflated, his shoulders sagging, Burt sits back and sighs, "Okay. Okay."

"Thank you for being so nice, Burt," I say, worried in a different direction now. "But what 'bout Aree?"

"Don't worry. I fibbed. Twice. She hasn't signed, although she is eager to. And I have only barely mentioned you to her."

"Burt, you shark," Richard laughs. "Prince and shark both."

"No, neither, actually. Just a guy trying to do the best for the college and everyone involved. I was testing the waters before telling you we can match their offer, or come pretty close."

Richard studies him thoughtfully. "Your last card?"

"Bottom of the deck."

"I'm flattered beyond belief. But no."

"Okay. That's it." Symbolically, Burt wipes his hands.

As they exchange stares and reach the final stages of their game, I press for an answer to my question. "And Aree?"

"We'll talk with her a final time and inform her of the entire picture. If she's still interested—and I think she will be —we'll make her an offer."

"You have 'nother lonely Thai woman on your hands then."

"Maybe. But she won't hunger for male attention. Like you, Dee, she's knockout. And *not* married."

"And I think my husband have monopoly on sweet talk!"

We all break up laughing; Richard and Burt rise simultaneously with a few more *bon mots* on their lips. I follow, and they are almost to the door, arms around each other's shoulders when Burt backs away and pauses thoughtfully for a moment, with his fingers at his lips.

"Ricky," he says, backing deliberately right up to the door, strangely, to—to what? Prevent our getting out? Or to keep the meeting strictly confidential to its end, although at this hour on a Saturday afternoon the closest human beings would be the students at the library or on the playing fields.

"Ricky," he repeats, weighing another decision to speak or not to speak a thought. "Too bad. I was looking forward to someday—someday smoking with you."

Richard freezes, and those two telltale little red spots rise to his cheeks like surfacing fish, as they do whenever he finds himself totally off guard, caught with his mental or emotional pants down.

"But Burt," he struggles, "I mean, you know I don't smoke. Just one of those cigarettes would wipe me out—I mean, the jogger in me, anyway."

"I'm not talking Marlboros," Burt, the black mountain man says, the one who listened to his new Hank Williams, Jr. disk at our house and surprised Richard by laughing heartily at Hank's "Country Boy Can Survive" line—"they can grow their own smoke."

Now he is amazing us, actually, and slightly disappointing me—*et tu*, Prince Burt? A metaphorical crack zigzags down the baked and shiny surface of your portrait.

All three of us know exactly what he is talking about. The American disease, here in the *halls of Academe*.

But what else do I expect?

"Well, okay," Richard says at length. "It is too bad. But I've just about quit."

"You won't be growing any more plants in the greenhouse?"

Richard's face gets *redder*. "Whoo-ee! How in the world —how did you know?"

"Hell, man, half the town does. Somebody—I think it was Stan—peeked over the patio fence when you went out of town once. Saw the stuff drying upside down in the sun."

At this point both our hearts stop, and I thank Jesus and Buddha both that there are no more plants, that there is practically no more habit. The jarred stuff in the refrigerator will have to go, too—and soon, very soon.

Apparently Richard is also thinking of that stuff; he looks suddenly stricken, short of breath—frightened, actually. "Can I—can I give you some good weed before we leave then? Several ounces? Oh, hell—all of it. I quit, man. I quit *here and now.*" He is visibly trembling.

Never before have his vocation and his avocation crossed paths as openly as this, and he doesn't like the feel of it at all.

"No," Burt says. "I wouldn't take it." He smiles. "I don't smoke."

But Richard is hardly listening. Weakly, but with firmness, he repeats, "I quit here and now. And that—that's a promise."

And, Buddha be praised, he means it—he means all his

promises, keeps every one he makes. He quits there and then, for good. For ever.

Down the disposal will go the stuff in jars. Not another puff, not another bite. Scared straight. *Shamed*, irony of ironies, out of his longstanding, very regrettable habit. The battle ended—in a matter of seconds.

The long and difficult war is over.

I nearly collapse, myself, right on the spot. But joy sustains me, a slowly spreading glow that warms all the way down to my shoes. It isn't exactly *my* victory, but that doesn't matter. I have been ready for years to take it any way it comes.

And does it feel *good!*

"Man," Richard says into the ensuing silence, "it's a weird feeling talking to your *boss* about this!"

"And listening, too," I chirp happily, nervously.

"And I'll tell you something else, Ricky," Burt says seriously. "I'm just not sure all dope—all of it and everything about it—isn't a device of the Devil, you know? Manna from Hell."

Richard studies him: "Spoken like a true Arkansan."

"You don't believe it's Satan's game?"

"I didn't say I don't."

"And you're not mocking your adopted state?"

"Hell, no. I've adopted more of it than you think."

A pause, conversation winding down.

Silence again. Staring at the floor, out the window.

"Well, look, you and Dee take care. We'll talk again before you leave. But not about your staying. Or about smoking."

"Yes, let's do that. Have a couple of brews."

We both shake his hand and leave.

Somehow, though, they never do get together before our departure. I never see Vera again either. Perhaps it is just that all was said on that last day of winter in Burt's office—nothing else needed.

CONFESSIONS OF A MAIL ORDER BRIDE

What will remain with me is the indelible memory of how Burt maneuvered Richard into a realization of how easily a bad habit can be known—and made public. Perhaps he was resigned to our leaving town and just didn't want Richard to blow his future somewhere else, at his age, on wacky weed.

When we walk out into the sunshine, I feel light and airy, as if a huge weight has finally been removed from my shoulders—as of course it has. When we get in the car, I lean over and kiss my strong American husband loudly on the cheek.

He grunts and, sticking the key into the ignition, pauses for a very long moment, staring hard, hard, hard through the windshield at nothing in particular—the sky maybe.

"Quite a guy," he says at last.

"He is."

Lips tight, face firmly set, he starts the car—but doesn't move just yet. "Manna from Heaven, Manna from Hell. I wonder, does he really believe that stuff?"

Now I see that other campaign, the one I thought I'd *never* get to, forming more clearly along the horizon of our future together. This new one is going to be comparatively easy, though—convincing the already half-convinced.

"You do. Deep down."

Backing away from the curb, he chooses not to respond.

I smile to myself. Everybody knows a grown man ought to believe in something—Christian doctrine, Buddhist thought, *something*.

And what's life without a little campaign?

Winter is over, but the wintry weather is not, not by a long shot—or a long trek.

On yet another cold day, an early-spring Saturday morning, we find ourselves low on groceries again after being snowed in since Thursday night. There is icy snow all over everything, and neither one of us feels like trying to drive half a block, much less three or four miles. We've had our fill of that.

"Let's *walk* to the Safeway," Richard proposes.

Our son looks up from the puzzle he is doing and rolls his eyes at his slightly crazy parents.

Great idea, I concur—but can we please wait until it warms up a few degrees? Even though I have never seen a single case of it, I understand the damage frostbite can do.

Richard guffaws. "It's well into the twenties now."

"Still sound cold to me."

"Thai gal. Of course."

But we do wait, and after a lunch pasted together from our few remaining comestibles, we head out, the three of us bundled and trundled together—a little domestic discovery company on an arctic sojourn.

What has begun as the thought of a hellish automobile trip is turning into one of those days so pleasantly adventure-some as to become fixed in the memory as a "good time."

It will also be, up to now, the single most thoroughly small town Middle-American thing I have done.

All it is, really, is a walk, a shopping trip in the snow. It probably does not mean one-tenth as much to Richard as it does to me, Rice Belt-born Siamese me. Nor can it mean a whole lot to James at seven years, nine months, except to give him the pleasure of an outing with Mom and Dad along with the mild discomfort of walking such a distance on such a young (but oh-so-long) pair of legs.

I never really liked winter before this day, this walk. Now I know I will never forget it.

For it is a perfect afternoon—probably more for me than for anyone within a hundred miles of us. There we are, making our way over and through packed snow and snowdrifts in a village winter wonderland, replete with icicles hanging from limbs and eaves, some of them (the ones in shade) a full two-feet long and as lethal-looking as Samurai blades.

The snow itself is perfect, and my mind arranges and rearranges the shapes into a gallery of sculpted ghost-images. It piles up cleanly and whitely against the sides of houses, humps itself over idle cars, rolls like a tide through the tall grasses of vacant lots, and here and there, underfoot, indifferently lets a street be shown, or a sidewalk, or even the tired brown grass of an incompletely inundated lawn.

Someday, I feel, I will be able to sculpt such a scene—a frieze chipped and created with a single chisel, the way ancient Siamese stone-masters are said to have done.

But they never did *snow*.

The sun, old friend from the tropics, stays out for the length of our trek and warms us despite a temperature that does not get above freezing. Mild and unobtrusive, the wind comes around now and then to remind us—through the tips of our noses, primarily—that this is indeed a "cold spell," as they call it in these parts, and that we are given passes for this one day only.

Tomorrow you better not loosen that collar, take off that scarf! And maybe not until next week! But, as for today— today is yours.

Carpe diem.

People at the market seem unusually cheerful and friendly as well. Beaming and excited, in part at least because of the brilliant weather, they joke and laugh with good humor. Richard speaks with one of his students, a supermarket stockboy, while James browses through the Poptarts and cake mixes.

When I have half-filled my basket, enough for a few days at least, I rein them back in, and we start for home.

It is four in the afternoon, and the sun has succeeded in melting the ice and snow off a few well-sited trees and building facades. Traffic, too, has worn the slush off the main streets; businesses hum with Saturday activity, people and vehicles in motion everywhere like the molecules of some gigantic, happy, weather-spawned organism. At that late afternoon hour, the town has taken on a sort of cold, golden aura, as if everything has been bronzed *in vivo*.

Admiring it all as we head back into the quieter haven of the residential section, I reflect on how American I have become. Nowhere in my mind do I lament and long for "home" any longer; this is home now. At this moment, I am as much American as anyone else on the streets. It brings euphoria to me, a lightheadedness that makes me want to skip down the snow-packed sidewalk instead of carefully negotiating it.

Rather than skipping, I verbalize my feeling to Richard as well as I can, which is substantially better than I was able to when I first landed in New York. That is another thing adding to my feeling at the moment, my maturing command of English: I can speak with anyone now, from delivery man to philosophy professor, without fear of missing more than a fraction of what is stated or implied. I can sit down and read the Rousersville *Times* or *Time* magazine or one of those professors' textbooks.

I can get along anywhere, with anyone, about anything, and I am as proud of that as I am of my American husband and my well-adapted Amerasian son.

"It is so nice," I say, and practice a simile: "Like piece of heaven in the streets."

"Today, yeah. Most days, too, as long as I have you and the boy nearby."

"Thank you. That is very sweet. But I mean today especially. It is beautiful, and so different from Thailand."

"Better, maybe? Like American Coca-Cola?"

I have told him how inferior the stuff we bottle under license is. But, for fun, I counter: "What about Thai silk?"

He's game. "American microcomputers. Apple? IBM?

"Hmmm . . . Thai tableware."

"Cigarettes."

"Porcelain."

"Automobiles."

"*Automobiles?*" I respond. He is cheating.

"Name a Thai one."

"Okay, we play dirty. Temples."

"Uhhhh . . ."

"Call it draw?"

"No draws. What about *America*—itself—today—right now?"

"Better now," I answer without hesitation, remembering his decision, the promise in Burt's office.

He knows what I mean. No doubt remains in our minds. But he feels like continuing, like *winning* this "better-than" game. "Come on, what could be better than the U.S. of A.—in what possible way?"

"Well . . . better *this* day, this afternoon outling."

"*Outing.*"

"*Outing.*"

"Admit it: better, overall, than Thailand." Frontal assault.

I stop in the middle of the sidewalk and listen to the wind rising in the wires overhead as the sun slants with an etching brilliance between the rows of houses down the street. A half-block ahead of us, secure and warm on this mid-American street, James plays in the snow. Suddenly a shivered memory of Sumwong, as stinging as the wind will be when the sun goes down, pierces my thoughts.

But, for the moment, this golden moment, I push it aside. At the very instant that I do, James looks up into my eyes. He smiles to see that we are still here, looking at him, and he waves.

"Better," I finally say, "than anything."

We continue up the street toward home, the three of us, humming a march that we all know, in time to the sound of our boots crunching through the crusts of snow.

Yankee Doodle Dandy.

EPILOGUE

In the spring of 1989, I return to Thailand for ten days after an absence of nearly thirteen years. Coincidentally, my trip ends at the first part of May, just after the 200th birthday of the American Constitution. It is thus the second Bicentennial for which I happen to arrive *late*.

Some habits are hard to break.

Nakhon Narai seems hardly to have changed at all. For better or for worse, let the same be said for any Sunbelt U.S. city over the span of thirteen years!

What is new is a large, modern hotel with air-conditioned rooms and an Olympic swimming pool. I learn that many Americans—tourists, military personnel, investors—

317

now stay there. My father was one of a half-dozen construction engineers consulted on the project.

Highways have been reconstructed for high-speed travel and city streets paved and even striped; the bus and train stations have been modernized. These are signs of the increasingly mobile, Western-style times, as are many huge new service stations for the vastly increased numbers of automobiles on the road.

Thailand is prospering as part of the Asian Revolution that has put Tokyo and Singapore and Hong Kong at the forefront of the world's financial and industrial picture. Bangkok is just a few steps behind—long steps, to be sure, but it is gaining all the time.

As for Bangkok itself—what little I could see of it from the windows of public transportation vehicles—it seems so much like an American city now as to be unrecognizable in some parts. There are multi-story buildings (after seeing the World Trade Center, I hesitate to call them skyscrapers) all over the place, and multi-lane highways (I cannot really call them *expressways)* lead in several directions out of the city.

Most telling of all are the shopping centers—and, yes, I can use that term—dominated by huge department stores with goods from all over the world, escalators to whisk people from one level to another, and shoppers by the thousands.

Thirteen years ago, fresh out of the Rice Belt, I could not have seen these changes coming at all. But that fact probably says more about me than about the progress.

Although I do not get to see them, I am told that the Royal Palace and the Emerald Temple are as they always have been—astonishingly beautiful symbols of traditional Siam. Village life, I am also told, has not changed all that much and perhaps never will. And, too, my native land still seems to be The Land of Smiling Faces.

EPILOGUE

It makes me feel good to know that a major part of what I left is still intact.

My parents show noticeable signs of having aged, yet still seem to me to be the same. This is a common phenomenon, I suppose; as we become adults, we fix images of our folks in our minds and freeze them in time like mementos in amber. Dad and Mom, with tears in their eyes and smiles on their faces, have both come to Don Meung to welcome their prodigal daughter back to Thailand.

The feelings run deep and are full of joy and relief—more than I am able to express either to myself or to them. We drink in each other for fifteen or twenty minutes before any of us is able to suggest getting the baggage and heading for the bus station.

When we get home after a comfortable (despite the traditionally insane driving) three-hour ride on a new style first-class bus—with air conditioning, pillow-soft ride, and a trip hostess—more family are waiting for me, including some I can barely remember. Among the guests are Veena and her three children, one of them, her boy, almost exactly James's age. Having read about him for years in her letters, I have been eager to meet him. Now I am proud to see that he lives up to her descriptions of a polite, handsome lad who looks very much "family."

The house, although smaller than I remember, is still basically the same. Dad has extended the ferroconcrete fence completely around the house. I do not ask him what he is trying to keep in now—or to keep out. He also has another new Japanese truck, his second since I left. It is the one luxury that he allows himself.

Mom, as always the sweetest soul in the world, has supervised the preparation of a huge meal of all my favorites, including *mee siam* and *gang gai*. When we arrive home, it is waiting for us in two dozen dishes, watched over and warmed by aunts and cousins, with auxiliary help from uncles, nieces, and nephews.

Because I am the star of the show, so to speak, "daughter home from America," I cannot give more than a fraction of my attention to the meal in the two hours it takes to consume it.

But everything is delicious, somehow even better than I remember. Especially the *mee siam* and *gang gai*.

And everyone is even nicer than I remember.

Veena's oldest boy is named Boon. He is much like James in personality—perhaps twelve-year-old boys are the same all over the world. He knows exactly where to go and what to do at all times, and takes enormous pride in that fact, even though he is sometimes wrong. (Of course, errors are never admitted and are subject to instant revision.)

Comparing his future with James's, I feel some regret for him that goes along with being thankful once again (as I will be a dozen times a day) to be an American and to have an American son. It is a bunch of little things—about his future especially—that add up to the one big thing about the U.S.A.: talk of decay and decline notwithstanding, it is still the place for opportunity.

At Veena's house, he shows me his new handheld calculator.

I think of the Apple computer Richard bought James last Christmas on which to do his homework and play games.

Veena says that Phat's marital service folded a few years ago. Phat is rumored to be dead. Also, she confides the rumors that Marree turned to prostitution in Bangkok in order to support her family. The city is becoming known as the Sex Capital

EPILOGUE

of Asia and, plying their trade among Americans, Australians, Europeans, and Japanese, Thai prostitutes can make up to $300 a week, practically all year round. The idea is deplorable but the lure, for many, irresistible.

On the plus side of the national moral ledger, King Phumiphon has decreed that poppy cultivation be curtailed and opium production eliminated along the Burmese border. He has dedicated thousands of soldiers and millions of dollars to this and other projects aimed at destroying the drug trade. Elusive though that goal may be, the massive commitment speaks for itself.

It is our good king's *campaign*.

Women are coming up in Thailand. In Nakhon Narai they comprise nearly one-fourth the doctors and three-fourths the bankers; moreover, they are now represented across a broad spectrum of business and professional positions. What this trend will do to traditional Thai family values is only just now coming under scrutiny; in fact, in my ten days I found no fewer than four newspaper and magazine articles on that subject, in addition to one TV editorial.

Only time will tell, they all say.

It seems that one key to the rise of women outside the home has been an increase in their opportunities to avail themselves of tests that measure and reward academic achievement and career potential. With that foot in the door, plus their durable patience and quiet determination, women have been able to advance into areas formerly restricted to men only.

There is still a long way for them to go to have the same chances in life that Western women have, but they are off and running. It is amazing what happens when you are able to let your light shine—even in as seemingly small a way as achieving a 10- or 20-point higher test score.

Both canoes are gone. Because no one was using it—kids nowadays want to ride Thai mopeds and Japanese motorcycles—Dad put his in the truck five years ago and took it down to Bangkok to give to a fellow worker on a government project.

A full seven years before that—not very long after my departure, in fact—Mom gave Sumwong's to a town family in need. It depressed her to see it each day and be reminded of losing him. They are still using it, I hear, to catch and sell fish along the Chao Phraya.

So it was not so badly made, after all.

During the days, I go for long walks to see places old and new with Veena's three kids and a few cousins. They all seem taller and healthier-looking than kids were in my day. Is this an illusion, or is the difference just one more fruit of progress?

We are strolling through a rebuilt—cleaner, fancier, and of course, more expensive—market a mile or so from home when I catch sight of a familiar face: Suwad, my former fiance.

People have been writing that he has become even heavier and more evil-tempered, but I am not prepared for a man who is fifty to seventy pounds overweight and appears ten to fifteen years older than he is. I know that he has failed in trying to establish several businesses of his own and that he and his family (wife, four kids) live off his parents' income. But it is an unpleasant shock to see what physical devastation time and temperament have brought to him.

Although I do not dwell on the thought that such are the terrible rewards of unpunished murder, I cannot help but consider the reasons for his long downhill slide. It all seems to have started with those three gunshots on that fateful day in Pak Nam thirteen years ago.

EPILOGUE

Our eyes meet for an instant. There is a flash of recognition, and I want to say something to him, and perhaps he to me. But a moment later he lowers his head and goes his way, and I go mine.

On the day before I depart for the States, I visit the Temple to say a final prayer for Sumwong. I am to leave his spirit behind me in Thailand, where it belongs. I will miss it, of course, but my brother must rest for good in his native land.

I go in the morning. With me in a little plastic bag are candles and incense to burn, and some tea and jackfruit for the monks. It pleases me to see that the Bo trees *(thon po)* on the temple grounds have remained extraordinarily healthy since I last saw them. This can be taken as an excellent sign, for it was a Bo under which Buddha sat when enlightenment came to him.

I follow the manicured gravel path to the temple entrance, where just outside the huge wooden door sit three monks, one of whom I recognize from many years ago. The only sign of aging in him is his eyes, which, nevertheless, do not seem so much older as wise. He accepts my gifts and bids me enter and pray.

Inside I light the candles and incense as an offering to Buddha, and I kneel before His gold-leafed statue. In my prayer, I ask for the happiness of all my family, including my dead brother whose spirit has been with me these many years. I tell Sumwong not to worry about me any longer.

As he knows, my husband has overcome his personal flaws and has God in his heart at last; occasionally he teaches church-sponsored classes to teenagers about that quick, deep trap of drugs into which the unsuspecting can fall before they even know it. Who better to speak against drugs than Ricky?

CONFESSIONS OF A MAIL ORDER BRIDE

Next year one of his students will be teenaged James, whose grades have already proven how well he can learn.

I have much to thank you for, my brother. And I can think of no better way than to ask the Enlightened One to place you in His care here forever.

At the moment I utter these words to myself, my head begins to swim and goosebumps arise all over my body. It lasts only a moment and is not at all unpleasant, but it overpowers me, taking my breath away. I rise and back slowly away from the statue with tears of emotion in my eyes.

Outside the temple, the sun is dizzyingly bright. I take a moment to steady myself, then walk over to the old monk.

He smiles as I tell him what happened to me inside the temple. He says not to be concerned; it means only that my prayer was heard by Buddha.

As I walk down the gravel path, a *nog kau* bird is singing melodiously at the very top of one of the Bo trees, and my heart is filled with peace.